Søren Kierkegaard was born in Copenhagen in 1813. He studied at the University of Copenhagen, and it was while he was there that he experienced a mental and moral crisis which precipitated his entire writing career. A devout Christian, he nevertheless decided not to take Holy Orders but to dedicate his life and writings to an ideal. Between 1842 and 1851 he wrote about thirty-five books and most of his twenty-volume journal. His philosophical and argumentative works were first published under a pseudonym but his religious discourses, written at the same time, appeared chiefly under his own name; this supports his claim that he was from first to last a religious author. He died in 1855.

P|Ph.

Religious Books in the Fontana Series

Edifying Discourses

A SELECTION

SØREN KIERKEGAARD

Edited with an
Introduction by
Paul L. Holmer

Translated by
David F. and
Lillian Marvin
Swenson

COLLINS

fontana books

This selection of *Edifying Discourses* is published by arrangement with the following publishers:

Princeton University Press for "The Unchangeableness of God" from *For Self-Examination*, and *Judge for Yourselves*, translated by David Swenson. © 1944 by Princeton University Press.

Augsburg Publishing House for the Preface and remaining Discourses from *Edifying Discourses* Vols. I, II, III and IV, *Thoughts on Crucial Situations* and *The Gospel of Suffering*, all translated from the Danish by David F. and Lillian Marvin Swenson, © 1941, 1943, 1944, 1945, 1948 by Augsburg Publishing House.

CONTENTS

INTRODUCTION BY
PAUL L. HOLMER

Thou plain man [wrote Kierkegaard toward the close of his life]!
The Christianity of the New Testament is infinitely high; but
observe that it is not high in such a sense that it has to do with
the difference between man and man with respect to intellectual
capacity, etc. No, it is for all. . . .

Thou plain man! I have not separated my life from thine;
thou knowest it, I have lived in the street, am known to all; . . .

Thou plain man! I do not conceal from thee the fact that,
according to my notion, the thing of being a Christian is infinitely
high, that at no time are there more than a few who attain it,
as Christ's own life attests, if one considers the generation in
which He lived, and as also His preaching indicates, if one takes
it literally. Yet nevertheless it is possible for all. . . .[1]

It is with this explicit appeal to plain people that all of the
discourses in this book were written. Each discourse is
calculated to bring the reader, whatever his æsthetic and
intellectual capacity, into conversation about religious and
Christian concerns. For this reason, among others, Kierkegaard suggests that they should be read in privacy and
preferably aloud. Their simplicity and repetitive style
make them extremely effective devotional essays.

Not every discourse, however, is equally adapted to every
reader. Kierkegaard therefore suggested in subtle ways
that the person whom he calls " with joy and gratitude,
'my' reader " will be self-chosen. Kierkegaard knew of
no way to assure himself of his audience; therefore, he
likens his discourses to the objects which the bird, his
reader, fixes with his eye, flies down to pluck off, and
takes away unto himself. It is a safe surmise that each
reader can easily enough discover those discourses which

[1] *Attack Upon " Christendom,"* translated by Walter Lowrie
(Oxford University Press, 1944), pp. 287-88.

are peculiarly adapted to his own interests and needs, and begin there.

Kierkegaard flatters his readers by supposing that they are willing and able to explore those needs and interests native to themselves. He seeks to address himself to the universally human in each of us. However, against those who have identified the universally human as rationality or as æsthetic sensibility or as an endowment with natural rights, Kierkegaard insists that the truly universal and distinctively human factor lies in subjectivity and inwardness. Furthermore, by developing our capacities for interest, for enthusiasm and passion, we become ethical and religious subjects. The discourses are efforts, then, to stimulate and also to discipline our feelings, wishes, and hopes. Kierkegaard does not try to convey results as much as to elicit in his reader a self-activity and a process of appropriation. His conviction is that every man is potentially a being of spirit. This means in effect that the awakening of inwardness is the beginning of the relationship to God.

If the reader should discover that these discourses speak poignantly to him, he may want to read more of them. The first eight discourses included in this selection are chosen from twenty-one printed in five small volumes: *Edifying Discourses* Vols. I-IV (Minneapolis: Augsburg Publishing House, 1943-1944) and *Thoughts on Crucial Situations* (same publisher, 1941); the next two, numbers IX and X, are from *The Gospel of Suffering* and *What We Learn From the Lilies of the Field and the Birds of the Air*, respectively, where ten discourses are published under the single title, *The Gospel of Suffering* (Augsburg Publishing House, 1948); the last discourse in this selection, "The Unchangeableness of God," accompanies Walter Lowrie's translation of *For Self-Examination* (Oxford University Press, 1941), another and substantial work in a religious mood. All of the above essays were translated by David F. Swenson or his wife and widow, Lillian Marvin Swenson.

The story of Kierkegaard's life is essentially the story of his authorship. His early years seem like the seedtime for a writing career; his last years, when his pen was relatively quiet, are like a benediction upon a work already done. The period between, about nine or ten years, is strenuous but resolute. From 1842 to 1851, Kierkegaard wrote about thirty-five books and the bulk of his twenty-volume journal. When giving an account of his literature, he said it was like a single movement, accomplished in one breath.[2]

Søren Aabye Kierkegaard was born in Copenhagen in 1813 and died in 1855. A desultory youthful period, including study at the University of Copenhagen, was climaxed by a broken engagement. This event, so common to the rest of the world, became for Kierkegaard in 1841 the precipitating cause of his entire authorship. By 1843 his writing career was launched and books began to pour forth in profusion. *Either/Or* in two volumes, *Fear and Trembling, Repetition, Philosophical Fragments, The Concept of Dread, The Stages on Life's Way* and the *Concluding Unscientific Postscript* were published within the thirty-six-month period ending in February, 1846. Besides being some of the finest literature penned in Scandinavia, if not all of Europe, these pages include as well the most discriminating philosophic reasoning.

Oddly enough, though, these are not all of Kierkegaard's works even for this brief period. For at intervals during these same months he also published seven smaller volumes of religious discourses. These accompanied in a certain manner the above-noted longer works. The first series of books were issued under pseudonyms, this not so much to secure anonymity as to fulfil a certain pedagogical intention. The second series, the religious discourses, were published under Kierkegaard's own name. Kierkegaard asserted that the use of his own name was crucial evidence, despite the somewhat ambiguous nature of his writings, that he was, from first to last, a religious author.

[2] *On My Work as an Author in The Point of View,* translated by Walter Lowrie (Oxford University Press, 1939), pp. 146-47.

The early literature from 1843 to 1846 has then two strands. The first which is pseudonymous is also philosophical and argumentative. In obedience to the pedagogical principle which says that one who teaches must begin where the learners are, Kierkegaard creates authors who are ideal representations of the kind of existence they describe. From *Either/Or* through the *Postscript,* a transition is effected, from an æsthetic view of life which is hedonistic and largely a quest for immediate satisfactions, through an ethical view which is dutiful and describes existence as a responsible and obliged sojourn, into the religious view. The *Postscript,* together with the *Fragments,* carries the depiction, again pseudonymously, from a mild kind of religiousness, perhaps akin to Ralph Waldo Emerson's Unitarian Christianity, to a more severe and demanding form of Christianity, that which is paradoxical and even entails suffering.

Kierkegaard likened himself to a missionary whose responsibility it was to reintroduce Christianity into Christendom. He attacked, as he said, from behind. His pseudonymous literature was his way of coming to grips with the philosophy and culture of his day in its own terms. Every book has a significance given by its role in his extended programme and, independently, an immediate and intrinsic importance. Following his literature beyond 1846, the reader discovers that the two strands seem to come together. The numerous books of the late forties (and they are as many as the earlier period from 1843 to 1846) articulate over Kierkegaard's name the details of the Christian view of life. The early literature is even conceived as a kind of introduction and preparation, a kind of softening up of the opposition, to this specifically Christian literature.

Only briefly is pseudonymity again invoked and this for a special purpose. It was when Kierkegaard came to the depiction of the most strenuous Christian categories, those growing out of the consideration of the vicissitudes of following Jesus, that he decided he had no right to attribute such holiness to himself as the use of his own name might suggest. It is interesting to note, too, that several of these later works, which again were somewhat argumentative and polemical, were also accompanied by more religious discourses, edifying in intent.

Kierkegaard wrote over eighty discourses in his lifetime. Most of them were published in books of substantial proportions; others were added to longer works, and a few were even published singly. No one can understand Kierkegaard's authorship unless he also fathoms these discourses, for here the litmus test of Kierkegaard's thought and conviction must finally be made. The discourses, especially the earlier ones, parallel his more technical and abstruse writings. In one sense, his literature moves through its numerous difficulties and niceties of argument for the purpose of showing why the simplicities of the sermon contain the highest wisdom.

In late 1854 and continuing through 1855, the last year of his life, Kierkegaard engaged in a most exacting pamphleteering attack upon the Lutheran Church of Denmark. Using every literary weapon at his disposal, irony, savage wit, and scorn, Kierkegaard heaped diatribe upon diatribe and applied relentlessly the categories articulated in his earlier literature to the particular empirical situation presented by the State Church of Denmark. His attack is as savage as any that has ever been composed. However, immediately after the most devastating articles and in the midst of his fiercest attack, he published another edifying discourse, "The Unchangeableness of God" (number xi in this volume).[3] This served again to call the attention of his contemporaries to the fact that despite the violent controversy, Kierkegaard was speaking from within the Christian community and not from without, as many assumed.

From first to last, Kierkegaard said, he was a religious

[3] *Cf. Attack Upon "Christendom,"* pp. 232-34, where the editor, Walter Lowrie, discusses this discourse and its place in Kierkegaard's literature.

author. His edifying discourses limn the author from his earliest days of authorship to the last. His philosophy succeeded in taking him out of the speculative, the poetic, and the aristocratic, back to the simple and the edifying. For this reason Kierkegaard could insist that the religious discourses, slight as they appear in comparison, nevertheless, enable the reader to interpret the more imposing philosophic works. Just as he had argued that philosophy could not really distill the gist of religion anyway, so, too, Kierkegaard's own literature is contrived so ironically that the simple discourses become more crucial and important to any reader who understands them than the profound and difficult philosophic pieces.

Therefore no reader should assume that these are lesser works. Even though few people noticed the discourses as they appeared, and even though *Either/Or,* the most popular and most spectacular of his pseudonymous works, got most of the attention, Kierkegaard could say:

> I held out *Either/Or* to the world in my left hand, and in my right the *Two Edifying Discourses*; but all, or as good as all, grasped with their right what I held in my left.[4]

It was the hope, often expressed by the author, that the readers would, instead, accept with their right hand what was offered with his right hand, and these were his edifying discourses.[5]

Kierkegaard developed very precise notions of why his religious essays were discourses and not sermons. Primarily it is that sermons are properly a work "absolutely and entirely through authority, that of Holy Writ and of Christ's Apostles."[6] They presuppose a priest who in virtue of ordination speaks categorically and definitively

---

4 *Point of View,* p. 20.
5 "Foreword" to *Two Edifying Discourses* in *Edifying Discourses,* Vol. III (Augsburg Publishing House, 1945), p. 5.
6 *The Journals of Søren Kierkegaard,* translated by Alexander Dru (Oxford University Press, 1938), entry no. 629, p. 192.

on God's behalf.[7] But discourses, or addresses as they may also be called, use as their point of departure, not the authoritatively given content, but the human situation. They deal with doubt, and, hence, they are not categorical and declaratory as much as they are accommodating to, and eliciting of, the religious potentiality in the listener or reader. Discourses are in a different tenor than sermons and can even be conceived and delivered by a layman.

Kierkegaard indicated that his early pseudonymous literature was conceived as a description of individual stages on the way toward a Christian religious existence. In an extended account of a contemporary effort in literature which is useful to his own purposes, " Johannes Climacus," the thirty-year-old pseudonymous author of the *Concluding Unscientific Postscript*, tells about discovering to his surprise the edifying discourses by Magister Kierkegaard. Climacus' comments, which for good reasons can be accepted also as Kierkegaard's judgments, are to the effect that the discourses are not sermons " since they employ only the ethical categories of immanence,"[8] and nowhere use the distinctively Christian concepts and categories.

Furthermore, the discourses are exploratory in a philosophical manner. They aim to tease out of the human being's ethical life those considerations which are upbuilding and regenerative. In contradistinction to sermons, which are edifying by reference to Jesus and God who are independent of the inner life, the discourse uses every device, æsthetic and poetic, to encourage the growth of inward propensities toward the good life and God. These early discourses abstain from all " Christian-dogmatic terminology, from mentioning the name of Christ, and so forth."[9] They are an illustration of the fact that the edifying is a wider category than the Christian. Kierke-

[7] *The Postscript,* translated by David F. Swenson (Oxford University Press, 1941), pp. 243-44.

[8] *Ibid.*, p. 229.

[9] *Ibid.*, p. 243. Also note *Journals,* entry 519, p. 140.

gaard insists that Christianity is edifying. By this he means that it too builds up or constitutes human beings as ethical subjects. Christian faith does have moral consequences; it makes an empirical difference in the lives of men. From such facts, however, it does not follow that every edifying truth is Christian.

Thus, in a precise sense, the majority of these discourses are not Christian, though they indeed are believed to be edifying. Neither are they non-Christian. They are conducive to, and preparatory of, Christian faith without quite presupposing it. The last three discourses in this selection, IX, X, and XI, are, however, distinctively Christian while also being edifying. They are later in Kierkegaard's authorship and actually use Christian categories. The mode of communication and style is still that of the discourse, however, and not that of the sermon.

In all of his writings Kierkegaard practises a deliberate kind of craftiness. Instead of becoming impatient with his devices it might be well for the reader, instead, to understand his point of view and ascertain whether or not he is correct in designing his literature as he did.

Early in his career Kierkegaard concluded that his entire age had been misled by the increase of knowledge. Unsuspecting people, almost overwhelmed by the sheer quantity of truths about almost anything you please, had come to the view that being even ethical or religious was a matter of " knowing " first and then " doing " subsequently. As the world says in our day, so it is said in his, namely, that it is first necessary to know what is what before any action can be contemplated.

Kierkegaard viewed this situation as at once tragic and comic. It was tragic because it meant that people had really forgotten what it means to exist. Personal living was made to appear as an addendum, a mere consequent to objective reflection about the world and things in it. It was comic because it meant that an extraordinary and utterly exaggerated significance had been given to knowledge and, by accident, to the professors. Kierkegaard said that it was so bad that even the clergy were rated on a scale which gave them greater eminence the closer they got to being professors of theology. All of this meant too that a person's subjectivity, his emotional cosmos of convictions, wishes, hopes, and feelings, his entire range of inward sensibility, was deemed a by-product of his knowledge. The upshot of such attitudes was that even religion was made a matter of objective faith.

> The objective faith, what does that mean? It means a sum of doctrinal propositions. . . . The objective faith—it is as if Christianity also had been promulgated as a little system, if not quite so good as the Hegelian; it is as if Christ—aye, I speak without offence—it is as if Christ were a professor, and as if the Apostles had formed a little scientific society.[10]

Such a mode of understanding profound ethical and religious problems has numerous advantages. It seems to convert the human condition into a manageable scholarly and scientific problem. Nowadays enthusiasts for such a point of view insist that all we need is sound human engineering and better social management. Kierkegaard's protest is both an ethical one, against the denigration of human personality which such a contention implies, and an intellectual one, against any interpretation of knowledge which understands it to invest men with omnicompetence.

Kierkegaard tells us that we have forgotten what it means to exist as human beings. In fear of subjectivity, in fear that something whimsical and fortuitous might mar our otherwise controlled objective temper, men have gone to another extreme. Instead of inwardness being aberrant, it has become non-existent. Another type of madness takes over, and it means the dehumanizing of people.

> One shrinks from looking into the eyes of a madman of the former type lest one be compelled to plumb there the depths of his delirium; but one dares not look at a madman of the latter type at all, from fear of discovering

[10] *Postscript,* p. 193.

that he has eyes of glass and hair made from carpet-rags; that he is, in short, an artificial product. If you meet someone who suffers from such a derangement of feeling, the derangement consisting in his not having any, you listen to what he says in a cold and awful dread, scarcely knowing whether it is a human being who speaks, or a cunningly contrived walking stick in which a talking machine has been concealed.[11]

Even the man who everlastingly repeats objectively true sentences about the world may betray by that fact that he is mad and even inhuman.

Therefore, Kierkegaard urged another consideration upon his age. He deliberately and carefully plotted his entire authorship to show his readers what it means to exist, and what inwardness and subjectivity signify. Almost incidental to this was his highly sophisticated analysis of the misunderstandings and mistakes concerning the relation between philosophy and Christianity. Such mistakes as he discerned were explicable on this same ground. Though his interest was religious and, perhaps, more specifically, Christian, he believed that men had forgotten not only what it means to exist Christianly, but also humanly. Therefore, he began way back, as he said he must, with the most rudimentary drives and satisfactions by which people forged a way of life.[12]

However, Kierkegaard was convinced that his task could not be done in any straightforward dogmatizing manner. He noted that a man with a doctrine which said a man ought not to have any disciples would be inconsistent if he had disciples; therefore, a man who said existing did not consist in getting to know something about this and that would be inconsistent if he conceived his task as one of communicating something in the form of knowledge. Any attempt at direct and immediate communication between

[11] *Ibid.*, p. 175.
[12] *Ibid.*, pp. 222-24. Also, "A Glance at a Contemporary Effort in Danish Literature," pp. 225-66.

such an author and his reader would result in a misunderstanding. Accordingly, Kierkegaard designed his works to beguile the reader into the truth.[18] The pseudonymous works created ideal authors who designed in turn a series of mirrorlike positions in which the reader sees himself reflected. No results are conveyed by the author in these works. Instead he endeavours to get the reader to make the decisions and achieve the results in his own personality. If there is any increment anywhere, it is in the reader, not in the author's work.

Kierkegaard's constant and lifelong wish, to which his entire literature gives expression, was to create a new and rich subjectivity in himself and his readers. Unlike many authors who believe that all subjectivity is a hindrance, Kierkegaard contends that only some kinds of subjectivity are a hindrance. He sought at once to produce subjectivity if it were lacking, to correct it if it were there and needed correction, to amplify and strengthen it when it was weak and undeveloped, and, always, to bring the subjectivity of every reader to the point of eligibility for Christian inwardness and concern.

But the *Edifying Discourses,* though paralleling the pseudonymous works, spoke a little more directly, albeit without authority. They spoke the real author's conviction and were the purpose of Kierkegaard's lifework. Whereas all the rest of his writing was designed to get the readers out of their lassitude and mistaken conceptions, the discourses, early and late, were the goal of the literature. Though they do not convey results either, they aim to elicit that specific kind of existing, that mode of subjectivity and inwardness, which is the truth for every reader.

Kierkegaard was a master at once in two different areas. On the one side, he was a dialectician. This means that he commanded the abilities to define a thought, to trace its implications and consequences, and to juxtapose it against differing views. On the other side, he was also skilled at

[18] *On My Work As an Author* in *Point of View,* p. 148.

depicting and creating pathos. Here he was a kind of poet, quick to catch and to express the nuances of mood and feeling that make up our inward life.[14]

Kierkegaard's philosophical and theological reflections, his dialectic as he called it, led him to say that religious and ethical truth for every man lay finally in subjectivity and inwardness. His literary talents, his poetic nature as he called it, caused him to describe the kinds of inwardness that belonged to human existing. He concluded that many of these kinds of inwardness were untrue and unworthy of a man. His *Edifying Discourses* are attempts to create that kind of subjectivity and pathos that is the truth for every reader. Perhaps the words of his pseudonym, a pastor, are conclusive:

Do not check your soul's flight, do not grieve the better promptings within you, do not dull your spirit with half wishes and half thoughts, ask yourself, and contrive to ask until you find the answer; for one may have known a thing many times and acknowledged it, one may have willed a thing many times and attempted it, and yet it is only by the deep inward movements, only by the indescribable emotions of the heart, that for the first time you are convinced that what you have known belongs to you, that no power can take it from you; for only the truth which edifies is truth for you.[15]

Kierkegaard was seeking to be a Christian. Christianity was the truth for every man, because it alone described and produced that kind of subjectivity which is sufficient to the human quest. It is toward such an end that his discourses lead his readers.

November, 1957

---

[14] *The Point of View,* pp. 82-88.
[15] *Either/Or,* Vol. II, translated by Walter Lowrie (Oxford University Press, 1944), p. 294.

PREFACE

Although this little book (which is called "discourses,"
not sermons, because its author has no authority to *preach;*
"edifying discourses," not discourses for edification, because the speaker does not claim to be a *teacher*) only
wishes to be what it is, something of a superfluity, and only
desires to remain in secret, as it came into existence in
secret, I still have not said farewell to it without an almost
fantastic hope. In so far as it, by being published, is, figura-
tively speaking, starting out on a kind of journey, I let my
eye follow it a little while. I saw, then, how it set out on its
solitary way, or solitary set out along the highway. After
one and another little misapprehension, when it was deceived by a fleeting resemblance, it finally met that individual whom with joy and gratitude I call *my* reader,
that individual whom it seeks, towards whom, as it were,
it stretches out its arms; that individual who is benevolent
enough to let himself be found, benevolent enough to receive it, whether in the moment of meeting it found him
happy and confident, or "melancholy and thoughtful."
On the other hand, in so far as, by being published, it in a
stricter sense remains quiet without leaving the place, I let
my eye rest on it for a little while. It stood there, then,
like an insignificant little blossom in its hiding place in the
great forest, sought for neither for its showiness nor its
fragrance nor its food value. But I saw also, or believed
that I saw, how the bird whom I call *my* reader, suddenly fixed his eye upon it, flew down to it, plucked it off,
and took it to himself. And when I had seen this, I saw
nothing more.   s.k.

Copenhagen, May 5, 1843
[*His thirtieth birthday*]

I

THE EXPECTATION OF FAITH

NEW YEAR'S DAY

But before faith came, we were kept under the law, shut up unto the faith which should afterwards be revealed. Wherefore the law was our schoolmaster to bring us unto Christ, that we might be justified by faith. But after that faith is come, we are no longer under a schoolmaster. For ye are all the children of God by faith in Christ Jesus. For as many of you as have been baptized into Christ have put on Christ. There is neither Jew nor Greek, there is neither bond nor free, there is neither male nor female: for ye are all one in Christ Jesus. And if ye be Christ's, then are ye Abraham's seed, and heirs according to the promise.

Galatians 3:23-29

It is on the first day of the year that we are gathered here, devout listeners to this address! The festival we celebrate to-day is one to which the Church has given no name; and yet is its celebration no less welcome, its challenge to quiet meditation no less solemn. It is in the house of God that we are gathered, where the subject of discourse is always the same, though varied in fashion according to times and circumstances. A year has passed, a new year has begun, though as yet there has nothing happened in it. The past is completed; the present is not; only the future is, which yet is not. In our daily life we are accustomed to wish each other one or another good. According to what we believe ourselves to know about a man's special circumstances, his thoughts and achievements, to that degree we deem ourselves capable of wishing for him some definite good, particularly suitable for him and for his life. On this day, too, we do not neglect to show other men our good will and sympathy by wishing them this or that good thing.

But since on this particular day the thought about the future and the inscrutable possibility involved in the future, rises vividly before us, our wish tends to take on a more general character, because we hope that the greater compass of the wish may better succeed in laying hold of the future's manifold variety; because we feel the difficulty, over against the indeterminate and the indeterminable, of wishing anything determinate. Nevertheless we do not permit this difficulty to repress our wish; we do not give the thought time to disturb the heart's mysterious and indeterminate impulses; we express a good will, which, even if it does not deserve to be honoured by the name of love, still ought not to be disparaged as thoughtlessness. Only with respect to an individual person do we make an exception. To him our heart clings more steadfastly, for his welfare we are more concerned. The more this is the case, the more conscious we become of the difficulty. When the thought now becomes absorbed in the future, it strays hither and thither in its restless efforts to force or coax from the mystery its explanation; like a spy it hastens from one possibility to another, but in vain; and under all this the wishing soul becomes sorrowful, sits there and waits for the thought to return and enlighten it as to what it might venture to wish with all its heart. What others do easily and without trouble seems to this man heavy and difficult; what he himself does easily in relation to others, he finds hard in relation to the one he loves most, and the more he loves the greater the difficulty becomes. At last he becomes irresolute; he does not wish to release the beloved from his own influence, to surrender him to the future's power, and yet he must; he will accompany him with all good wishes, but he has not one single, exclusive wish.

If a man's troubled mind felt itself ensnared like a prisoner in this difficulty, he would doubtless recollect the testimonies he had heard in these sacred places; he would perhaps go to one of them again in order to inquire as to whether there might not be a wish which was so safe that he dared pour the whole of his soul's fervency into it, without holding back any part of it for another wish, also of importance to the beloved; so certain and so sure that he almost feared that he did not have enough inwardness to wish it as it ought to be wished; a wish that needed not to be accompanied by new wishes relative to its permanence; a wish which did not guilefully continue after he had ceased to wish it; a wish that did not concern some one particular thing, lest he might have forgotten some other particular thing, which later might disturb his peace; a wish that did not confine itself to the present, but was suited to the future, as this was the occasion for his wishing. If such a wish could be found, then he would be free and glad, glad in his wish, and still more glad that he could wish it for the other.

And in these sacred places many good things are mentioned. There is mention of worldly goods, of health, good times, wealth, power, fortune, a glorious fame; and the listener is warned against them; for he who has them is warned not to trust in them; he who does not have them is warned not to set his heart upon them. About *Faith* a different kind of speech is heard. It is said to be the highest good, the most beautiful, the most precious, the richest of all blessings, not to be compared with anything else, not replaceable by anything else. Is it then so different from the other goods because it is the highest good, but, for the rest, of the same kind as those, transient, unstable, conferred only upon the chosen few, seldom for the whole life? If this were so, then it would be inexplicable that in these sacred places there is always one thing, and only one, said about faith, that it is again and again eulogized and commended. He who would speak about it must either be in possession of this good, or feel the lack of it. If he possessed it, then he would probably say: " I readily admit that it is the highest good of all, but praise it to others—no, I cannot do that, for that would make it harder for those who do not have it; besides, there is a secret pain connected with its possession which makes me more lonely than do the greatest sufferings." And this would be a very noble and benevolent thought on his part. But he who did not have faith could hardly admit it. So then the opposite of what happens would happen; faith would be the only good which was never mentioned in the holy places; for it would be too great for a man to dare warn against it, too glorious for one to dare to praise it, for fear there might be someone present who did not have it and could not get it. Consequently faith has a different quality; it is not only the highest good, but it is a good in which all can share; and he who rejoices in his possession of it, rejoices also on behalf of countless generations of men; "for what I possess," he says, "that every man possesses or may possess." He who wishes it for another man, wishes it for himself; he who wishes it for himself, wishes it for every man; for that quality by virtue of which a man has faith is not one in which he is different from another man, but that wherein he is identical with him; that whereby he possesses it is not something in which he differs from others, but something in which he is absolutely identical with everyone else.

There was then such a wish as that bewildered man sought; he could wish it for another man with all his heart and with all his might and with all his soul, could dare to continue to wish it more and more heartily, as his love became more fervent. So, then, he would wish it.

If there was a man who went to another man and said to him: " I have often heard faith extolled as the highest good; I certainly feel that I do not have it; the complexity of my life, my troubles, my numerous affairs and many other things interfere; but this I know, that I have one wish and only one, that I may have a share in this faith." If it was a benevolently inclined man he went to, he would answer: " That is a beautiful and a devout wish which you ought not to relinquish, and it will surely be fulfilled."—Is it not true that it would seem to him an acceptable speech, to which he would gladly listen, for we are all willing to hear one who speaks about the fulfillment of our wish. Still time went on, and he got no farther.

Then he went to another man, confided to him, too, his concern and his wish. The man looked earnestly at him and said : "How can you be so in error? Your wish is not only pious and beautiful, but for no price should you relinquish it; you are much nearer to its fulfillment than you yourself believe; it is your duty to have faith, and if you do not have it, then it is your fault and a sin."

He would perhaps be startled by this speech, he would perhaps think : "So this faith is not as glorious as it was described, since it is acquired so easily; that would be absurd. For other good things one travels out into the wide world; they are concealed in distant places which are only accessible to men through great perils; or if this is not the case, then it is with their distribution as with the water at the pool of Bethesda, about which we read in the sacred Scriptures : At times an angel went down and troubled the water, and whoever came first, aye, he who came first, he was fortunate. With faith, on the contrary, with the highest good, should not this also be the case; should there be no difficulty connected with its acquisition?" However, he would still certainly think earnestly upon this matter, and when he had rightly considered it, he might perhaps say : "He was right, it is so; it was a bold speech in which there was sense and meaning; that is the way a man should speak; for the wish profits nothing." Then would he quietly review his inner emotions; and every time his soul allowed itself to rest on a wish, he called it to him and said : "You know you must not wish"; and in so doing he made progress. When his soul became fearful he called it to him and said : "If you are anxious, it is because you are wishing; for fear is a form of wishing, and you know you must not wish"—and so he went on. When he was near despair, when he said : "I cannot, all other men can except myself. Oh, that I never had heard that speech, that I had gone my way through life undisturbed, with my sorrow—and with my wish." Then he called upon his soul and said: "Now you are being crafty; for you say that you wish, and pretend that the speech was about something external, which one can wish, while you know that it is something internal, which one can only will; you delude yourself, for you say: 'All other men can, only not I,' and yet you know that that whereby other men can do it, is that in which they are absolutely identical with you, so that if it really is the truth that you can not do it, then neither can the others do it. So you betray not only your own case, but, insofar as it depends on you, the case of all men; and when you humbly exclude yourself from their number, then you slyly destroy their power!"

Then he went on. When he was then being slowly educated over a longer time under a schoolmaster, he was perhaps nearer to the faith. "Was being educated," as if it were another man who was doing it. Still this is not the case; it is only a misunderstanding, only an appearance. One man can do much for another man, but he cannot give him faith. We hear various stories in the world. One says: "My being what I am is my own work; I owe no man anything"; and he thinks it something to be proud of. Another says: "That distinguished man was my teacher, and I count it an honour to dare call myself his disciple"; and he believes it something to take pride in. We shall not decide how far such a speech is legitimate; but for it really to mean anything, it can only be applied to the specially gifted: those who either were inherently talented, or else so favoured that they could become disciples of the distinguished man. We, on the other hand, my hearers, we who were too insignificant to become disciples, what shall we say? If a man were to say: "When men rejected me, then I went to God; He became my schoolmaster, and this is my happiness, my joy, my pride," would this be less beautiful? And yet every man can say it, dares to say it, can say it in truth, and if he does not say it in truth, then it is not because the thought is not true, but because he distorts it. Every man dares say it. Whether his forehead was flattened almost like a beast's or arched more proudly than the heavens; whether his arm was outstretched to rule over kingdoms and countries, or to gather up the necessary gifts which fell from the rich man's table; whether his gesture was obeyed by thousands, or there was not a soul who paid attention to him; whether eloquence blossomed on his lips or only unintelligible sounds passed over them; whether he was the powerful man who defied the storm, or the defenceless woman who only sought shelter against the storm—it has nothing to do with the matter, my hearer, absolutely nothing. Every man dares say it when he has faith; for this is precisely the glory of faith. And you know it, my hearer, you do not become afraid when it is mentioned, as if it thereby took something from you, as if you first savoured its bliss in the moment of its departure. Or do you not know it? Alas! then were you very unfortunate. You could not grieve and say: "The giver of good gifts passed by my door"; you could not grieve and say: "The tempest and the storms took it from me"; for the giver of good gifts did not pass by your door; the tempest and the storm did not take it from you, for they could not do it.

So there was, then, a wish quite as that bewildered man had hoped for; he was no longer in distress. Yet there now appeared a new difficulty; for as he was wishing it, it became clear to him that that good could not be obtained through a wish; he could not even get it himself by wishing it, although this concerned him less, but neither could he give it to another by wishing it to him; only by himself willing it, could the other get it. So then it was again necessary to set him free, necessary to leave him to himself, his wish for him was as impotent as before. And yet this was not his intention. He wished to do everything for him; for when I wish a man something, I do not require his co-operation. The bewildered man had also considered it in this way. He would, as it were, say to the beloved: "Just be quiet and unconcerned, you have nothing at all to do except to be glad, satisfied, and happy with all the good things I shall wish you. I shall wish, I shall not grow weary of wishing; I shall move the all-bountiful God who bestows the good gifts, I shall move Him by my prayers; and so you shall have everything." And lo, as he mentioned the individual good things, they seemed to him so questionable that he dared not wish them for the other; when he finally found what he sought, what he might confidently wish for, lo, it was something that could not be wished.

He was again bewildered, again concerned, again ensnared in a difficulty. Is then the whole of life only a contradiction; can love not explain it, but only make it more difficult? That thought he could not endure; he must seek a way out. There must be something wrong in his love. Then he perceived that however much he had loved the other man, he still had loved him in the wrong way; for if it had been possible to procure for him all the good things, and also the highest good, faith, then he would by this very fact have made him into a more imperfect being. Then he found that life was beautiful, that it was a new glory in faith that no man can give it to another; but that what is highest, noblest, most sacred in man, that every man has; it is inherent in him, every man has it if he wills to have it; and this is the glory of faith, that it can only be had on this condition; therefore it is the only unfailing good, because it can only be had through being constantly acquired, and can only be acquired through being constantly developed.

The bewildered man was then reassured; but perhaps a change had taken place in him as well as in the one for whose welfare he was so concerned—in their relation to each other. They had become separated, in that one, so to speak, was established in his right, the other certain within his own limits. Their lives had become more significant than before, and yet they had become almost strangers to one another. His heart, which before was so rich in wishes, had now become poor; his hand, which formerly was so willing to help, had now learned to be quiet; for he knew he could not help. It was truth he had recognized, but this truth had not made him happy. So life is then a contradiction, the truth can not explain it, but can only make it more painful; for the more profoundly he recognized the truth, the more he felt himself separated, the more powerless in his relation to the other. And yet he could not wish that it was untrue, could not wish that he had remained unconscious of it, although it had separated them for all eternity, as death itself could not have separated them. This thought he was not able to endure; he must seek an explanation; and then he perceived that his relation to his friend had now acquired its true significance. "If I," said he, "with my wish or with my gift could present him with the highest good, then could I also take it from him, even if he need not fear this; aye, what is worse, if I could do this, then I should in the same moment that I gave it to him, take it from him; for in the fact that I gave him the highest good, I took the highest good from him; for the highest would be that he should give it to himself. Therefore I will thank God that this did not happen; my love has only lost its anxiety and gained gladness; for I know that with all my efforts I still should not have been able to preserve this good for him as certainly as he himself can keep it. He will not have to thank me for it, not because I set him free, but because he owes me nothing at all. Should I then be less glad with him, less glad that he now owns the most precious of all goods? Nay, I will only be the more happy; for if he owed it to me, it would disturb our relation. And if he is not in possession of it, then I can be very helpful to him; for I will accompany his thought, and urge him to perceive that it is the highest good, and I will prevent it from escaping into some hiding place where it might become obscure to him, whether he can understand it or not; with him I will penetrate every irregularity, until, if he does not have it, there is but a single expression which explains his failure—that he did not will it; this he cannot endure, then he will acquire it. On the other hand, I will praise the glory of faith to him, and as I assume that he possesses it, I bring him to will to own it. So to-day on the first day of the year, when the thought of the future tempts us with its manifold possibilities, I will show him that in faith he possesses the only power which can triumph over the future, I will speak to him about the expectation of faith."

My hearers, shall we not do the same, and according to the opportunities of this festal occasion, speak with one another about

THE EXPECTATION OF FAITH.

When we speak about the expectation of faith, we also speak about expectation in general; when we speak about expectation, then we naturally think of ourselves as talking to those who expect something. But those who have expectations are the happy and the successful. Are they then the proper persons to be addressed in these sacred places, and not rather the unsuccessful, those who have already made up their account with life and who expect nothing? Aye, the speech could well be addressed to them if our voice were capable of it. It could be said to them that it was a very wretched wisdom they had found, that it was easy enough to harden the heart; the pillow of sloth on which they would drowse away their lives in idleness could be taken away from them; it could be said that it was a proud distinction they had acquired in life, that while all other men—however successful or however troubled they had been in the world—were still always ready to recognize that God could indeed make up the reckoning, that while all other men confessed that on the day of judgment they would not be able to answer one to a thousand, they made it a condition that they should be in possession of a just demand on life which could not be redeemed, a demand which in its time would make the reckoning difficult enough—but not for them. They might be addressed thus; still we prefer to speak to those who still expect something.

As the number of those who expect something always constitutes the majority of the world, so too their expectations can be so various that it is very difficult to mention all of them. Yet all of them have one expectation in common, that they all expect some future; for expectation and the future are inseparable thoughts. He who expects something is preoccupied with the future. But to occupy himself with it, is perhaps not right. The complaint which is often heard, that men forget the present in their preoccupation with the future, is perhaps well founded. We shall not deny that this has happened in the world, even if more seldom in our time, but neither shall we fail to recall that it is precisely man's greatness, the proof of his divine heritage, that he can occupy himself with the future; for if there were no future, neither would there have been a past, and if there were neither past nor future, then would man be enslaved like the beasts, his head bent toward the earth, his soul ensnared in the service of the moment.

In that sense one might not, indeed, wish to live for the present; nor in that sense might one have meant it when he recommended the present as the great thing. But where shall we set our limits, how much do we dare to occupy ourselves with the future? The answer is not difficult: until we have conquered it, until we are able to return to the present, until our life finds significance therein. Still it is indeed an impossibility; the future is everything, the present is a part of it; how could we have conquered the whole before we have even reached the first part of it; how return from this victory to that which went before? Is it not so; is it an ill-timed difficulty the thought raises? By no means. It is precisely as here stated; for we dare not commend every occupation with the future. He who absolutely relinquishes it, becomes only in an unworthy sense strong in the present; he who does not conquer it, has one enemy more who will make him weak in the fight against the present. Consequently, not until he has conquered the future does his present life become sound and strong.

The fact of being able to occupy himself with the future is then an indication of man's nobility; the conflict with it is most ennobling. He who strives with the present strives with a single thing against which he can use his entire strength. If therefore a man had nothing else to strive against, it would be possible for him to go victoriously through life without learning to know himself or his own strength. He who fights with the future has a more dangerous enemy, he can never remain ignorant about himself; for he fights with himself. The future is not; it borrows its strength from the man himself, and when it has tricked him out of this, then it appears outside of him as the enemy he must meet. Let a man then be as strong as he will, no man is stronger than himself. Therefore we frequently see those who in life conquered in every battle; when it was a future enemy they had to deal with, they became powerless, their arms paralyzed. While they were perhaps accustomed to challenge the whole world to battle, they had now met an enemy, a vague figure, who was able to terrify them. Therefore, perhaps frequently the men whom God called to be tested in battle went from a worse fight into that battle which to men seemed so terrible; perhaps they sometimes smiled in the heat of conflict when they considered the invisible fight which had taken place before. They were admired in the world, because people thought they had conquered in the most dangerous fight, and yet that fight seemed to them like a childish game in comparison with the fight which had gone before, which no man saw. It would naturally be true that he who is stronger than others conquers in the conflict with these; but it is also natural that no man is stronger than himself. When a man strives with the future, then he learns that however strong he is compared with the rest, there is one enemy who is stronger, that is himself; one enemy he cannot conquer by himself, that is himself.

Yet why describe this conflict with the future as so dangerous? "Whether old or young, we have all of us had some experience, the future is not entirely new; for there is nothing new under the sun; the future is the past. Old or young, we have all had experience, we will put it on, we will follow the trail of conjecture and the guidance of the supposition; by the power of the conclusion will we overcome it, and thus armed go confidently forth to meet the future." And it is indeed well that a man be armed when he goes into a conflict; still better that he be armed according to the nature of the conflict. If a man who would compete on the running-track were to put on heavy armour, he would indeed be armed, but his armour would scarcely be advantageous to him. Is not the case the same in the matter of equipment for one who would strive with the future? For experience as a friend has a double tongue which says now one thing, now another; and guessing is a deceitful guide who deserts one when one needs him most, and the supposition is a vague glance which does not look very far, and the conclusion is a sling wherein a man more often catches himself than the other. In addition, those weapons are difficult to use; for with guessing goes fear, with conjecture apprehension, with the conclusion disquiet, since the questing soul does not remain unmoved by the experience. So we might be well-armed when we had put on experience, but not for the kind of conflict we go to meet, the conflict with the future; we sought to transform this into something present, something individual; but the future is not an individual part but the whole.

How should we then go to meet the future? When the sailor is out upon the sea, when everything is changing about him, when the waves are constantly born and die, then he does not stare down into the depths of these, for they change. He looks up at the stars : and why? Because they are faithful; as they stand now, they stood for the patriarchs, and will stand for the coming generations. By what means does he then conquer the changing conditions? Through the eternal. Through the eternal can one conquer the future, because the eternal is the foundation of the future; therefore through this one can understand that. What then is the eternal power in man? It is faith. What is the expectation of faith? Victory, or as the Scriptures have so earnestly and so movingly taught us, it is that all things must work together for good to those that love God. But an expectation of the future which expects victory has indeed conquered the future. The believer is therefore done with the future before he begins on the present; for what one has conquered no longer has power to disturb one, and this victory can only make one more powerful for the present.

Then the expectation of faith is victory! The glad heart which had not yet tasted of life's adversities, which was not educated in the school of sorrow, which was not shaped by the dubious wisdom of experience, assists this expectation with all its might; for it expects victory in everything, in every conflict and exertion, or rather, it expects to conquer without conflict. We would not choose to be the austere figure which would halt the young on his way; we would rather be considered as a consolation to him when he has learned that this expectation, however beautiful it was, was still not the expectation of faith; we would rather be the one who should call him to the conflict when he feels himself powerless; rather be the one who will let victory beckon to him when he believes everything lost. On the other hand, the troubled one, who has scarcely dried his tears over the present loss, pictures the future differently, and that future is indeed light and ephemeral, more flexible than any sickle; so everyone fashions it according to the way he himself is fashioned. The troubled one does not expect victory, he has felt his loss too keenly; and even if it happened in the past, he still keeps it with him; he expects that the future will at least grant him peace for the quiet occupation with his pain.

The experienced man disapproves of both modes of conduct. When one has almost every good one could desire, then one ought to be prepared to have the troubles of life also visit the home of the fortunate; when one has lost everything, then one ought to consider that time conceals much precious healing power for the sick soul; that the future, like a loving mother, also conceals good gifts. In success a man ought, to a certain degree, to be prepared for failure; in failure, to a certain degree, for success. And the counsel of the man of experience is not in vain; for both the one who was happy, if he was not thoughtless, and the troubled man, if he was not in despair, will readily heed his words; both will willingly arrange their lives according to his advice. The successful man inspects the goods he possesses. Some of them he thinks he could lose without pain; others are such that he could easily recover from the pain of their loss. Only one single good he can not lose without losing his gladness, he cannot lose it to a certain degree without losing it absolutely, and with it his joy. He will then be prepared to lose his goods, and in this way he is, according to the advice of the man of experience, prepared for a certain degree of misfortune. Still the experienced man said : to a certain degree. This word might also apply to that one good he could not lose without losing his happiness; not lose to a certain degree without losing it entirely. The man of experience will not interpret his words, he repeats them unchanged, unshakable; he leaves the explanation and the application to the one whom they would guide. So then the successful man, no less than the troubled one, becomes bewildered. This expression : to a certain degree, which should set them free, becomes the binding power which ensnares them, and the word continues to sound, shows no sympathy, is not concerned about their strenuous efforts to understand it, pays no attention to their prayers for an explanation. The experience which should guide them, gives birth to doubt; the experienced man's advice was questionable advice.

On the contrary, the believer says: "I expect victory." Nor is this a vain speech. For both the fortunate man who was not thoughtless and the troubled man who was not in despair will readily listen to his words. Gladness returns again to the glad heart, victory is its expectation, victory in every conflict, in every temptation; for experience taught that there might be talk about a conflict. Still by the help of faith it expects victory in everything; only for a moment does it pause: "It is too much," it says, "it is impossible, life cannot be so glorious; however rich youth was in its extreme happiness, this is even more than the most joyous hope of youth." Aye, it is certainly more than the gladdest hope of youth, and yet it is so, even if not quite as you think. You speak about many victories, but faith expects only one, or rather, it expects victory. If there was a man who had heard of a belief which was able to give everyone the thing he needed, and he were to say: "That is impossible—all the necessities for a man, as now for me, all the much which I need"; then would the one who referred him to the Holy Scriptures, rightly dare to testify about them, that he would find in them the thing needed, but the seeker would find that it did not turn out quite as he had expected. The Scriptures say: "One thing is needful." So too with faith; when you speak about many victories you are like one who talks about many things being needed. Only one thing is needful, and faith expects victory.

But it expects victory, and therefore it is glad and confident, and why should it not be since it expects victory! Still I am sensible of a voice which you also know well, my hearer. It says: "This is good to listen to, these are great words and agreeable modes of speech, but truly the earnestness of life teaches something different." What then did life's earnestness teach you, you who speak in this way? Is it not true that it taught you that your wishes would not be fulfilled, your yearnings not sated, your cravings not heeded, your desires not satisfied? It taught you this, all this, of which we do not speak at all; and in addition it taught you with deceitful lips to come to men's assistance, to suck faith and confidence out of their hearts, to do this in the sacred name of earnestness. Why did it teach you this? Could it not have taught you something else?

When two men learn different things from life, it may be because they experienced it differently; but it can also arise from the fact that they themselves were different. If two children were brought up together and shared everything in common, so that if one was singled out for commendation, the other was also; if one was rebuked, the other was likewise; if one was punished, the other was also; still it would be true that they might learn absolutely different things. For the one might learn, whenever it was commended, not to become proud; every time it was rebuked to humble itself under the admonition; every time it was punished to profit by the suffering. The other might learn, when it was commended, to become arrogant; when it was rebuked, to harbour resentment; whenever it was punished to store up secret anger. So also with you. If you had loved men, then perhaps life's earnestness had taught you not to be vociferous, but to be silent, and when you were in distress like one at sea, and saw no land, then at least not to drag others into your distress. Perhaps it taught you to smile, at least as long as you believed that someone sought an explanation, a testimony in your appearance. Life might then perhaps have afforded you the melancholy gladness of seeing others succeed where you had not succeeded; the consolation that you had gained through stifling the shriek of anguish in your heart, so that it might not be disturbing to others. Why did you not learn this?

Since you did not learn it, we cannot pay attention to what you say. We are not judging you because you doubt; for doubt is a cunning passion, and it may well be very difficult to free one's self from its snares. What we do demand of the doubter is that he shall be silent. He certainly realized that doubt did not make him happy; why then confide to others what will make them equally unhappy? And what does he gain by telling them? He loses himself, and makes others unhappy. He loses himself, whereas by keeping silent he might perhaps have found peace, had he preferred quietly to bear his pain in solitude rather than to become noisily important in the sight of men by coveting the honour and distinction so many desire—of doubting, or at least of having doubted. Doubt is a profound and cunning passion, but he whose soul it did not grip so intensely that he became speechless, only falsely imputes this passion to himself; what he says, therefore, is not only untrue in itself, but especially so on his lips. Consequently, we pay no attention to him.

The expectation of faith, then, is victory. The doubt which comes from without does not disturb it; for it dishonours itself by speaking. Still doubt is crafty. In its secret way it sneaks about a man, and when faith expects victory, then it whispers that this expectation is a delusion. "An expectation whose time and place are not determined, is only an illusion; thus one can always continue to expect; such an expectation is an enchanted circle from which the soul cannot escape." Certainly the soul, in the expectation of faith, is prevented from falling out of itself into the manifold; it remains in itself; but it would be the greatest evil which could befall a man if he escaped from this circle. From this it by no means follows that the expectation of faith is a delusion. It is true that he who expects something in particular, may be disappointed; but this does not happen to the believer. When the world begins its sharp testing, when the storms of life snap the vigorous expectation of youth, when existence, which seems so loving and so gentle, transforms itself into a merciless proprietor who demands everything back, everything which he gave so that he could take it back, then the believer looks with sadness and pain at himself and at life, but he still says: "There is an expectation which all the world can not take from me; it is the expectation of faith, and this is victory. I am not deceived; for what the world seemed to promise me, that promise I still did not believe that it would keep; my expectation was not in the world, but in God. This expectation is not deceived; even in this moment I feel its victory more gloriously and more joyfully than all the pain of loss. If I lost this expectation, then would everything be lost. Now I have still conquered, conquered through my expectation, and my expectation is victory."

Was it not so in life? If there was a man to whom you felt yourself so strongly attracted that you dared say : I trust him, is it not true that when everything went in accordance with your wish, or if not entirely so, yet so that you could easily bring it into agreement with your ideas, then you trusted him, as others also trusted him; but when the inexplicable happened, the incomprehensible, then the others fell away, or rather (not to confuse the language) they showed that they never had trusted him? Not so with you. You felt that it was not on the fact that you could explain what happened, that you had based your faith; for then it would have been based on your insight, and far from being resignation, it would rather have been self-confidence. It seemed to you that it would be a disgrace to give it up; for as you had believed that these words from your mouth : I trust him, had signified something different from their meaning when others said them, so you felt it impossible that the change could bring you to act as did the others, unless your faith originally had not signified more than theirs. You continued to trust. Perhaps you did wrong in doing so; not in trusting, not in trusting in this way, but in trusting a man in this way. Perhaps the inexplicable was easily explained; perhaps there was a distressing certainty that witnessed so strongly that your belief became only a beautiful conceit that you ought rather to give up. We do not know. Still we do know this, that if in this faith you forgot that there was a higher faith, then it was, in spite of its beauty, only a means of perdition to you. If, on the other hand, you put your faith in God, how could your faith then ever be changed into a beautiful conceit which you ought rather to relinquish? Could He be changed with whom there is no variableness, neither shadow of turning? Should He not be faithful, through whom every man who is so is faithful? Should not He be without deceit in whom you yourself had faith? Could there ever be an explanation which could explain anything other than that He is truthful and keeps His promises? And yet we see that men forget this.

When everything succeeds for them, when they see good days, when in a wonderful manner they feel themselves in harmony with everything about them, then they believe; in their gladness they do not always forget to thank God; for every man will readily be thankful for the good he receives, but every man's heart is also weak enough to wish to determine for itself what the good is. When everything changes, when sorrow replaces gladness, then they fall away, they lose their faith, or rather, for let us not confuse the language, they show that they never had it. Do not behave in this way, my hearer. When you caught yourself being changed by everything changing about you, then you said : " I confess that now I see that what I called my faith was only a delusion. That the highest one man can do in his relation to another is to believe him; that what is even higher, more beautiful and more blessed than language can describe—to believe God—that I have presumptuously imagined myself to have done; to all the rest of my gladness I have also added this; and yet my faith, as I now see, was only a fleeting emotion, a reflection of my earthly happiness. But I will not edify myself by presumptuous, meaningless speech; I will not say that I have lost faith, will not lay the blame upon the world, nor upon men, nor even accuse God." In this way, my hearer, you sought to halt yourself when you would go astray in sorrow; you did not harden your heart; you were not foolish enough to wish to imagine that if particular things had not happened, then you would have preserved your faith, nor wretched enough to wish to seek fellowship with this wisdom. Lo, therefore you won, even if slowly, again to the expectation of faith. Then when you failed in everything, when what you had slowly built up was blown away in a moment, and you must toilsomely begin again from the beginning; when your arm was weak, your step wavering, then you still held fast to your expectation of faith, which is victory. You did not even reveal it to others lest they mock you, because in all your wretchedness you still expected victory, in your inmost heart you still hid your expectation. "The joyful days are indeed able to embellish my faith," you said. "I adorn it with the garlands of gladness, but prove it I cannot; the gloomy times can indeed bring tears to the eyes and sorrow to the heart, but they still cannot deprive me of my faith." And even if the adversity continued, your soul became gentle. "It is still beautiful," you said, "that God will not thus appear to me in the visible things; we were separated in order to meet again; I still could not wish always to be a child, who every day requires proofs, signs, and wonderful deeds. If I continued to be a child, then I could not love with all my might and with all my soul. Now we are separated, we do not meet daily, only secretly we meet in the triumphant moment of believing expectation."

The expectation of faith is then victory, and this expectation cannot be disappointed unless a man disappoints himself by depriving himself of expectation; like the one who foolishly supposed that he had lost faith, or foolishly supposed that some individual had taken it from him; or like the one who sought to delude himself with the idea that there was some special power which could deprive a man of his faith; who found satisfaction in the vain thought that this was precisely what had happened to him, found joy in frightening others with the assurance that some such power did exist that made sport of the noblest in a man, and empowered the one who was thus tested to ridicule others.

Yet perhaps one or another says: "This speech is in-

deed coherent and consistent; but through it one gets no
farther, and in so far it is a foolish and meaningless speech."
One gets no farther. Could a man then wish to get farther
than to conquer? Then he must also lose the victory.
Would it be so foolish and insignificant a thing for a man
really to become conscious of whether he had faith or not?
But when I say : I believe, then it can only too often be
very obscure to me what I really mean by that. Perhaps I
am mistaken, perhaps I am only creating a conception
about the future; perhaps I am wishing, hoping, perhaps
longing for something, desiring, coveting; perhaps I am
certain about the future, and when I am, it seems to me
that I believe, although I really do not. On the other
hand if I confront myself with the question : Do you
expect victory? then every obscurity becomes more difficult. Then I perceive that not only does he not believe
who expects absolutely nothing, but also he who expects
some special thing, or he who bases his expectation on
something special. And should this not be of importance,
since not until a man is finished with the future can he be
entirely and undividedly in the present? But only by
conquering it, is one finished with the future, and faith
does exactly this, for its expectation is victory. Every time
then that I catch my soul not expecting victory, I know
that I do not believe; when I know that, then I know too
what I have to do; for it is by no means an easy matter to
believe. The first condition for my coming to believe, is
that I become conscious of whether I do believe or not.
For that reason we so often fall into error because we look
for an assurance of our expectation, instead of an assurance of faith that we believe. The believer demands no
proof for his expectation : " for," he says, " if I could
assume something to be a proof, then, when it proved my
expectation, it would also disprove it. My soul is not
insensible to the joy or pain of the individual, but, God be
praised, it is not thus that the individual can prove or disprove the expectation of faith. God be praised! Nor can
time prove or disprove it; for faith expects an eternity.

And to-day on the first day of the year, when the thought about the future thrusts itself upon me, I will not satiate my soul with various expectations, nor dissipate it in manifold ideas; I will rally it, and, sound and happy, if possible, go forth to meet the future. It brings what it will and must bring; many expectations disappointed, many fulfilled, so it will happen, as experience has taught me; but there is an expectation which will not be disappointed; experience has not taught me this, nor has it authority to deny it; it is the expectation of faith, and this is victory."

There is a little word sufficiently familiar to the congregations even if not always heeded by them; little and insignificant it seems, and yet so rich in content; quiet and yet so moving, calm and yet so filled with longing. It is the word : at last; for many of the sacred collects which are read in our churches end in this way : " and at last be saved." The older man among us, who stands almost at the end, looks back in his thought over the way he has travelled; he remembers the course of events; the shadowy figures from the past again become living before him; he is overwhelmed by the varied content of what he has lived to see; he is weary and he says : " and so at last be saved." The younger, who even now stands at the beginning of the way, looks ahead in thought over the long road. In thought he experiences what is to come : the painful bereavements, the quiet concerns, the sad longings, the fearful anxieties; he is wearied at the thought and says : " and so at last be saved." It would indeed be a great gift if a man could rightly use this word; but no man learns this from another, but severally only from and through God. Therefore will we commit to Thee, Father in heaven, our heart and our thought, so that our soul may never be so ensnared by the joys of life or by its sorrows, that it forgets this liberating word; but so that it may not too often be impatience and inner disquiet which bring this word to our lips; so that when, like a faithful friend, it has accompanied us through all the many relations of life, has accommodated itself to us, yet without being false to itself, has been our consolation, our hope, our gladness, our cause of rejoicing; has sounded to us solemnly and inspiringly, softly and soothingly; has spoken to us warningly and admonishingly, cheerfully and invitingly; that then our soul in its last hour may be carried away from the world on this word, as it were, to that place where we shall understand its full significance. So we may understand that the same God who by His hand led us through the world, now withdraws it and opens His embrace to receive the longing soul. Amen.

II

EVERY GOOD AND EVERY PERFECT GIFT IS FROM ABOVE

Every good gift and every perfect gift is from above, and cometh down from the Father of lights, with whom is no variableness, neither shadow of turning. Of his own will begat he us with the word of truth, that we should be a kind of first fruits of his creatures. Wherefore, my beloved brethren, let every man be swift to hear, slow to speak, slow to wrath: for the wrath of man worketh not the righteousness of God. Wherefore lay apart all filthiness and superfluity of naughtiness, and receive with meekness the engrafted word, which is able to save your souls.

James 1:17-22

Every good and every perfect gift is from above and cometh down from the Father of lights, with whom is no variableness, neither shadow of turning. These words are so beautiful, so eloquent, so moving, that it was certainly not the fault of the words if they found no entrance to the listener's ear, no echo in his heart. They are by an apostle of the Lord, and in so far as we ourselves have not felt their significance more deeply, we still dare have confidence that they are not loose and idle words, not a graceful expression for an airy thought, but that they are faithful and unfailing, tested and proved, as was the life of the apostle who wrote them. They are said not incidentally but with special emphasis, not in passing but accompanied by an earnest admonition : Do not err, my beloved brethren. We dare then set our confidence in their having not only power to lift up the soul, but also strength to sustain it, these words which sustained an apostle through a stormy life. They are spoken in connection with other words; it is in order to warn against the fearful error of believing that God would tempt a man, in order to warn against the foolishness of a heart that would tempt God,

45

that the apostle says : Do not err, my beloved brethren. We dare then assure ourselves that the word is also mighty in explaining the folly, mighty in halting the erring thought.

Every good and every perfect gift is from above, and cometh down from the Father of lights, with whom is no variableness, neither shadow of turning. These words are again and again repeated in the world, and yet many go on as if they had never heard them, and it would perhaps have affected them disturbingly if they had heard them. Carelessly they go on their way, a friendly fate makes everything so easy for them, every wish is fulfilled, all their undertakings are successful. Without knowing how it comes about, they are in the midst of the life movement, a link in the chain which connects a future with a past. Unconcerned about how it happened they are borne along on the wave of the present. Resting in the natural law that lets a human life develop in the world in the same way that it spreads a carpet of flowers over the earth, they live happy and satisfied amid the changes of life, wishing at no moment to extricate themselves from it, giving everyone his honest due : thanksgiving to the one to whom they ascribe the good gifts; help to the needy in the way they believe is useful to him. That there are good and perfect gifts they know well; they also know whence these come; for the earth gives its increase, and heaven sends the early and the late rain, and family and friends consider it best for them; and their plans, wise and intelligent, succeed as is natural since they are wise and intelligent. For them life holds no riddle, and yet their life is a riddle, a dream, and the apostle's earnest admonition : Do not err, does not make them pause; they have no time to pay attention to it nor to the words, any more than the wave gives heed as to whence it comes or whither it goes. Or if some individuals among them, considering higher things, gave heed to the apostle's words, they would soon be through with them. They let their thought for a moment occupy itself with the words, and then they said : " Now we have understood them, bring us some new thoughts which we have not understood." Nor would they have been wrong; for the apostle's words are not difficult, and yet they proved thereby, in that after having understood them they wished to abandon them, that they had not understood them.

Every good and every perfect gift is from above, and cometh down from the Father of lights, with whom is no variableness, neither shadow of turning. These words are so soothing, so comforting, and yet how many were there who really understood how to suck the rich nourishment from them, how to appropriate them! Those concerned, those whom life did not permit to grow up and who died as babes, those whom it did not suckle on the milk of prosperity, but who were early weaned from it; the sorrowing, whose thought attempted to penetrate through the changing to the permanent—those were conscious of the apostle's word and gave attention to them. The more completely they could sink their souls in them, could forget everything in them, the more they felt themselves strengthened and made confident. Still it soon appeared that this strength was a delusion; no matter how much confidence they gained, they still did not gain the strength to comprehend life; sometimes the troubled mind and the bewildered thought resorted again to that rich consolation, sometimes they felt again the contradiction. At last perhaps it seemed to them that these words were almost dangerous to their peace of mind. They awakened a confidence in them which was constantly being disappointed. They gave them wings which could indeed lift them up to God, but which could not help them in their walk through life. They did not deny the inexhaustible comfort of the words, but they almost feared this comfort even when they praised it. If a man owned a magnificent jewel, a jewel which he never denied was magnificent, he might take it out from time to time, and rejoice over it; but soon he would say : I cannot adorn myself with this for daily use, and the festal occasions on which it would really be appropriate, I wait for in vain. So then he would put the jewel away, and would sadly consider the fact that he owned such a jewel, but that life gave him no opportunity to find happiness in displaying it.

So they sat in their quiet sorrow; they did not harden themselves against the consolation of the word; they were humble enough to acknowledge that life is a dark saying, and as in their thought they were swift to listen to see if there might be an explanatory word, so were they also slow to speak and slow to wrath. They did not presume to give up the word; they longed only for the opportune hour to come. If that came, then they would be saved. Such was their belief. And it might happen, you said, my hearer. Or is there only a spirit who bears witness in heaven, but not spirit who bears witness on earth? Heaven only knows, and the spirit which flees from earth, that God is good; the earthly life knows nothing about it! Is there then no mutual harmony between what happens in heaven and what happens on the earth? Is there joy in heaven, only sorrow on earth, or is it only said that there is joy in heaven? Does God in heaven take the good gifts and hide them for us in heaven so that we may some time receive them in the next world? Perhaps you spoke in this way in your heart's bewilderment. You did not demand that for your sake there should be given signs and wonderful manifestations, you did not childishly demand that every one of your wishes should be fulfilled; only you begged for a testimony early and late; for your troubled soul treasured a wish. If this were fulfilled, then everything would be well; then would your thanks and your praise be unceasing, then would the festal occasion come, then would you with all your heart bear testimony to the word, that every good and every perfect gift comes from above. But lo, that was denied you; and your soul became restive, tossed about by the passionate wish. It became defiant and angry. You did not impatiently cast off the leading-strings of humility, you had not forgotten that you are on earth and God in heaven. With humble prayers and burning desires you sought, as it were, to tempt God : This wish is so important to me; my joy, my peace, my future, all depend on this; for me it is so very important, for God it is so easy; for He is all-powerful. But the wish was not fulfilled. Vainly you sought rest; you left nothing untried in your unfruitful restlessness; you ascended the dizzy heights of anticipation to see if a possibility might not appear. If you believed that you saw such a possibility, then you were immediately ready with prayers, that by the help of these you might create the actual from the apparent. Still it was an illusion. You descended again, and gave yourself up to the stupefying exhaustion of sorrow, while time went on as it always does. And the morning came, and the evening, but the day you desired did not dawn. And still you made every effort, you prayed early and late, more and more fervently, more and more temptingly. Alas, it still did not come to pass ! And you gave up, you would dispose your soul to patience, you would wait in quiet longing, if only your soul might be assured that eternity would bring you your wish, bring you that which was the delight of your eyes and your heart's desire. Alas, this certainty too was denied you. But when the busy thoughts had worked themselves weary, when the fruitless wishes had exhausted your soul, then perhaps your being became more quiet, then perhaps your heart, secretly and unnoticed, had developed in itself the meekness which received the word which was implanted in you, and which was able to save your soul, that every good and perfect gift cometh from above.

Then you acknowledged in all humility that God had certainly not deceived you, since He accepted your earthly wishes and foolish desires, exchanged them for you, and gave you instead heavenly consolation and holy thoughts; that He did not treat you unfairly when He denied you your wish, but for compensation created this faith in your heart; when instead of the wish, which even if it could do everything, was at most able to give you the whole world; He gave you a faith through which you gained God and overcame the whole world. Then you recognized with humble gladness that God was still the almighty Creator of heaven and earth, who had not only created the world out of nothing, but had done the even more miraculous—out of your impatient and unstable heart He had created the incorruptible essence of a quiet spirit. Then ashamed you confessed that it was good, so very good for you, that God had not permitted Himself to be tempted; then you understood the apostle's admonition, and its relation to the error that wishes to tempt God. Then you perceived how foolish your conduct had been. You wished that God's ideas about what was profitable to you might be your ideas, but you also wished that He might be the almighty Creator of heaven and earth, so that He might rightly fulfil your wish. And yet if He were to share your ideas, then must He cease to be the almighty Father. You would in your childish impatience, as it were, corrupt God's eternal Being, and you were blind enough to delude yourself, as if it helped you if God in heaven did not know better what was profitable to you than you yourself; as if you would not sometime discover with terror that you had wished what no man would be able to bear if it came to pass. For let us for a moment speak foolishly and with human wisdom. If there was a man in whom you rightly had confidence, because you believed he wished for your welfare; but you had one conception about what would be advantageous to you, he another—is it not true, you would then seek to persuade him, you would perhaps beg and adjure him, to fulfil your wish; but if he continued to deny you, you would cease to beg him, you would say: If now I influenced him by my prayers to do what he does not regard as right, then it would be even more terrible that I had been weak enough to make him equally weak, since then I should have lost him and my confidence in him, even if, in a moment of intoxication, I had called his weakness affection.

Or perhaps this was not the case with you; you were perhaps too old to cherish childish conceptions about God, too mature to think humanly about Him; you would perhaps influence Him by your defiance. That life was a dark saying you readily confessed, but you were not, in accordance with the apostle's warning, swift to hear whether there might be an explanatory word; you were, contrary to his admonition, swift to wrath. If life is a dark saying, then let it be so, you would not concern yourself about the explanation—and your heart was hardened. Your appearance was perhaps calm, perhaps friendly, your speech even benevolent, but in your heart, in the secret workshop of your thoughts, you said—no, you did not say it, but you heard a voice which said : God does tempt a man. And the coldness of despair chilled your spirit, and its death brooded over your heart. If sometimes life again stirred within you, then there raged wild voices, voices which did not belong to you, but which still sounded from within you. For why was your complaint so violent, why was your shriek so penetrating, why were even your prayers so challenging? Or was it not because you believed that your sufferings were so great, your sorrows so crushing, and because of this your complaint so just, your voice so mighty, that it must resound through heaven, and call God forth from His hidden depths, where, as it seemed to you, He sat calm and indifferent, paying no attention to the world and its fate? But heaven is closed to such presumptuous speech, and it is written that God is tempted of no man. Impotent was your speech, impotent as your thought, as your arm was impotent; and heaven did not hear your prayer. But, then, when you humbled yourself under God's powerful hand and, crushed in spirit, groaned : " By God, my God, great is my sin, greater than can be forgiven," then heaven again opened, then did God, as a prophet writes, look down upon you from the window of heaven and say : Yet a little while; yet a little while, and I will renew the forms of earth—and lo, your form was renewed, and God's merciful grace had produced in your barren heart the meekness which receives the word. Then you humbly acknowledged before God that God tempts no man, but that everyone is tempted when he is seduced and drawn away by his own desires, just as you were tempted by proud and arrogant and defiant thoughts. Then you were terrified at your error in thinking that the idea that God tempts a man could make life inexplicable; for then life would become to you a dark saying, as you listened to this explanation, which, as you must confess, simply made everything inexplicable. Then you acknowledged, humbled and ashamed, that it was well that God did not allow Himself to be tempted, that He was the almighty God, able to crush every presumptuous thought; well that you, in your despair, should not have found an explanation of life's dark saying which any man would be able to insist upon.

Every good and every perfect gift is from above, and cometh down from the Father of lights, with whom is no variableness, neither shadow of turning. These words are so comprehensible, so simple, and yet how many were there who rightly understood them, rightly understood that they were a badge of honour, more glorious than all the treasures of the earth, but that they were also small change, useful in the daily relationships of life?

"Every good and every perfect gift is from God." The apostle uses two expressions. "Every good gift," he says, and indicates thereby the inmost nature of the gift, that it is a sound and blessed fruit which hides no unsound and injurious decay within itself. "Every perfect gift," says the apostle, and indicates thereby the closer relation in which the good gift, through God's assistance, stands to the particular man who accepts it, so that what is good in itself does not become a detriment and a loss to him. These two expressions are analogous to two others. "The gift is from above, and comes down from the Father of lights." "It is from above," says the apostle, and in this way he directs the believer's thought up toward heaven where everything good has its home, the blessing that satisfies the mouth, and the one which satisfies the heart; up to heaven from which the good spirits issue forth for the deliverance of men; up to heaven from which the good intentions return as heavenly gifts. "From the Father of lights," says the apostle, and means thereby that God with His eternal clarity penetrates everything, so that He understands the thoughts of men from afar, and knows clearly all their ways; that His eternal love hastens forward and prepares everything, and thus makes the "good gift" into a "perfect gift." For God in heaven is not like a man who, if he had a good gift to give, still gave it in darkness and in uncertainty, glad indeed because it was a good gift and he a glad giver, but also sorrowful because he did not know whether it actually became a good gift for the other or not. "Every good and perfect gift," says the apostle; "every," what does this mean? Does the apostle mean by this that the firmament of heaven is a great store-room, and that all the things which heaven contains are good gifts? Does he mean that God brings things out from this rich store, and sends them, according to time and opportunity now and then, sometimes to one, sometimes to another, to the one many, to another fewer, to a particular individual nothing at all, but that what He sends is good and perfect? Let us notice the words which follow: "with whom is no variableness, neither shadow of turning." If the apostle had wished to express this, then in place of this word he would have added: from the God of love, the God of mercy and consolation, the Giver of good gifts, or however else he would have expressed it, better and more emphatically than we are able to do; he would next have admonished the believers to thanksgiving according to time and opportunity, in proportion to the good gifts bestowed upon them. He did not do this. He did warn against the error of thinking that God would tempt a man, the error of believing that God would allow Himself to be tempted. That which he emphasizes is that God is constant, that He remains the same while everything else changes; that which he admonishes us to do is to love God, so that our being may come into likeness with His own, in order that we may win God in constancy, and save our souls in patience. He says nothing in this word about the quality of the particular gifts, but he speaks about God's eternal relation to the believer. When gladness explains life, and everything is delightful and clear, then he warns against this explanation, and admonishes us to refer it to the Father of lights, with whom is no variableness, nor shadow of turning. When sorrow casts its shadow over our lives, when despondency veils our sight, when the clouds of anxiety take God away from before our eyes, then sounds the apostolic warning, that with God there is no shadow of turning. That which the apostle warns against is the disturbing of God's blessed Being through the unrest of temptation, as if His heart had either become cold or weak. That which he emphasizes is that as God's all-powerful hand made everything good, so He, the Father of lights, still constant, makes everything good in every moment, everything into a good and perfect gift for everyone who has the heart to humble himself, heart enough to be confident.

Still doubt is cunning and wily, by no means vociferous and defiant, as it is sometimes claimed to be; it is unobtrusive and crafty, not impudent and arrogant, and the more unassuming it is, the more dangerous it is. It does not deny that those words are beautiful, nor that they are comforting. If it did this, then would the heart rebel against it; it merely says that the words are difficult, almost mysterious. It wishes to help the troubled mind to understand the apostolic saying, that every good and every perfect gift is from God. "What does this mean? What else than that everything which comes from God is a good and a perfect gift, and that everything which is a good and perfect gift is from God." This explanation is so simple and so natural, and yet doubt has cunningly hidden itself within it. It continues therefore: "Consequently, for a man in his lifetime to be able to find peace in these words, he must either be able to determine what it is which comes from God, or what may rightly and in truth be called a good and perfect gift. But how is this possible? Is then every human life a continuous chain of miracles? Or is it possible for a man's understanding to make its way through the interminable ranks of derived causes and effects, to penetrate all the intervening events, and thus find God? Is it possible for a man's understanding to determine with certainty what constitutes for him a good and perfect gift? Is it not stranded again and again on this? How often has mankind, how often has every individual man, learned by painful experience that to wish to venture on what had been denied to man is a folly that will not go unpunished?" Thus doubt was ready with an explanation of the meaning of the words, and also ready with words. It had changed the apostolic exhortation into mere words that passed from mouth to mouth, without sense or meaning. It was modest enough not to demand that the words should be erased or consigned to eternal oblivion; it tore them out of the heart, and left them on the lips.

Could it be this way, my hearer? Was an apostle of the Lord perhaps not responsible for these words? Were perhaps those spiritual hosts beneath heaven responsible for them? Was there a curse which rested upon them, so that they should be homeless in the world, and find no dwelling place in the heart of man? Was it their intention to confuse men? Is it not possible to check these anxious meditations in which the thought exhausts itself, and yet never makes any progress? Was it still perhaps true that God does tempt a man, if in no other way, then by preaching a word whose only effect is to confuse his thought?

The apostle Paul says : "All of God's creation is good, if it is received with thankfulness." It is principally in order to warn against an earthly prudence which would enslave the believer in the service of ceremonial, that the apostle says these words. Meantime, what is the apostle doing? He is raising the believer's mind above earthly and finite concerns, above worldly prudence and doubt, by a godly reflection that one ought always to thank God. For the thanksgiving the apostle speaks about is not the gratitude which is offered by one man to another; and those teachers of false doctrines believed, too, that the believers, by transgressing ceremony, sinned against God. Would not the same hold true of every man's relation to God, that every gift is a good and perfect gift when it is received with thanksgiving?

Is it not true, my hearer, that you interpreted those apostolic words in this manner, and you were not perplexed as to what was a good and perfect gift, or whether it came from God? For, you said, every gift is good when it is received with thanksgiving from the hand of God, and from God comes every good and every perfect gift. You did not anxiously ask what it is which comes from God. You said gladly and confidently: this, for which I thank God. You did not concern your mind with reflections on what constitutes a good and a perfect gift; for you said confidently, I know it is that for which I thank God, and therefore I thank Him for it. You interpreted the apostolic word; as your heart developed, you did not ask to learn much from life; you wished to learn only one thing: always to thank God, and thereby learn to understand one thing: that all things serve for good to those that love God.

Is then the apostolic word, that every good and every perfect gift is from above, and comes down from the Father of lights, a dark and difficult saying? And if you believe that you cannot understand it, dare you assert that you have wished to understand it? If you doubted whether it came from God, or whether it was a good and perfect gift, have you dared to make the test? And when the easy play of happiness beckoned you, have you thanked God? And when you were so strong that it seemed as if you needed no assistance, have you thanked God? And when your allotted share was small, have you thanked God? And when your allotted share was suffering, have you thanked God? And when your wish was denied you, have you thanked God? And when you must deny yourself your wish, have you thanked God? And when men did you wrong and offended you, have you thanked God? We do not say that the wrong done you by men thereby ceased to be a wrong, for that would be an untrue and foolish speech! Whether it was wrong, you must yourself decide; but have you referred the wrong and the offence to God, and by your thanksgiving received it from Him as a good and perfect gift? Have you done this? Then surely you have worthily interpreted the apostolic word to the honour of God, to your own salvation; for it is beautiful for a man to pray, and many promises are held out to the one who prays without ceasing; but it is even more blessed to return thanks. Then have you worthily interpreted that apostolic word, more gloriously than if all the angels spoke in glowing tongues.

Still, who had such courage and such faith, who loved God in this way? Who was the joyful and resolute and devout warrior who stood so persistently at his post in life that he never slumbered? And if you did it, my hearer, have you not secretly done it for yourself? Have you said to yourself : " I certainly understand the apostolic word, but I also understand that I am too cowardly, or too proud, or too sluggish rightly to wish to understand it "? Have you admonished yourself? Have you considered that timidity, even if it seems like a hard saying, that timidity also has a deceitful heart, and is not a sincere lover? Have you considered that there is a judgment upon the despondent, but the humble heart comes not to judgment? Have you considered that the sorrowful does not love God with his whole heart, but that he who is glad in God, has overcome the world? Have you at least watched over yourself? Have you held the apostolic word sacred? Have you hidden it in a pure and clean heart, and for no price, for no crafty bribery of prudence, would ransom yourself from the deep pain of having repeatedly to confess that you have never loved as you were loved? That you were faithless when God was faithful; that you were lukewarm when He was ardent; that He sent good gifts which you yourself perverted; that He questioned you, but you would not answer; that He called to you, but you would not hear; that He spoke kindly to you, but you did not listen; that He spoke earnestly to you, but you misunderstood it; that He fulfilled your wish, and you for thanks brought new wishes; that He fulfilled your wish, but you had not wished rightly, and you were swift to wrath? Have you really deeply felt the sadness since, in order to describe your relation to God, you need so many words? Have you at least in this way been sincere toward yourself and toward God in your relation to Him? Have you not deferred the reckoning, not wishing to shame yourself in your solitude? Have you been swift to endure the pain of the reckoning, have you considered that He first loved you? Have you been swift to judge yourself, so that He should not continue to love you, while you were slow to love in return? If you have done this, then you will now and then gain courage to be thankful, also then, when what happens is wonderful in your eyes, you will gain courage to understand that every good and every perfect gift is from above, courage to explain it in love, faith to accept this courage; for it, too, is a good and a perfect gift.

Every good and every perfect gift is from above, and cometh down from the Father of lights with whom is no variableness, neither shadow of turning. These words are so refreshing, so healing, and yet how often did the penitent soul understand how to let himself be healed by them, how often did he understand their condemning earnestness but also their merciful grace?

Or, my hearer, was there perhaps no occasion in your life when you found these words difficult? Were you always satisfied with yourself, so satisfied that you perhaps thanked God that you were not like other men? Had you perhaps become so clever that you understood the profound meaning in the meaningless saying that it was glorious not to be like other men? . . . What was it, then, that made them difficult for you? If a man himself were a good and a perfect gift, if he only were receptive and accepted everything from God's hand, how then, indeed, could he receive other than good and perfect gifts? But when you submitted to the common lot of man, then you confessed that you were neither good nor perfect, that you not only withheld yourself, but that everything you received underwent a change. Can then the like be understood by other than the like; can the good remain good in other than the good; can wholesome food preserve its wholesomeness in the sick soul? A man does not merely refrain from receiving, he is also communicative, and it became difficult for you to understand how the unsoundness which came from you could be anything but injurious to others. You certainly understood that it was only through your thanksgiving to God that everything became for you a good and perfect gift; you are convinced that in the same way the other man must appropriate everything himself. But was, then, even the love which gave rise to thanksgiving pure; did it not change the recipient?

Can then a man do more than love? Have thought and language any higher expression for the fact that loving is always thanking? By no means. It has a lower, humbler one; for even the one who is always willing to return thanks, still loves according to his perfection, and a man can truly only love God when he loves Him according to his own imperfection. What is this love? It is the love born of repentance, which is more beautiful than all other love; for in it you love God! It is more faithful and more inward than all other love; for in repentance it is God who loves you. In repentance you receive everything from God, even the gratitude which you bring Him, so that even this is what the child's gift is in the eyes of the parent, a jest, a receiving something one has himself given. Was it not this way, my hearer? You always wished to thank God, but even this thanks was so imperfect. Then you understood that God is the one who does everything for you, and then grants you the childish joy of having Him regard your thanksgiving as a gift from you. This joy He grants you, if you did not fear the pain of remorse, nor the deep sorrow in which a man becomes joyful as a child in God; if you did not fear to understand that this is love, not that we love God, but that God loves us.

And you, my hearer, you who in a more simple and humble manner understood the profound meaning of the thought that you were not like other men, was it as easy not to misunderstand the apostolic word? You certainly fully understood that every good and every perfect gift comes from God. Alas! but you could not understand that the gift good for you might be injurious to another. Dew and rain are good gifts from above, but if the harmful weed understood itself and could speak, then it would perhaps say: "Oh, stop, return to heaven again, that I may perish of drouth; do not revive my root so that I may thrive and grow, and become even more harmful!" And you did not understand yourself, nor the apostolic word; for if that were true, then it would not be true that every good and every perfect gift comes from God, then would God not be greater than a man's troubled heart, and how, then, could all good and perfect gifts come from Him?

Perhaps there was something in your life you wished undone; if this were possible, then would you with glad thanksgiving take every perfect gift from God's hand. Your joy even at the thought of it, was so great that it was as if it would tempt God, so that He would make the thing done undone. But God is tempted of no man. You endeavoured to forget it, so that your thanksgiving might not be weak, and like smoking flax. Alas; and if you could forget it, how would it then be possible for you to understand the apostolic word? If it were possible for you to forget it, then every good and every perfect gift would not come from God; you had excluded yourself from the blessing, not by what you had done, but by your poor, selfish, and arbitrary understanding of the word, so that, if your wish was denied, it would exclude you from the blessing, through your being willing to believe that the denied wish was not also a good and a perfect gift, even if it seemed to you far harder than to him who dared to understand it.

You perhaps understood the apostolic word differently, that punishment from God is also a good and perfect gift. The wrath in your heart joined, as it were, the divine wrath in helping that the punishment might consume you, and yet the punishment you suffered was different from what you had thought it to be. It perhaps included more than yourself, and yet you were the only one guilty; it was perhaps more comprehensive, and yet you were the only one who should have been its object. Even if in your quiet thought you recognized that the divine guidance knows how to overtake a man, knows how to make itself intelligible to him, even if no one else understood it, the apostolic word remained obscure to you; it was as if the punishment itself became a new temptation. You became doubtful as to what was punishment, and what was incident; if it was only incident, then your soul demanded punishment; if it was entirely punishment, then you could not put it on. You would renounce everything, every wish, every desire; you would give up the idea that the best you had done in the extreme exertion of your soul, was an assurance that it was good, that it was anything else than folly and sin; you would suffer every punishment, but the *more* which was connected with this, you could not bear. Was it also a good and a perfect gift? Then your soul became darkened; you could not understand the word. But what did you do? Did you give up the word? Oh, no, you held fast to it in all your need. And when all the devils stood ready to save your soul from the insanity of despair by explaining that God is not love, is it not true that you clung fast to the word, even if you did not understand it, because you still cherished a vague hope, and felt that to let it go was more terrible than anything else?

Did you do this, my hearer? Then, although the outward man perished, the inward man was renewed. Then you understood that every good and every perfect gift is from above if it is received with thankfulness; you understood that repentance is a returning of thanks not only for punishment but also for the dispensation of Providence, and that he who in his repentance will only suffer punishment, will still not, in the deepest sense, love according to his imperfection. As the Lord Himself says: Yet to-day, so the apostle of the Lord says: Yet to-day is every good and every perfect gift from above, and comes down from the Father of lights, with whom is no variableness, neither shadow of turning; yet to-day, and that although He is the same to-day as He was yesterday.

Every good and every perfect gift is from above and cometh down from the Father of lights, with whom is no variableness nor shadow of turning. These words are so beautiful, so eloquent, so moving; they are so soothing and so comforting, so simple and comprehensible, so refreshing and so healing. Therefore we will beseech Thee, O God, that Thou wilt make the ears of those who hitherto have not regarded them, willing to accept them; that Thou wilt heal the misunderstanding heart by the understanding of the word, to understand the word; that Thou wilt incline the erring thought under the saving obedience of the word; that Thou wilt give the penitent soul confidence to dare to understand the word; and that Thou wilt make those who have understood it more and more blessed therein, so that they may repeatedly understand it. Amen.

III

LOVE SHALL COVER A MULTITUDE OF SINS

But the end of all things is at hand: be ye therefore sober, and watch unto prayer. And above all things have fervent love among yourselves: for love shall cover the multitude of sins. Use hospitality one to another without grudging. As every man hath received the gift, even so minister the same one to another, as good stewards of the manifold grace of God. If any man speak, let him speak as the oracles of God; if any man minister, let him do it as of the ability which God giveth: that God in all things may be glorified through Jesus Christ, to whom be praise and dominion for ever and ever. Amen.   I Peter 4:7-12

What is it that makes a man great, admired by his fellows, acceptable in the sight of God? What is it that makes a man strong, stronger than the whole world, what is it that makes him weak, weaker than a child? What is it that makes a man immovable, more immovable than the rock, what is it that makes him soft, softer than wax? It is love! What is it that is older than everything else? It is love! What is it that outlives everything else? It is love. What is it that cannot be taken, but itself takes everything? It is love. What is it that cannot be given, but itself gives everything? It is love. What is it that endures when all else disappoints? It is love. What is it that comforts when all comfort fails? It is love. What is it that persists when all else changes? It is love. What is it that remains when the imperfect is abolished? It is love. What is it that bears witness when prophecy is silent? It is love. What is it that does not end when the vision ceases? It is love. What is it that explains when the dark saying is ended? It is love. What is it that bestows a blessing on the abundance of the gift? It is love. What is it that gives emphasis to the speech of angels? It is love. What is it that transforms the widow's mite into an abundance? It is love. What is it that turns the words of the simple man into wisdom? It is love. What is it that never changes when all else changes? It is love; and only that is love which never becomes anything else.

For the pagans also praised love, its beauty and its power; but that love could become something else, which they praised even more highly. Love was beautiful, more beautiful than anything else; but revenge was sweet, sweeter than all else. And so foolish was the pagan thought about love and about the heavenly, so selfish was everything both in heaven and on earth, that the power which benevolently bestowed the joy of love on mankind, enviously reserved revenge for itself, because it was the sweeter.

What wonder then that the idea of revenge was concealed in all pagan love, that fear was not cast out, even if it was forgotten; what wonder that the enemy worked in stillness, even when love slept soundest; what wonder that resentment secretly lay in wait and watched for an opportunity; what wonder that it suddenly burst forth in all its fierceness; what wonder that it completely filled the pagan soul which imbibed its forbidden sweetness, and thereby assured itself of its kinship with the heavenly! What wonder that no love was happy, as no man was in paganism, until his last hour was come, which again could only bitterly mock a man with the idea that he had been happy! What wonder that sorrow was mingled in every joy, that even in the moment of gladness the next moment constantly loomed as alarmingly as the shadow of death! How then could a pagan be able to overcome the world? But if he could not do this, how could he be able to gain the world?

What is it that is never changed when all else changes? It is love, and only this is love which never becomes something else. For the pious Jew also bore witness to love, but his love was the child of mutability and change, and he knew how to hate his enemy. He even ascribed vengeance to the Lord, because he himself had it; his own soul was not unacquainted with its sweetness. Then, too, was this consciousness sweet, that the Lord's vengeance is more terrible than human vengeance, that a man curses his enemy, but the Lord curses the ungodly and the family of the ungodly through many generations. What wonder then that fear always kept one eye open even when love was least concerned; what wonder that resentment quietly sat and reckoned up the things given and the things received, the thine and mine, even when love least dreamed of it! What wonder that no love was happy until the last hour came, because not till then was love's uncertain demand perfectly redeemed.

What is it that is never changed, even if all else changes? It is love. And only this is love which never becomes something else, this which gives *everything* and *because of this* demands nothing, this which demands nothing, and therefore has nothing to lose, this which blesses, and blesses when it is cursed, this which loves its neighbour, but whose enemy is also his neighbour, this which leaves vengeance to the Lord, because it comforts him to believe that the Lord is even more merciful than he himself is.

It is this love the apostle Peter speaks about in the text we read, and as this love many times and in many ways received the testimony of the apostle, so here again he bears witness to its power when he says: Love shall cover a multitude of sins.

It is this word, this testimony, we shall examine a little more carefully, as we reflect on

HOW LOVE COVERS A MULTITUDE OF SINS.

Still, how ought we to speak about these words? Shall we speak hastily, not giving ourselves time to dwell on the meaning of them, because the mere sound of them contains a quiet reproach which awakens grief, which calls forth a striving toward that goal which is set for every man to strive after? Shall we speak in such a way that, if possible, the individual, even at this hour, may resolve to buy the opportune moment; so that, if possible, the word may influence one whom it met standing idle to begin the race; him whom it came across on the way to accelerate his speed; him whom it met in the race to hasten to finish it? Shall we speak thus as to the imperfect? Shall we recall how rarely even one is found who either has never known or has absolutely forgotten those rudiments of worldly wisdom, that revenge is sweet? Shall we recall that every man, if he is honest, only too often catches himself tediously, earnestly learning to interpret this sorry truth, that revenge is sweet? Shall we recall how rarely there is even one who left vengeance to the Lord, confident that He had an even milder explanation of the guilt, an even more merciful judgment upon it; that He is greater than the heart of man? On the contrary, how often must every honest man confess that he really did not relinquish the idea of revenge because he left it to the Lord? Shall I recall how rarely there was even one who forgave in such a way that the repentant enemy really became his neighbour; one who in his forgiveness actually broke down the wall between them, and was conscious of no difference because he himself was called in the early morning, his enemy at the eleventh hour, nor that he was owed only fifty pennies, his enemy five hundred? Shall I recall how seldom there was even one who loved so much that his ear, when his enemy was prosperous, was sensible of no whisper of envy, because his heart was free from envy; who loved so much that " his eye did not begrudge forgiveness " when fortune favoured his enemy; one who loved so much that when it went hard with his enemy, he had forgotten that it was his enemy? Shall we warn against that which in the eyes of men is a lesser fault, against a certain shrewd commonsense which cunningly knows how to discover a man's fault, and which does not indeed misuse its knowledge in judging, yet through its curiosity does not so much harm the neighbour as retard itself. Shall we admonish everyone to aim at that Christian love, because every man so often needs forgiveness himself? Shall we admonish every man to judge himself, and in so doing forget to judge others; admonish against judging and condemning, because no man can entirely understand another, because it still sometimes happens that the wrath of heaven did not consume the one upon whom one called it down, but that that Lord, gracious and gentle, secretly delighted in him? Shall we admonish everyone not to be too zealous in invoking the wrath of heaven upon another, lest through his unforgivingness he call down a more terrible wrath upon himself on the day of judgment?

Shall we speak in this way? Certainly, to speak in this way would indeed very frequently be profitable to us, but to do it is so very difficult that not even the speaker himself is able to act in accordance with the speech in judging others. Certainly, even in speaking it is very difficult to judge oneself, so that the speaker does not become entangled in a new misunderstanding, and thereby confuse others. Therefore we choose the easier task; we shall lay the emphasis on the words themselves, and, as all other kinds of love have been praised in the world, we shall explain and praise the love which has power to perform the miraculous, to cover a multitude of sins. We shall speak as to the perfect. If there should then be one who did not regard himself as perfect, the speech would make no difference. We shall let our soul rest in the apostolic word, which is not a deceitful, poetic mode of expression, not a bold outburst, but a trustworthy thought, a perfectly valid testimony, which to be understood must be taken at its face value.

Love shall cover a multitude of sins. Love is blind, says an old proverb, but it does not thereby mean that this is an imperfection in the lover, or that he was born blind; for not until love won a place in his soul did he become blind, and then, as love triumphed more and more within him, he became more and more blind. Or did love become more imperfect when, after having first deceived itself by not wishing to see what it actually saw, at last it did not even see it any more? Or who concealed it best, he who knew that he had forgotten something, or he who had even forgotten this? To the pure all things are pure, is an old saying which does not indicate an imperfection in the pure that might gradually disappear; on the contrary, the more perfect he becomes, the purer everything seems to him. Or was it an imperfection in the pure, that after having saved himself unspotted by the impurity through not wishing to know what he really did know, he at last finished by not knowing it any longer?

It depends, then, not only on what a man sees, but what a man sees depends on how he sees it; for all observation is not only a receiving, a discovery, but also a creation, and in so far as it is that, the crucial thing is what the observer himself is. Thus, when one person sees one thing and another another in the same object, then the one discovers what the other conceals. In so far as the object of contemplation belongs to the external world, the nature of the observer is a matter of relative importance, or rather, it is then, as a necessary object of reflection, something the observer's deeper nature is unconscious of; on the contrary, the more the object of contemplation belongs to the spiritual world, the more important becomes the question of what the observer is in his inmost being; for all things spiritual are appropriated only in freedom; but what is appropriated in freedom must also be produced in freedom. The difference then does not depend on externals but on the inward condition, and from within goeth forth everything which makes a man unclean, and his thoughts unclean. What the eye sees externally is of no importance, but from within " proceedeth the evil eye." But an evil eye discovers much that love does not see; for an evil eye even regards the Lord as unrighteous when He is good. When evil dwells in the heart then the eye sees evil, but when purity abides in the heart, then the eye sees the finger of God; for the pure always see God, " but he who does evil, does not see God."

What is in a man, then, decides what he discovers and what he conceals. When the lust of sin dwells in the heart, then the eye discovers the multitude of sins, and makes them even more numerous; for the eye is the light of the body, but if the light that is in a man be darkness, then how great is that darkness! When the apprehension of sin dwells in the heart, then the ear discovers the variety of sin, and makes it even more manifold, and how is such a man helped by being blind? For a rascal casts his eyes down, and listens with his rascally ears. When love dwells in the heart, then the eye closes, and does not discover the manifest acts of sin, even less those that are concealed; for " he who winketh with the eye " has an evil mind; but he who understands the invitation of the eye is not pure. When love abides in the heart, then the ear is closed and does not hear the worldly speech, the bitterness of its blasphemy; for he who says Raca to his brother, is guilty before the council, but who hears it, when it is said to him, is not perfect in love. When there is precipitancy in the heart, then is a man quick to discover the multitude of sin, then he is excellently able to understand a half-uttered word, hastily understand it from a distance, almost before it is spoken. When love dwells in the heart, then a man comprehends slowly, and does not hear at all the hasty word and does not understand its repetition, because he ascribes to it a good intention and a good meaning; does not understand the long, angry or derisive speech, because he still expects one word which will give meaning to the speech. When fear dwells in the heart, then a man easily discovers the multiplicity of sin—weakness and deceit and faithlessness and scheming, so that

> Every heart is like a trap,
> Every rogue like a child,
> Every promise but a shadow.

But the love which covers a multitude of sins is never deceived. When the heart is niggardly, when one gives with one eye and with seven eyes looks to see what one will get in return, then one easily discovers a multitude of sins. But when the heart is filled with love, then the eye is never deceived; for love when it gives, does not scrutinize the gift,

but its eyes are fixed on the Lord. When the heart is filled
with envy, then the eye has power to call forth uncleanness
even in the pure; but when love dwells in the heart, then
the eye has power to foster the good in the unclean; but
this eye does not see the evil but the pure, which it loves
and encourages by loving it. Certainly there is a power in
this world which by its words turns good into evil, but
there is a power above which turns the evil into good;
that power is the love which covers a multitude of sins.
When hate dwells in the heart, then sin lies at a man's
door, and its manifold desires exist in him; but when love
dwells in the heart, then sin flees far away, and he sees it
no more. When disputes, malice, wrath, quarrels, dissen-
sions, factions fill the heart, does one then need to go far
in order to discover the multitudinousness of sin, or does a
man need to live very long to produce these outside of
himself? But when joy, peace, longsuffering, gentleness,
goodness, faith, meekness and temperance dwell in the
heart, what wonder, then, that a man, even if he were surrounded by a multitude of sins, remains an alien, a
stranger, who understands only a very little about the cus-
toms of the country, even if these were explained to him?
Would not this, then, be a covering of the multitude of
sins?

Or is it not this way? Should we shrewdly say: The
variety of sin in the world is and remains equally great
whether love discovers it or not? Should we permit the
apostolic word, and with it the love which is described, to
remain ambiguous, a graceful turn of expression which is
not able to endure the test of an investigation? But then
did the intelligence really understand love as well as it
understood the manifold of sin! Or would it admit the
opposite, that the manifold of sin remained equally great
whether the intelligence discovered it or not, and not
rather commend its own ingenuity in discovering and trac-
ing the hiding place of sin? But then it became equally
true that the intelligence discovered the manifold of sin,
and that love concealed it; but the one was no truer than

the other. Or was there not still a third way in which one without being sensibly conscious of it, nor lovingly unconscious of it, was still conscious of the manifold of sin; was not such a knowledge a superhuman knowledge? It is not, then, merely a rhetorical expression that love covers a multitude of sins, but it is the very truth, and this is the power of the Christian love, which is not great through unusual achievements, as other love is, but greater in its quiet miraculousness.

Happy that man who saw the world in all its perfection when everything was very good; happy that man who with God was a witness to the glory of creation; more blessed the soul who was God's collaborator in love; blessed the love which covers a multitude of sins.

Love shall cover a multitude of sins. A *multitude* of sins, that is an appalling word, and readily recalls another connection in which the word is frequently used: the multitude of created beings wherein we contemplate the countless hosts of generations, the innumerable multitude of living beings, which cannot be reckoned in numbers, because no number is vast enough, and because there is no moment when one can begin to count; for every moment an innumerable number is born. But this is not the case with the multitude of sins. As it is said that to him who hath shall be given, and he shall have in abundance, so, too, is sin very fruitful, and one sin breeds many, and becomes more and more multitudinous. But love covers a multitude of sins. If the eye of love had not closed, if it had not even hidden the multitude of sins from its view, how could it then venture to check the power of sin! So then love really covers a multitude of sins through the fact that it has covered them before.

An ancient sage has said: Prevent boredom and you will diminish sin. But one who reduces the number of sins, covers a multitude of sins, and conceals them doubly by not sinning himself, and by preventing another from sinning. And yet he who prevents boredom keeps a man from sinning only for a moment; perhaps the same man will seek boredom in another direction; but he who converteth a sinner from the error of his way, as the apostle James says, he covers a multitude of sins.

Still is it possible to explain correctly how love covers a multitude of sins, or is not love even more manifold than sin is? When love sees the bruised reed, then it knows how to cover the multitude of sins, so that the reed is not crushed under the burden. When love sees the smoking flax, then it knows how to cover the multitude of sins, so that the flame is not quenched. When love has triumphed over the multitude of sins, then it knows how to hide again the multitude of sins, then it prepares everything festally for the reception, as the father of the prodigal son did; then it stands with open arms and awaits the erring, then has it forgotten everything and causes him to forget everything, as it again hides the multitude of sins. For love does not even weep over the multitude of sins; if it did this, then it would have seen the sins, but it covers their multitude. And when sin offers resistance, then love becomes even more manifold, never weary of faithfully pulling in an unequal yoke with it, never weary of believing all things, hoping all things, enduring all things. When sin hardens itself against love, and wishes to be rid of it, when it rewards kindness with abuse and scorn and ridicule, then love does not requite abuse with abuse, then it blesses and curses not. When sin enviously hates love, when it would maliciously cause love itself to sin, then it finds no deceitfulness on its lips, but only prayer and admonition. But when prayers and warnings only inflame the sin, and become a new occasion for multiplying the sins, then is love silent, but not the less faithful; steadfast as a woman, it saves, as a woman does—" without words." Sin thought that it would soon bring about the parting of their ways, but lo, love remained with it. And sin would thrust love away from it; it forces love to go a mile with it, but lo, love goes two; it struck love on the right cheek, but lo, love turned the other to it; it took away love's coat, but lo, love gave its cloak also. Already sin feels its impotence, it cannot hold out against love, it will then tear itself away from it. Then it injures love as deeply as possible; for even love itself, sin believes, cannot forgive more than seven times. But lo, love could forgive seventy times seven, and sin sooner became tired of needing forgiveness than love did of forgiving. Yes, as there is a power of sin which has the power to consume every better feeling in a man, so, too, is there a heavenly power which starves out the manifold of sin in a man. This power is the love which covers a multitude of sins.

Or is it not this way? Should we rather praise a cleverness which knows how to describe the multitude of sins even more terribly? Or ought we not rather to ask this cleverness where it gets such knowledge? Certainly, if it could convince love that such is the case, then love would never begin, and would accomplish nothing. But because of this, love begins by hiding a multitude of sins, and therefore it ends where it began, by hiding a multitude of sins.

Blessed the man whose sins are hidden; more blessed the love which hides a multitude of sins.

Love shall cover a multitude of sins. If love had triumphed in the world, then would all the multitude of sins be hidden, and everything would be perfect in love. If the hosts of love were numerous in the world, if their number were equal to that of the enemy, so they could fight man to man—then, how could love do other than conquer since it is the stronger! If, on the contrary, the servants of love are but a small host, if each one is only a solitary man, then will love actually be able to cover a multitude of sins? Or is the apostolic word, in so far as we wish thereby

to consider its zeal within its own limits, anything more
than the pious ignorance of love; is not the apostolic utter-
ance in such a case a beautiful but still a meaningless
expression? Ought we not to regard the apostolic expression as an enthusiastic bit of foolishness, and rather commend the cleverness which says: The way of life follows
an appointed course; let love live next door to ungodliness,
the ungodliness gains no advantage from it? Would the
reason be equally prompt to assert the opposite, that it
makes no difference if ungodliness does dwell with love?
Will the reason deny that in life the innocent must often
suffer with the guilty?

Let us interrogate the reason. An ancient pagan, who
in pagandom was renowned and praised for his wisdom,
sailed on the same ship with a wicked man. When the ship
was in distress the wicked man lifted up his voice in prayer,
but the wise man said to him: "Keep quiet, my friend; if
heaven discovers that you are on board, the ship will go
under." Thus is it not true that the guilty may be the
occasion for the destruction of the innocent? But is not
the opposite equally true? Perhaps then the understanding
lacked only the courage to believe this, and while it had
sufficient distressing cleverness to discover the wretchedness
of life, it did not have the courage to apprehend the power
of love. Is this not true? For the reason still merely makes
a man despondent and faint-hearted, but love gives courage freely, and because of this every apostolic word is
always confident.

If, instead of there having been a wicked man on board
that ship, there had been a righteous man, if there had been
an apostle! And did this not happen? A pagan ship
sailed from Crete bound for Rome, and the ship was in
distress, and for many days they saw neither sun nor
stars. On board that ship there was an apostle; and Paul
came forward and said to them who were with him in the
ship: "Men, I admonish you to be of good courage; for
not one soul among you shall perish." Or should unright-

eousness really have greater power than love; should the fact that a wicked man was on board have power to alter the circumstances for the others on the ship, but an apostle not have power to do this? Or does not the Lord Himself say that for the sake of the elect the days of distress shall be shortened?

Is this an unworthy conception of God to believe that love thus hides a multitude of sins? Do we perhaps forget in our speech and in our reflection that God in heaven is not hindered by any illusions, that His thought is vivid and present, that He penetrates everything and judges the designs of the heart? Would one be right in reminding us, when we wished to extol love, rather to restrict ourselves to telling the truth, that it is beautiful and lovely that love should wish to cover the multitude of sins and avert wrath, than to exaggerate by saying that love does cover a multitude of sins? Has he who speaks thus not forgotten, what we do not forget, that love prays for the sins of others; has he not forgotten that the prayer of a righteous man availeth much?

When Abraham spoke earnestly to the Lord and begged for Sodom and Gomorrah, did he not then conceal a multitude of sins? Or is it perhaps a commendable sophistry for someone to say that by his prayer he recalled the multitude of sins and proclaimed the judgment, just as his own life was already a judgment, which, if it had power to impose a condition, made the judgment, if anything, even more terrible? How did Abraham pray? Let us speak about it from the human point of view! Did he not, as it were, carry the Lord along with him in his course of reasoning, did he not cause the Lord to forget the multitude of sinners in order to count the number of the righteous, whether there might be fifty, forty-five, forty, thirty, twenty, aye, whether there might be even ten innocent men? Did not Abraham then conceal a multitude of sins? Does the destruction of the cities prove the converse, or prove anything except that there were not ten righteous men in Sodom? And yet what was Abraham in comparison with an apostle, what was his confidence in comparison with an apostle's?

Great is a man, in that his life, if he is upright, shall even judge angels; more blessed the love which covers a multitude of sins.

We have praised the power of love to cover a multitude of sins. We have spoken as to perfection. If there was someone who did not feel himself perfect, the speech made no difference. Let us once more dwell upon this love in order to observe the image of it which clearly presents itself to the soul. Should there be one who by observing himself in this mirror ascertained his own unlikeness, should this be the case with everyone, the speech makes no difference.

When the scribes and the Pharisees had taken a woman in open sin, they brought her into the midst of the temple before the face of the Saviour; but Jesus bowed down and wrote with His finger on the ground. He who knew everything, knew also what the scribes and the Pharisees knew, before they told Him. The scribes and the Pharisees soon discovered her guilt, which was indeed easy since her sin was open. They also discovered a new sin, one of which they made themselves guilty, when they artfully laid snares for the Lord. But Jesus bowed down and wrote with His finger upon the ground. Why, I wonder, did He bow down; why, I wonder, did He write with His finger upon the ground? Did He sit there like a judge who listens attentively to the story of the accusers, who, listening, bows down and jots down the principal points so that he may not forget them, and may judge strictly; was the woman's guilt the only thing which was noted by the Lord? Or did not He who wrote with His finger on the ground rather write it down in order to erase it and forget it? There stood the sinner, surrounded perhaps by those even more guilty, who loudly accused her, but love bowed down and did not hear the accusation, which passed over His head into the air; He wrote with His finger in order to blot out what He himself knew; for sin discovers a multitude of sins, but love covers the multitude of sins. Yes, even in the sight of the sinner, love covers a multitude of sins. For by one word from the Master the Pharisees and the scribes were struck dumb, and there was no longer an accuser, no one who condemned her. But Jesus said to her: "Neither do I condemn thee, go and sin no more," for the punishment of sin breeds new sin, but love covers a multitude of sins.

IV

THE LORD GAVE, AND THE LORD HATH TAKEN AWAY, BLESSED BE THE NAME OF THE LORD

Then Job arose, and rent his mantle, and shaved his head, and fell upon the ground and worshipped, and said: Naked came I out of my mother's womb, and naked shall I return thither: the Lord gave, and the Lord hath taken away; blessed be the name of the Lord.   Job 1:20-21

Not only do we call that man a teacher of men who through some particularly happy talent discovered, or by unremitting toil and continued perseverance brought to light one or another truth; left what he had acquired as a principle of knowledge, which the following generations strove to understand, and through this understanding to appropriate to themselves. Perhaps, in an even stricter sense, we also call that one a teacher of men who had no doctrine to pass on to others, but who merely left himself as a pattern to succeeding generations, his life as a principle of guidance to every man, his name as an assurance to the many, his own deeds as an encouragement to the striving. Such a teacher and guide of men was Job, whose significance is by no means due to what he said but to what he did. He has indeed left a saying which because of its brevity and its beauty has become a proverb, preserved from generation to generation, and no one has been presumptuous enough to add anything to it or to take anything away from it. But the expression itself is not the guidance, and Job's significance does not lie in the fact that he said it, but in the fact that he acted in accordance with it. The expression itself is truly beautiful and worthy of consideration, but if another had used it, or if Job had been different, or if he had uttered it under different circumstances, then the word itself would have become something different—significant, if, as uttered, it would otherwise have been so, but not significant from the fact that he acted in asserting it, so that the expression itself was the action. If Job had devoted his whole life to emphasizing this word, if he had regarded it as the sum and fulfilment of what a man ought to let life teach him, if he had constantly only *taught* it, but had never himself practised it, had never himself acted in accordance with what he taught, then Job would have been a different kind of man, his significance different. Then would Job's name have been forgotten, or it would have been unimportant whether anyone remembered it or not, the principal thing being the content of the word, the richness of the thought it embodied.

If the race had accepted the saying, then it would have been this which one generation transmitted to the next; while now, on the contrary, it is Job himself who guides the generation. When one generation has served its time, fulfilled its duty, fought its battle, then Job has guided it; when the new generation, with its innumerable ranks and every individual among them in his place, stands ready to begin the journey, then Job is again present, takes his place, which is the outpost of humanity. If the generation sees only happy days and prosperous times, then Job faithfully goes with them, and if, nevertheless, an individual in his thought experiences the terrible, is apprehensive because of his conception of what life may conceal of horror and distress, of the fact that no one knows when the hour of despair may strike for him, then his troubled thought resorts to Job, dwells upon him, is reassured by him. For Job keeps faithfully by his side and comforts him, not as if he had thus suffered once for all what he would never again have to endure, but he comforts him as one who witnesses that the terror is endured, the horror experienced, the battle of despair waged, to the honour of God, to his own salvation, to the profit and happiness of others. In joyful days, in fortunate times, Job walks by the side of the race and guarantees it its happiness, combats the apprehensive dream that some horror may suddenly befall a man and have power to destroy his soul as its certain prey.

Only the thoughtless man could wish that Job should not accompany him, that his venerable name should not remind him of what he seeks to forget, that terror and anxiety exist in life. Only the selfish man could wish that Job had not existed, so that the idea of his suffering might not disturb with its austere earnestness his own un-substantial joy, and frighten him out of his intoxicated security in obduracy and perdition. In stormy times, when the foundation of existence is shaken, when the moment trembles in fearful expectation of what may happen, when every explanation is silent at the sight of the wild uproar, when a man's heart groans in despair, and " in bitterness of soul " he cries to heaven, then Job still walks at the side of the race and guarantees that there is a victory, guarantees that even if the individual loses in the strife, there is still a God, who, as with every human temptation, even if a man fails to endure it, will still make its outcome such that we may be able to bear it; yea, more glorious than any human expectation. Only the defiant could wish that Job had not existed, so that he might absolutely free his soul from the last vestiges of love which still remained in the plaintive shriek of despair; so that he might com-plain, aye, even curse life; so that there might be no con-sonance of faith and confidence and humility in his speech; so that in his defiance he might stifle the shriek so that it might not even seem as if there were anyone whom it defied. Only the effeminate could wish that Job had not existed, so that he might relinquish every thought, the sooner the better; might renounce every emotion in the most abhorrent impotence and completely efface himself in the most wretched and miserable oblivion.

The expression which, when it is mentioned, at once reminds us of Job, immediately becomes vividly present in everyone's thought, is a plain and simple one; it conceals no secret wisdom that must be unearthed from the depths. If a child learns this word, if it is entrusted to him as an endowment, he does not understand for what purpose he will use it; when he understands the word, he understands essentially the same thing by it as does the wisest. Still, the child does not understand it, or rather he does not understand Job; for what he does not comprehend is all the distress and wretchedness with which Job was tested. About that the child can have only a dark premonition; and yet, happy the child who understood the word and got an impression of what he did not comprehend, that it was the most terrible thing imaginable; who possessed, before sorrow and adversity made its thought cunning, the convincing and childishly vivid conviction that it was in truth the most terrible. When the youth turns his attention to this word, then he understands it, and understands it essentially the same as do the child and the wisest. Still he perhaps does not understand it, or rather, he does not understand Job, does not understand why all the distress and wretchedness should come in which Job was tried; and yet, happy the youth who understood the word and humbly bowed before what he did not understand, before his own distress made his thought wayward, as if he had discovered what no one had known before. When the adult reflects on this word, then he understands essentially the same by it as did the child and the wisest. He understands, too, the wretchedness and distress in which Job was tried; and yet perhaps he does not understand Job, for he cannot understand how Job was able to say it; and yet, happy the man who understood the word, and steadfastly admired what he did not understand, before his own distress and wretchedness made him also distrustful of Job. When the man who has been tried, who fought the good fight through remembering this saying, mentions it, then he understands it, and understands it essentially the same as the child and as the wisest understood it; he understands Job's misery, he understands how Job could say it. He understands the word, he interprets it, even though he never speaks about

it, more gloriously than the one who spent a whole lifetime in explaining this one word.

Only the one who has been tried, who tested the word
through himself being tested, only he interprets the word
correctly, and only such a disciple, only such an inter-
preter, does Job desire. Only such a one learns from Job
what there is to learn, the most beautiful and blessed truth,
compared with which all other art and all other wisdom is
very unessential. Therefore we rightly call Job a teacher
of mankind, not of certain individual men, for he offers
himself to every man as his pattern, beckons to everyone
by his glorious example, summons everyone in his beautiful words. While the more simple-minded man, the one
less gifted, or the one less favoured by time and circumstances, if not enviously yet in troubled despondency, may
sometimes have wished for the talent and the opportunity
to be able to understand and absorb himself in those things
which scholars from time to time have discovered, may
also have felt a desire in his soul to be able to teach others,
and not always be the one to receive instruction, Job does
not tempt him in this way. How, too, could human wisdom help here? Would it perhaps seek to make that more
intelligible which the simplest and the child easily understood, and understood as well as the wisest? How would
the art of eloquence and fluency help here? Would it be
able to produce in the speaker or in some other man what
the simplest is able to do as well as the wisest—action?
Would not human wisdom rather tend to make everything
more difficult? Would not eloquence, which, despite its
pretentiousness, is nevertheless unable to express the differences which always dwell in the heart of man, rather
benumb the power of action, and allow it to slumber in
extensive reflection? But even if this is true, and even if,
as a result of this, the speaker endeavours to avoid intrud-
ing disturbingly between the striving individual and the
beautiful pattern which is equally near to every man, so
that he may not increase sorrow by increasing wisdom;
even if he takes care not to ensnare himself in the splendid

words of human persuasiveness, which are very unfruitful, still it by no means follows that the reflection and the development might not have their own significance. If the one reflecting had not hitherto known this word, then it would always be an advantage to him that he had learned to know it; if he had known it, but had had no occasion to test it, then it would always be an advantage to him, that he had learned to understand what he perhaps might some time have to use. If he had tested it, but it had deceived him, if he even believed that it was the word which had deceived him, then it would be advantageous to him that he had previously reflected upon it, before he fled from it in the unrest of the strife and the haste of battle! Perhaps the reflection would sometime become significant to him; it might perhaps happen that the reflection would become vividly present in his soul just when he needed it in order to penetrate the confused thoughts of his restless heart; it might perhaps happen that what the reflection had understood only in part, would sometime gather itself regenerated in the moment of decision; that what reflection had sowed in corruption would spring up in the day of need in the incorruptible life of action.

So let us endeavour to understand Job better in his beautiful words: *The Lord gave, the Lord hath taken away; blessed be the name of the Lord!*

In the land toward the east there lived a man whose name was Job. He was blessed with lands, innumerable herds, and rich pastures; "his words had lifted up the fallen, and had strengthened the feeble knees"; his tent was blessed as if it rested in the lap of heaven, and in this tent he lived with his seven sons and three daughters; and "the secret of the Lord" abode there with him. And Job was an old man; his joy in life was his pleasure in his children, over whom he watched that no evil might come upon them. There he sat one day alone by his fireside, while his children were gathered at a festival at the oldest brother's house. There he offered burnt offerings for each one individually, there he also disposed his heart to joy in the thought of his children. As he sat there in the quiet confidence of happiness, there came a messenger, and before he could speak there came another, and while this one was still speaking, there came a third, but the fourth messenger brought news concerning his sons and daughters, that the house had been overthrown and had buried them all. "Then Job stood up and rent his mantle and shaved his head, and fell down upon the ground and worshipped." His sorrow did not express itself in many words, or rather he did not utter a single one; only his appearance bore witness that his heart was broken. Could you wish it otherwise! Is not that one who prides himself on not being able to sorrow in the day of sorrow put to shame by not being able to rejoice in the day of gladness? Is not the sight of such imperturbability unpleasant and distressing, almost revolting, while it is affecting to see an honourable old man, who but now sat in the gladness of the Lord, sitting with his fatherly countenance downcast, his mantle rent and his head shaven! Since he had thus surrendered himself to sorrow, not in despair but stirred by human emotion, he was swift to judge between God and himself, and the words of his judgment are these: "Naked I came forth from my mother's womb, and naked shall I return thither." With these words the struggle was decided, and every claim which would demand something from the Lord, which He did not wish to give, or would desire to retain something, as if it had not been a gift, was brought to silence in his soul. Then follows the confession from the man whom not sorrow alone but worship as well had prostrated on the ground: "The Lord gave, and the Lord hath taken away. Blessed be the name of the Lord!"

The Lord gave, the Lord took. What first arrests the attention is that Job said, "The Lord gave." Is not this word irrelevant to the occasion; does it not contain something different from what lay in the event itself? If a man in a single moment is deprived of everything dear to him, and deprived of the most precious of all, the loss will perhaps at first so overwhelm him that he will not even trust himself to express it, even if in his heart he is conscious before God that he has lost everything. Or he will not permit the loss to rest with its crushing weight upon his soul, but he will put it away from him, and in his heart's agitation he will say, " The Lord took." And thus to humble one's self before the Lord in silence and humility is indeed worthy of praise and emulation, and in the struggle such a man saves his soul though he loses all his gladness. But Job! At the moment when the Lord took everything, he did not say first, " The Lord took," but he said first, " The Lord gave." The word is short, but in its brevity it perfectly expresses what it wishes to indicate, that Job's soul is not crushed down in silent submission to sorrow, but that his heart first expanded in gratitude; that the loss of everything first made him thankful to the Lord that He had given him all the blessings that He now took from him. It did not happen with him, as Joseph predicted, that the abundance of the seven fruitful years would be entirely forgotten in the seven lean years. The nature of his gratitude was not the same as in that long vanished time when he accepted every good and perfect gift from the hand of God with thanksgiving; but still his gratitude was sincere, as was his conception about the goodness of God which now became living in his soul. Now he is reminded of everything which the Lord had given, some individual thing perhaps with even greater thankfulness than when he had received it. It was not become less beautiful to him because it was taken away, nor more beautiful, but still beautiful as before, beautiful because the Lord gave it, and what now might seem more beautiful to him, was not the gift but the goodness of God. He is reminded again of his abundant prosperity, his eyes rest once more upon the rich pastures, and follow the numerous herds; he remembers what joy there was in having seven sons and three daughters, who

now needed no offering except that of thankfulness for
having had them. He is reminded of those who perhaps
still remembered him with gratitude, the many he had
instructed, "whose weak hands he had strengthened, whose
feeble knees he had upheld." He is reminded of the glorious days when he was powerful and esteemed by the
people, "when the young men hid themselves out of rever-
ence for him, and the old men arose and remained standing." He remembers with thankfulness that his step had
not turned away from the way of righteousness, that he had
rescued the poor who complained, and the fatherless who
had no helper; and therefore, even in this moment, the
"blessing of the forsaken" was upon him as before.

The Lord gave. It is a short word, but to Job it signified so very much; for Job's memory was not so short, nor
was his thankfulness so forgetful. While thankfulness
rested in his soul with its quiet sadness, he bade a gentle
and friendly farewell to everything at once, and in this
farewell everything disappeared like a beautiful memory;
moreover, it seemed as if it were not the Lord who took it,
but Job who gave it back to Him. When therefore Job
had said, "The Lord gave," then was his mind well prepared to please God also with the next word, "The Lord
took."

Perhaps there might be someone who on the day of
sorrow was also reminded that he had seen happy days,
and his soul would become even more impatient. "Had
he never known happiness, then the pain would not have
overcome him, for what is pain, after all, other than an
idea which he does not have who knows nothing else, but
now happiness had so educated and developed him as to
make him conscious of the pain." Thus his happiness
became pernicious to him; it was never lost but only lacking, and it tempted him more in the lack than ever before.
What had been the delight of his eyes, he desired to see
again, and his ingratitude punished him by conjuring it
up as more beautiful than it had formerly been. What his
soul had rejoiced in, it now thirsted for again, and his

ingratitude punished him by painting it as more desirable than it had previously been. What he had once been capable of doing, that he now wished to be able to do again, and his ingratitude punished him with visions that had never had reality. Thus he condemned his soul to living famished in the never satisfied craving of want.

Or there awakened a consuming passion in his soul, because he had not even enjoyed the happy days in the right way, had not imbibed all the sweetness from their voluptuous abundance. If there might only be vouchsafed to him one little hour, if he might only regain the glory for a short time so that he might satiate himself with happiness, and thereby learn to disregard the pain! Then he abandoned his soul to a burning unrest; he would not acknowledge to himself whether the enjoyment he desired was worthy of a man; whether he ought not rather to thank God that his soul had not been so extravagant in the time of joy as it had now become in his unhappiness; he was not appalled by the thought that his desires were the cause of his perdition; he refused to be concerned by the fact that more wretched than all his wretchedness was the worm of desire in his soul, which would not die.

Perhaps there might be another man who at the moment of loss also remembered what he had possessed, but who had the audacity to try to prevent the loss from becoming intelligible to him. Even if it were lost, his defiant will would still be able to retain it as if it were not lost. He would not endeavour to bear the loss, but he chose to waste his strength in an impotent defiance, to lose himself in an insane preoccupation with the loss. Or in cowardice he immediately avoided humbly attempting to understand it. Then oblivion opened its abyss, not so much to the loss as to him, and he did not so much escape the loss in forgetfulness as he threw himself away. Or he lyingly sought to belittle the good which he had once enjoyed, as if it never had been beautiful, had never gladdened his heart; he thought to strengthen his soul by a wretched self-deception, as if strength lay in falsehood. Or he irrationally assured himself that life was not so hard as one imagined, that its terror was not as described, was not so hard to bear, if one, as you will remember that he did, began by not finding it terrifying to become such a person.

In fact, who would ever finish, if he wished to speak about what so frequently has happened, and will so frequently be repeated in the world? Would he not tire far sooner than would passion of that ever new ingenuity for transforming the explained and the understood into a new disappointment, wherein it deceives itself!

Let us rather, therefore, turn back to Job. On the day of sorrow when everything was lost, then he first thanked God who gave it, defrauded neither God nor himself, and while everything was being shaken and overthrown, he still remained what he had been from the beginning— "honest and upright before God." He confessed that the blessing of the Lord had been merciful to him, he returned thanks for it; therefore it did not remain in his mind as a torturing memory. He confessed that the Lord had blessed richly and beyond all measure his undertakings; he had been thankful for this, and therefore the memory did not become to him a consuming unrest. He did not conceal from himself that everything had been taken from him; therefore the Lord, who took it, remained in his upright soul. He did not avoid the thought that it was lost; therefore his soul rested quietly until the explanation of the Lord again came to him, and found his heart like the good earth well cultivated in patience.

The Lord took. Did Job say anything except the truth, did he use an indirect expression to indicate what was direct? The word is short, and it signifies the loss of everything; it naturally occurs to us to repeat it after him, since the expression itself has become a sacred proverb; but do we just as naturally link it to Job's thought? For was it not the Sabeans who fell upon his peaceful herds and killed his servants? Did the messenger who brought the news say anything else? Was it not the lightning which destroyed the sheep and their shepherds? Did the messenger who brought the news mean something else, even though he called the lightning the fire from heaven? Was it not a wind-storm from out of the desert which overturned the house and buried his children in the ruins? Did the messenger mention some other perpetrator, or did he name someone who sent the wind? Yet Job said, "The Lord took"; in the very moment of receiving the message, he realized that it was the Lord who had taken everything. Who told Job this? Or was it not a sign of his fear of God that he thus shifted everything over to the Lord, and justified Him in doing it; and are we more devout, we who sometimes hesitate a long time to speak thus?

Perhaps there was a man who had lost everything in the world. Then he set out to consider how it had happened. But everything was inexplicable and obscure to him. His happiness had vanished like a dream, and its memory haunted him like a nightmare, but how he had been cast off from the glory of the one into the wretchedness of the other, he was unable to understand. It was not the Lord who had taken it—it was an accident. Or he assured himself that it was the deceit and cunning of men, or their manifest violence, which had wrested it from him, as the Sabeans had destroyed Job's herds and their keepers. Then his soul became rebellious against men; he believed he did God justice by not reproaching Him. He fully understood how it had happened, and the more immediate explanation was that those men had done it, and furthermore it was because the men were evil and their hearts perverted. He understood that men are his neighbours to his injury; would he perhaps have understood it in the same way if they had benefited him? But that the Lord who dwells far away in heaven might be nearer to him than the man who lived next to him, whether that man did him good or evil, such an idea was remote from his thought. Or he fully understood how it had happened, and knew how to describe it with all the eloquence of horror. For why should he not understand that when the

sea rages in its fury, when it flings itself against the
heavens, then men and their frail accomplishments are
tossed about as in a game; that when the storm rushes forth
in its violence, human enterprises are mere child's play;
that when the earth trembles in terror of the elements and
the mountains groan, then men and their glorious achievements sink as nothing into the abyss. And this explanation
was adequate for him, and, above all, sufficient to make his
soul indifferent to everything. For it is true that what is
built on sand does not even need a storm to overthrow it;
but would it not also be true that a man cannot build and
dwell elsewhere and be sure his soul is safe? Or he understood that he himself had merited what had befallen him,
that he had not been prudent. For had he rightly calculated in time, it would not have happened. And this
explanation explained everything by first explaining that
he had corrupted himself and made it impossible for him
to learn anything from life, and especially impossible for
him to learn anything from God.

Still who would ever finish if he tried to explain what
has happened and what will frequently be repeated in
life? Would he not become tired of talking before the
sensual man would weary of deluding himself with plaus-
ible and disappointing and deceptive explanations? Let us
therefore turn away from that which has nothing to teach
us, except in so far as we knew it before, so that we may
shun worldly wisdom and turn our attention to him from
whom there is a truth to be learned—to Job and to his
devout words, " The Lord took." Job referred everything
to the Lord; he did not retard his soul and extinguish his
spirit in reflections or explanations which only engender
and nourish doubt, even if the one who dwells on them
does not realize it. In the same instant that everything
was taken from him he knew that it was the Lord who
had taken it, and therefore in his loss he remained in
understanding with the Lord; in his loss, he preserved his
confidence in the Lord; he looked upon the Lord and
therefore he did not see despair. Or does only that man

see God's hand who sees that He gives; does not that one also see God who sees that He takes? Does only that one see God who sees His countenance turned towards him? Does not that one also see God who sees Him turn His back upon him, as Moses always saw only the Lord's back? But he who sees God has overcome the world, and therefore Job in his devout word had overcome the world; was through his devout word greater and stronger and more powerful than the whole world, which here would not so much carry him into temptation but would overcome him with its power, cause him to sink down before its boundless might. And yet how weak, indeed almost childishly so, is not the wild fury of the storm, when it thinks to cause a man to tremble for himself by wresting everything away from him, and he answers, " It is not you who do this, it is the Lord who takes!" How impotent is the arm of every man of violence, how wretched his shrewd cleverness, how all human power becomes almost an object of compassion, when it wishes to plunge the weak into the destruction of despair by wresting everything from him, and he then confidently says, " It is not you, you can do nothing—it is the Lord who takes."

Blessed be the name of the Lord! Hence Job not only overcame the world, but he did what Paul had desired his striving congregation to do : after having overcome everything, he stood. Alas, perhaps there has been someone in the world who overcame everything, but who failed in the moment of victory. The Lord's name be praised! Hence the Lord remained the same, and ought He not to be praised as always? Or had the Lord really changed? Or did not the Lord in truth remain the same, as did Job? The Lord's name be praised! Hence the Lord did not take everything, for He did not take away Job's praise, and his peace of heart, and the sincerity of faith from which it issued; but his confidence in the Lord remained with him as before, perhaps more fervently than before; for now there was nothing at all which could in any way divert his thought from Him. The Lord took it all. Then Job gathered together all his sorrows and "cast them upon the Lord," and then He also took those from him, and only praise remained in the incorruptible joy of his heart. For Job's house was a house of sorrow if ever a house was such, but where this word is spoken, " Blessed be the name of the Lord," there gladness also has its home. And Job indeed stands before us the image of sorrow, expressed in his countenance and in his form; but he who utters this word as Job did still bears witness to the joy, even if his testimony does not direct itself to the joyous but to the concerned, and yet speaks intelligibly to the many who have ears to hear. For the ear of the concerned is fashioned in a special manner, and as the ear of the lover indeed hears many voices but really only one—the voice of the beloved, so the ear of the concerned also hears many voices, but they pass by and do not enter his heart. As faith and hope without love are only sounding brass and tinkling cymbals, so all the gladness in the world in which no sorrow is mingled is only sounding brass and tinkling cymbals, which flatter the ear but are abhorrent to the soul. But this voice of consolation, this voice which trembles in pain and yet proclaims the gladness, this the ear of the concerned hears, his heart treasures it, it strengthens and guides him even to finding joy in the depths of sorrow.

My hearer, is it not true? You have understood Job's eulogy; it has at least seemed beautiful to you in the quiet moment of reflection, so that in thinking of it you had forgotten what you did not wish to be reminded of, that which indeed is sometimes heard in the world in the day of need, instead of praise and blessing. So let it then be forgotten, you will deserve, as little as I, that the memory of it should again be revived.

We have spoken about Job, and have sought to understand him in his devout expression, without the speech wishing to force itself upon anyone. But should it therefore be entirely without significance or application, and concern no one? If you yourself, my hearer, have been tried as Job was, and have stood the testing as he did, then it truly applies to you, if we have spoken rightly about Job. If hitherto you have not been tested in life, then it indeed applies to you. Do you think perhaps that these words apply only under such extraordinary circumstances as those in which Job was placed? Is it perhaps your belief that if such a thing struck you, then the terror itself would give you strength, develop within you that humble courage? Did not Job have a wife, what do we read about her? Perhaps you think that terror cannot get as much power over a man as can the daily thralldom in much smaller adversities. Then look you to it that you, as little as any man, do not become enslaved by some tribulation, and above all learn from Job to be sincere with yourself, so that you may not delude yourself by an imagined strength, through which you experience imaginary victories in an imaginary conflict.

Perhaps you say, if the Lord had taken it from me, but nothing was given to me; perhaps you believe that this is by no means as terrible as was Job's suffering, but that it is far more wearing, and consequently a more difficult struggle. We shall not quarrel with you. For even if this were true, the quarrel would still be unprofitable, and increase the difficulty. But in one thing we are in agreement, that you can learn from Job, and, if you are honest with yourself and love humanity, then you cannot wish to evade Job, in order to venture out into a hitherto unknown difficulty, and keep the rest of us in suspense, until we learn from your testimony that a victory is also possible in this difficulty. So if you then learn from Job to say, "Blessed be the name of the Lord," this applies to you, even if the preceding is less applicable.

Or perhaps you believe that such a thing cannot happen to you? Who taught you this wisdom, or on what do you base your assurance? Are you wise and understanding, and is this your confidence? Job was the teacher of many. Are you young, and your youth your assurance? Job had also been young. Are you old, on the verge of the grave? Job was an old man when sorrow overtook him. Are you powerful, is this your assurance of immunity? Job was reverenced by the people. Are riches your security? Job possessed the blessing of lands. Are your friends your guarantors? Job was loved by everyone. Do you put your confidence in God? Job was the Lord's confidant. Have you reflected on these thoughts, or have you not rather avoided them, so that they might not extort from you a confession, which you now perhaps call a melancholy mood? And yet there is no hiding place in the wide world where troubles may not find you, and there has never lived a man who was able to say more than you can say, that you do not know when sorrow will visit your house. So be sincere with yourself, fix your eyes upon Job; even though he terrifies you, it is not this he wishes, if you yourself do not wish it. You still could not wish, when you survey your life and think of its end, that you should have to confess, "I was fortunate, not like other men; I have never suffered anything in the world, and I have let each day have its own sorrows, or rather bring me new joys." Such a confession, even if it were true, you could still never wish to make, aye, it would involve your own humiliation; for if you had been preserved from sorrow, as no other had, you would still say, "I have indeed not been tested in it, but still my mind has frequently occupied itself seriously with the thought of Job, and with the idea that no man knows the time and the hour when the messengers will come to him, each one more terrifying than the last."

V

REMEMBER NOW THY CREATOR IN THE DAYS OF THY YOUTH

Remember now thy Creator in the days of thy youth, while the evil days come not, nor the years draw nigh when thou shalt say, I have no pleasure in them.   Ecclesiastes 12:1

There is a truth whose greatness, whose sublimity, we are accustomed to extol by saying that it is an *objective* truth, that it is equally valid whether anyone accepts it or not; indifferent to the special circumstances of the individual, whether he is young or old, happy or depressed; indifferent to its own relation to him, whether it benefits him or injures him, whether it restrains him from something or helps him attain it; equally valid whether he subscribes to it with his whole heart, or professes it coldly and unemotionally, whether he lays down his life for it, or uses it merely as a means of gain; whether he himself discovered it, or he merely repeats it by rote. And only that man would have the true understanding of it, the legitimate admiration, who understood that this objectivity is the main thing, and who allowed himself to be shaped in conformity with this into an objectivity toward that which concerns himself or some man as man, or particularly as man.

There is another kind of truth, or if this is more unassuming, another kind of truths, which we might call the *concerned* truths. Their life is not so exalted, perhaps because abashed, as it were, they are themselves conscious that they are not quite appropriate for all general occasions, but only specially for individual occasions. They are not indifferent to the particular condition of the individual, whether he is young or old, happy or depressed; for this decides for them whether they may be truths for him. Nor do they at once release the individual and abandon him, but they continue to be concerned about him until he completely frees himself, and not even this is a matter of indifference to them, although he is still not able to make them doubtful about themselves.

Such a truth is not indifferent as to how the individual accepts it, whether he appropriates it with his whole heart, or whether it merely becomes idle words to him, for this difference proves exactly whether he is jealous for himself. Such a truth is not indifferent as to whether it becomes a blessing or a curse to the individual, for the converse decision precisely testifies against the equal validity. It is not indifferent as to whether he sincerely has confidence in it, or self-deceived wishes to deceive others, for its avenging wrath proves conclusively that it is not indifferent. Such a concerned truth is not indifferent as to who has proclaimed it; on the contrary he continues to be constantly present with it, in order that it may again concern itself about the individual.

One such concerned truth is that tested admonition, repeated for hundreds of years, which we have read. And if you could have heard the voice of him who uttered it, then you would certainly realize how moved he was personally. And if you could see his face, and you yourself were a young man, then you would be gripped by the solicitude with which he concerned himself about you, while, at most, he could still only arouse you to concern about yourself. Who, then, was the man who uttered these words? We do not know. But if you are young, even if you stood next in succession to the throne and your thoughts were such as would be inspired by the expectation of dominion, then we are told that this man, too, wore the kingly purple, although, notwithstanding all this, he believed that the thought about the Creator was the best thought of youth. And if you are young, even if your life is impoverished, untempted by any glittering prospects, you still have his royal word, that, notwithstanding all this, the thought about the Creator is still the most beauti-

ful excellence of youth. Therefore, even if the story about
a king having spoken these words is only a pious wish
which wishes to reconcile the greatest inequalities in the
simple understanding of the same word, the word itself in
different ways is troubled about the inequalities.

For when one who is royal born and will sometime rule
over kingdoms and countries, sees upon the wall of a
humble cottage a picture such as might be expected in
such humble circumstances, a picture whose crudities almost provoke a smile, and he comes closer to it and reads
those words in the inscription on the picture, then the
Preacher speaks to him, but the Preacher was also a king.
And when the son of the poor man stands astonished in
the palace, when unclarified thoughts awaken in his soul,
as awe-struck he beholds the kingly majesty, then the
Preacher speaks to him, and the Preacher was also a king.
Then reconciled he returns home to his humble dwelling
and to his poor picture on the wall.

Is there then no compromise? Or will you assume the
appearance of contentment in order to seek untimely
quarrels to prove that you do not covet the splendour of a
king—but that neither are you satisfied with thinking
about your Creator! As if that self-created satisfaction
were not an arbitrary merit for which you dare not praise
yourself, aye, what is worse, a sign of your paltriness, which
only testifies against you! Is there anything indeed in the
wide world which is able, any more than the world itself
is able, to compensate a man for the injury he would
inflict upon his soul if he gave up the thought of God?
But the one who, blinded as he was, demanded the highest,
he still let it be understood that in a certain imperfect
sense he grasped the significance of that which he relin-
quished.

Or was it perhaps otherwise with you? You were perhaps unwilling to consent to a compromise, just because it
was a king who had spoken these words, and "a king
always gets everything he points at; after he has followed
the ways of pleasure to the uttermost limit of enjoyment,

E.D.   D

what wonder that his view of life suddenly undergoes a change?" The words would certainly have significance, but the admonition could not be accepted; because the words are certainly concerned, but not concerned about any individual; they were indeed words of concern, they were indeed reconciled with life, in so far as it had been softened by sorrow, but nevertheless only a sigh from the recesses of sadness, a sigh at the moment when the wearied soul bids the world farewell, but still only a bubble that bursts, no matter from what depth it rises. For there is a wisdom which almost prefers the concealment of madness, and in the sight of men affords satisfaction to everyone by its strange actions. But the sigh itself and the outburst and the emotion concern no one, no one in the whole world, not even the one from whose heart the sigh issues. Such a brief word, in which the heart would break, such a language of the heart, not emphatic like the language of thought, but trembling in earnestness, is sometimes heard in the world. It will not illuminate anyone's way; for the sun lights a man's way by day, and the moon will shine for him at night, but the will-o'-the-wisp in the fogs of night does not furnish light, not even for itself.

When a man's life draws toward evening, when, weary and thoughtful, he holds intercourse with death as his only confidant; when his spirit has lost the power to make up the reckoning in earnest, and death has become the comforter; when the will and the purpose desire nothing more, but the thought hazily centres about past experiences; while oblivion like a busy journeyman works early and late in the service of consolation—and youth slips past the soul like a dream, then such a man says to himself, as his mind dwells on the most beautiful significance of life, as this once appeared to him : "Happy the man who is done with it!"

But if a young man stood by his side upon whom life still had all its claims, then he would not speak in this way. Only when he sits alone, sunken like a ruin, lost in sadness, only then he says it, not to some man, not to his own soul, but he says it as to the air : "Happy the man who is done with it." And as the physician recognizes the sign of death in the face, so the psychologist knows that this outbreak indicates that the spirit wishes to be extinguished. The outburst may well have its own significance, but one will seek vainly in it for the strength of the admonition because there is no faith in it, faith in oneself's having perfected the good, or in another's having succeeded in doing so. And he who eagerly listens to such words, is, as often as not, himself in a similar condition, or at least in a sadly suspicious realization that something similar may befall him, and therefore they both find relief and alleviation in swooning in that weakness where neither the admonition disturbs them, nor the blessing of the admonition rests upon them.

"All is vanity and vexation of spirit," says the Preacher, and the light-minded regard such an expression as an ingenious triviality, the thoughtless as an unsolved riddle, and the melancholy as a stupefying drink, which makes the last condition worse than the first. The Preacher has spoken many such words, all of which would be profitable if they could help anyone to save himself from going through the same experience, or, at least, could help him to renounce the vain desires which constantly become more and more ingenious. But are the words we read of such a nature? I wonder if the Preacher has not said all that precedes for the sake of this and similar words; and I wonder if he would not readily have refrained from saying all the rest, if only someone would accept this word!

For the Preacher actually says that "childhood and youth are also vanity," and in so far, even to have done what he encourages one to do, "to let the heart cheer him in the days of youth, and to walk in the ways of the heart, and in the sight of the eyes," would be vanity; but has the Preacher ever said that to consider the Creator in youth is vanity and vexation of spirit; or that to have considered Him in youth would also sometime appear to have been vanity? Has he mingled the word about this in with

the rest? Or is not the manner in which he says this as far
removed from the manner in which he says the rest as
heaven is from earth? Has he not precisely resolved everything into vanity in order that the blessed and eternal
significance of this thought may rightly appear, so that it
may bind the wandering soul in obedience under the admonition?

He does not say, as ordinarily: "*So* rejoice in your
youth, *so* put sorrow from you," where the expression
itself, by casually disposing of the matter, indicates that
what he speaks about is of no concern to anyone. He has
omitted this little casual word, and as the discourse about
vanity goes on, and will, as it were, carry everything away
in vanity, the Preacher stands up to resolve the confusion,
so that it does not go beyond its limits; to check the vanity
by a definite expression of admonition: "*Therefore,* consider thy Creator."

He does not speak as if this thought were merely a
youth's thought, which still would sometime be outgrown;
he does not speak about it as about something past which
had once had significance; not as about something past,
of which it was desirable that it should once have had
significance; no, the youth's significance is exactly this
thought's significance, and it is precisely by means of this
thought that youth must be assured against being vanity,
assured against sometime seeming to be vanity. He does
not speak like a man who wishes, or like one who longs, or
like one who swoons; but with the power of conviction,
with the authority of experience, with the reliability of
complete knowledge, with the glad confidence of liberty,
with the emphasis of earnestness, with the concern of
admonition, he speaks to the young.

He does not speak vaguely about youth in general, but,
as the individual does not understand in general that he is
young, for such an understanding really belongs to a later
age, he understands it as a matter for his own personal
concern, and it is just in this way that the Preacher wishes
to have the admonition understood. For this is the solici-

tude in the admonition, that although it can be repeated again and again and concern an innumerable multitude, yet each time it speaks to the individual, since it is as if it spoke to him alone, as if it were only for his sake, as if it were unconcerned about all the rest of the world, but the more concerned about him; moreover, as concerned as if the youth were conferring a favour by accepting it. This is the way the word is spoken, and if you thoughtlessly or sadly were to attempt to deceive the Preacher, or to trick him out of the admonition, which would certainly be a distressing thing to do, you would not be able to do it; for the Preacher has been guilty of no ambiguity.

Thus the Preacher speaks admonishingly, and if you are young, even if you have earlier dedicated yourself to the pursuit of wisdom, he still speaks to you. And if you are young, even if you are among the more simple, you still need not stand begging at the door of that wisdom, for the Preacher's concern is for you also and he not only says you may consider your Creator, but he exhorts you to do so. And if you are young, if you are happy, if you are distressed, if you are unconcerned, if you are despondent at being what you are, it is still you, just you to whom he speaks, you to whom the admonition applies, as does also the reason for the admonition—" before the evil days come, and the years draw nigh, when you shall say : ' I have no pleasure in them.' " Therefore, in what he said earlier he sought to drive your soul up from its security to see the vanity of life; he prevented it from " believing in vain," for otherwise his admonition, however well-meant it was, would always remain a vanity, or rather, a serious matter which was always taken in vain. Youth does not think of the evil days, and does not understand what it means to say that the " sound of the grinding is low, and all of the daughters of music are brought low," and prevents itself from doing what it emphatically understands for some other age. And when the evil days come, and " the sound of the grinding is low, and the daughters of music are brought low," then if one has not remembered his Creator in his youth, he has not only lost his youth, but the understanding of youth's thought about the Creator.

Thus the Preacher addresses his admonition to the young. But he who wishes to speak about the passage we read, should endeavour not only to make the thoughts contained in the passage explicit, but to make the speech itself explicit; for "if the trumpet give forth an uncertain sound, who shall prepare himself for battle?" But to make the speech explicit—what else does this mean than that it should concern some particular individual, that it should speak to some man for his edification? Now it is certainly true that the concerned truth of the admonition addresses itself to the individual according to the special circumstances of his life; but the speech about this truth must still guard itself against conditioning the edification through the accidental; must certainly guard against the accidental enviously coming into conflict and contradiction with what is otherwise edifying; for then the edification is untrue, and naught but an unwholesome diversion, brought about by a preference or a mistaken wish which foolishly desires this.

Thus if someone wished to be edified by the thought about old age, but in so special a manner that youth could not be edified by the same thought, then the edification itself would be irrational. If one were to say, for the edification of an old man, that everything would soon be over, might he not by this speech disturb the young? For why would he not become despondent and tired of life long before his time, if the best one could say of it at its end was that everything would soon be over? But such an edification is a deception, a deceitful compromise, for being old is no advantage, and there is just as little advantage in being young. If a man wishes to believe that youth is an advantage, then he rejects the edification, and will only listen to the worldly speech of the like-minded, his fellow-conspirators, about how pleasant it is to be young. If one wishes to believe that youth itself with respect to this thought about the Creator, has a decided opportunity

which can never later be repurchased: who would dare to
say this to himself, who would dare say it to another, for
fear lest it might be too late, for fear lest the edifying
thought might transform itself into a terrifying one. But it
is not so. When, therefore, the Holy Scriptures make this
a condition for entering into the kingdom of heaven, that
a man should become a child again, then this speech is
really edifying, because it addresses itself to every man,
while otherwise understood it would be the most foolish
and disheartening speech the world has ever heard; for the
child itself does not know what it means to be a child.

What is true about childhood is also true about youth,
but with this difference, that in so far as youth is past, it
can also be lost or greatly neglected. So the speech about
youth can indeed occasion the individual concern, but if it
makes it impossible for this concern to become profitable
for his reassurance, to become a regret for the past which
effects his improvement, then the speech is not edifying,
but worldly-minded, contentious, and confused.

On the other hand, if the speech may also influence a
single youth to anticipate the painful aftercost of this
neglect, it will indeed imbue him with the significance of
youth, even if the speech concerning authority only
vouches for it.

REMEMBER THY CREATOR IN THE DAYS OF THY YOUTH

Remember thy Creator in the days of thy youth; for in
youth one does it best and most naturally, and if a man
throughout all the rest of his life preserved the thoughts
of youth, then he would accomplish a good work. Let this
be our eulogy of youth, even if it is more rarely heard,
although youth is praised often enough. Moreover, as it
might be injurious for the tiny babe to be handled too
much, so it seems that too much praise might be detri-
mental to the wholesomeness of youth. For when the false
or injudicious friendship of dejection is the spokesman,
will it not besmirch with its fiery unwholesomeness, will
it not bring a darting unrest and craving into the careless

confidence of youth? Because despondency is envious of youth, must we therefore make youth envious of itself and perplexed about itself? As one does not pay too much attention to the tiny babe, so let us not pay too much attention to youth, but neither let us, therefore, do the opposite : let us not make it old before its time, lest it drain the bitterness; nor keep it from being young when it is, so that it may not a second time drain the bitterness of not having been young when it was young.

Nor does the Preacher counsel thus. When a youth is joyful and happy at a banquet, then the Preacher is not a disconsolate figure who wishes to tear him away from the wild passion and enjoyment of the moment; not an alarming spectre who wishes to forget himself in the circle of youth; not a fool who imagines that, although advanced in age, he is still young; but neither is he a carping and irritable critic who cannot rejoice with the happy. He accompanies the happy, and when the youth has enjoyed himself with all his heart, when he has danced himself weary, not exactly of life, for youth ought not to do that, but for the evening, then the Preacher sits down in a room off the ballroom, and speaks more seriously. But he makes the transition as naturally as does the youth; for youth can do this with a smile upon his lips and exultation in his bearing, worthy to listen to the talk about high and holy things. So, then, let youth " wear the garlands of rosebuds before they be withered "; but let no one teach youth this —teach youth to " use creation as youth's possession," and in this or some other way cause it to " reason wrongly " as if this were the only thing it had to do. For the thought about the Creator is still the most beautiful glory of youth, a rosebud that does not wither.

And in youth one does it *most naturally*; for a man thinks most naturally who can think this thought in conjunction with all the other things he thinks; and he thinks it most naturally who does not himself have to be changed in order to think it, and who does not need to have the thought changed in order to think it, because in the thought he finds the childlike simplicity which makes the game the best. So that word of the Preacher is from the beginning a proof that this thought must be most natural for youth. If he had not been speaking to youth, he might perhaps have made lengthy preparations. He might perhaps have proved that God exists; and after he had kept the learner busier than the Jews in Goshen in slaving for the truth under his supervision, he would perhaps give him to understand that he might finally get to the point where God became the Creator.

And so it goes. When one grows older, then everything becomes so wretched. God in heaven must sit and wait for the fates to decide whether He exists, and finally He comes into being by means of some proofs; men must put up with waiting until the matter is decided. Suppose one dies before that time; suppose that by the time the matter is decided, someone had grown unaccustomed to thinking of God as the Creator, and the joy in the thought was past! The Preacher does not speak in this way, but as a friendly man predicts a happy future for the child in its cradle, so the Preacher uses the word, and the youth understands it at once. He understands immediately that a God exists, for to the young God's house lies next door to his father's yard, and it seems quite natural to him to be there. But when one becomes older, then the way to church is often very long; when the wind is severe in winter, then it is cold in the church; when the birds sing in the woods in the summer time, the church does not lie in the direction he is going. To youth God dwells close at hand; in the midst of sorrow and joy he hears God's voice calling; if he does not hear it, then he misses it at once, if he has not learned evasion, if he does not know how to hide himself—until he hears it again. When one becomes older, then it is far to heaven; and the earthly noises make it difficult to hear the voice; and if one does not hear it, then the earthly noises make it easy for one not to feel the want of it.

Youth understands it at once. Is not this wonderful! But is the fact that it is wonderful not also a clarification!

There was a thinker, whose memory is revered, who believed that wonder was a characteristic of the Jewish people, that this wonder, in a peculiar manner, overleaped the intervening causes to arrive at God. But, if we wish to select a youth who was not brought up among that people, I wonder if the miraculousness of wonder might not again appear. And then I wonder what essentially belongs to youth, and what, not as the accidental, belongs to an individual nation; I wonder if manhood dares to forget this completely. But when we become older, then come the intervening causes; and if someone reaches God by the long way of these intervening causes, then he can say that he comes from afar—if he reaches God, for many doubtless perish on the way. Is this the fault of the intervening causes or of the pilgrims?

Youth understands at once that God is the Creator, that He has created "the heavens and the earth, and all that in them is." "All that in them is"—is not this a great word, is it not becoming to youth? What has youth really seen? It has merely glanced at the world. What does it understand about the world in comparison with one who has circumnavigated the globe? But youth understands about God, and since He is never far away, if one is to find Him he should not look for Him far away.

There was a thinker who became a hero by his death. He had said that from a single straw he would prove the existence of God. Let the thinker keep his proof; give youth the straw, he can—not prove it. But why, too, is proof needed, when one has the straw and—God! When one becomes older, then the proof comes, and the proof is a distinguished traveller whom all regard with admiration. Youth understands that God has created the world, and yet that was six thousand years ago. But he understands it at once—what wonder, indeed; for how does six thousand years to youth differ from yesterday when it is past. When one becomes older, then six thousand years are many years; then one realizes that it is six thousand years since the world was created—and also six thousand years since everything was very good.

But as the youth quite naturally thinks that God is the Creator, so he just as naturally thinks what follows from that; and since he does not need to waste his time in understanding the first, he can at once begin on the last. But what does follow from this? Moreover, when one becomes older and very intelligent, then extremely strange things result from it. Then one repudiates an earlier thinker, becomes a disciple of a later one, or gives others the name of that one, and does other similar things which concern neither God nor one's self, but only the judgment of the world. On the contrary, youth has with the first already begun on the last; for what indeed follows farther from that except that which lies so near that it does not seem to result from it, even less to follow farther from it. And what is this other except thanksgiving in quiet humility, confidence resting in a childlike intimacy, the pain over the interruption of the harmony so deep that peace cannot long remain away, the concern so childlike that youth does not need to go far in order again to live and move and have his being in God.

And in youth one does it *best*; for he really thinks a thought best who has it always near at hand, and yet hides it the deepest; he, who does not have to seek among many things to find it, does not seek in out of the way places in order to find it.

Youth does not have many thoughts, but from that it merely follows that he can better cherish the one he has, even if he is constantly using it. When one gets older, then one has many thoughts; and if one of them is lost, then, like that woman, one lights a candle and goes and searches for it, and in the meantime allows the other ninety-nine to shift for themselves. Or it sometimes seems to someone that one of his thoughts was lost, and time is wasted in looking for it, for it was a delusion. Such things cannot happen to youth; for when one has but one thought, how could he lose it? When one has many thoughts, he is like one who has many suits of clothes. Sometimes he wears one suit, sometimes another. But youth has just one thought, which always clothes him equally well, and he does not waste time in choosing. On the other hand, youth has always the same place to hide his thoughts as does the older man, and scarcely less room. But when one has only one thought, then one can always get a good and ample place.

Youth does not see many men, but from that it does not follow that he cannot cling with his whole heart to man and to the human.

There was a pagan sage. Ridiculed by many, he thought he would ridicule the others. He went about with his lantern by day, seeking a *man*. One ought not to ridicule him; for whoever while young has not found a *man*, may indeed need a lantern. When one becomes older, then one sees many men, individually and collectively, but if from his youth up, one has not found a *man*, then what does one find? And he who does find one, whom does he find except the preacher and the schoolmaster, his equals, and all the rest he has known so well at home? And whatever he finds which replaces the best, that he gradually loses. So, too, with the thought about God. When the older man finds this thought again, what does he find different from that which he had found in his youth! He thought it in his youth, and the first time he thought it, it was as if he had already thought it an eternity. Compared with such an imperishable memory, the years think it with more difficulty. When one is older, then this thought has frequently only its own season, and this is as it must be. Other thoughts have their times and seasons, and everything is parcelled out. And if in other respects one has an abundance, with respect to this thought one often lives meagrely enough. But youth is the time of abundance. When one grows older, then one ceases to grow, but youth is the season of growth, and he grows together with his one thought, like the lovers who grew together. When one becomes older, then one often reflects on one's thoughts, and becomes absorbed in them. For one grows best in concealment, and, physically speaking, one never grows as much as during the nine months when he lies in his mother's womb; and, spiritually speaking, never so much as in the secret life of youth, when he grows to a divine stature. The older one becomes, the more complicated the reckoning becomes, and yet that thought of the Creator is the one which the schoolmaster of childhood talked so much about; it is the number to carry, and if one ever forgets the number to be carried, then is one's whole calculation wrong.

So let childhood then keep the angels who always behold the face of God; but grant to youth, O God, a friendly care, which will prevent it from losing the best. Woe to the one who defrauds the widow and the fatherless, but woe also to the one who defrauds youth of this thought, even if he gave it everything else! Woe to the one who removes the landmarks of the poor, but woe also to the one who removes the landmarks of youth!

Remember thy Creator in the days of thy youth; for this thought comes repeatedly, and it may sometime later help you to think best and most naturally about the Creator; how it may help you in a more intimate way, must be determined individually.

It is hard, men say, to separate those who were formerly united; but how much harder is it not, when these are thus separated : the thought of youth about the Creator and the Creator? Human language says little about this concern, for not only men's speech but practically their language is selfish; it speaks only about their own affairs, little about God's, whose concern the separation is.

But what is it, then, which separates them? My hearer, ought you not yourself to know what it was which separated you, and ought not the individual to know what it was which separated him from God, even if the cause of the separation differed for different individuals! Perhaps it was age which separated them, in that he grew old while God always remained the same. He was not to blame for growing older; on the contrary it is worthy of commendation, if a man in this respect recognizes the time and the hour; and nothing is more disgusting than to see the unhappy beggar whose eyes and expression beg everyone for the flattering untruth that he still seems young. Or that wretched one who, although advanced in years, still fortifies himself by means of the lie that he still retains his youth. Or that helpless one who has no other defence against the years except the impotent wish that he might still be young. On the contrary, he who recognizes the time and the hour and the opportunity, to him the separation is least noticeable, and he is farthest from having forgotten his youth, which that man has indeed done who spends his days and nights in wishing it back. Whether a man will succeed in becoming older in such a way that he never notices the separation, which would provide another kind of understanding, we do not know; but it happens with most men, that, as they are separated from what belonged to their youth, as they leave their father's house and their mother's solicitude, the more they are separated from these, the more, too, are they separated from God.

Hence, perhaps a man became older, and with the years came understanding, and with understanding knowledge, and with knowledge sorrow, and with increased knowledge increased sorrow. But as he was thus developed and educated, the simple became to him more difficult, and since without this guidance he must act for himself, everything became more and more complicated. Perhaps he chose the guidance of thought, and in order not to owe anyone anything, he let this propagate itself, and the one thought develop out of another, until at last the infinite appeared before him and made him giddy. The more he stared at it, the more his eye lost the power of vision to find its way back in the finite. Perhaps pleasure blinded him, life became a jest, and he let God sorrow in heaven while he chose gladness, and let enthusiasm talk in vain about battle and conflict, about courage in danger, patience in affliction, love in life, victory in death, rewards in heaven, while he permitted every day to have its own pleasure.

Perhaps worldly concern about food and clothing diverted his mind, so that he did neither one thing nor the other. Perhaps he subjected himself to a sorrowful earnestness which transformed life down here into slavery, God in heaven to a strict task-master, His will into a terrifying law, and so he wandered about in a wilderness without finding any refreshment.

Perhaps it was sin and perdition which lay divisively between him and his youthful thought about God, and his resentment at the separation seemed to make an understanding impossible. We might, indeed, carry this course of reasoning farther, but to what end? When the separation exists, then it is not so important to scrutinize the reason for it as to sorrow over the separation which may appear in so many different ways, when the evil days come, about which the Preacher speaks, or when the *retreat* must begin. For as the first book in the Old Testament is called the Birth, the second the Departure, so we might certainly say that there is a third book in human life which is called the Retreat. Hence there appears to be a necessity to return to what was once so beautiful, but which later came to be despised, forgotten, overlooked, polluted, and yet to which everyone, with a certain degree of shamefacedness, resorts for refuge. And the shame is certainly a cheap price for him to pay, in that he, whatever the error of his way had been, experimented with everything before he resolved to return. But then was it not a blessing that he had something to which he could return? Was it not fortunate that the blind man had a child who could lead him? And so one goes his little hour like a blind man who is led by a child.

We do not deny that the return of one person can be very different from that of another; that of the one may be a more peaceful return, that of the other an escape from a pursuing terror; but it is the Preacher who says: "Remember therefore thy Creator in the days of thy youth, remember Him for the sake of the return." Even if the moment when the retreat must begin is sufficiently terrifying, even if a man, at enmity with himself, has destroyed much of what lay behind him: merely a memory of this thought must always help him somewhat. Perhaps there was someone who, reduced to the last extremity, only endeavoured to concentrate his bitterness, his wrath, in a single passionate outburst, and sought vainly in the shrewdness which ordinarily understands life's emptiness and nothingness, until at last he burst forth: "Oh, the world and the lust thereof perish!" but lo, this word then awakened like a memory in his soul; and with it awakened a saving recollection, which still called to him with the faithfulness of youth: "but God's word endureth forever." Thus the youthful memory helped him when there was no other help, thus it does help him. It dissolves the spell of brooding earnestness, so there is again joy in heaven and on earth; it disperses the mists of the busy concern in a resigned freedom from care; it dissolves the troublesome evil in quiet wonder over the dark saying of hoping against hope; it saves the despairing soul from seeing the despair through the frankness which understands nothing, which does not understand the specious assertion of self-accusation, but understands only God's mercy.

Perhaps there was someone who had pondered deep and long about the divine, while he still sometimes even understood what he had found out far more simply than he had discerned it, until at last, as he sat thoughtful and brooding, he could smile at his long meditation by giving heed to the memory of youth, which whispered the simple truth to him, and thus through its intervention transformed for him the beautiful earnestness into a still more beautiful jest.

Perhaps there was one whose plans always gained the victory for him and the adulation of men, while he himself, when he compared the results with his calculations, always discovered a little irregularity, until at last, as he stood there austere and dominating, he was softened by listening to the memory of youth which softly hummed the simple truth to him and, by entwining itself within it, transfigured his beautiful earnestness into an even more beautiful jest.

We do not praise the retreat, as if this were the sole significance of life, as if memory were everything in life. We do not speak presumptuously and slightingly about the truth which the more mature human wisdom discovers; or about the beauty which human art produces; even less do we disparage the honest work of manhood; we speak only about the beautiful significance of the retreat for human life, and we speak about how to have remembered the Creator in the days of youth is the angel of salvation of the retreat.

So let a man's work exact from him what belongs to it, his time and his industry; but in the advancing years, O God, preserve Thou a memory of his youth which preserves for him the youthful thought about the Creator. Woe to him who separates what God has joined together; woe to him who separates manhood from its youth.

If there be someone whom this meditation merely painfully reminds of his own lack, then it would in truth be unseemly and unworthy to be an edifying discourse; especially unfortunate for itself, if it were without sympathy; for then it would not be edifying, and would not have found the universal truth, but would have been deceived by the accidental. It is indeed seldom that a man can truly feel this lack, and perhaps he sometimes deceives himself, repels the sense of guilt, maintains his soul in cowardice, deceives it with good intentions, and chooses the pain of want instead of the sorrow of repentance.

If this is the case, then the discourse is reassured. Even if such a man will not understand himself, the discourse has certainly understood him.

If, on the contrary, there was a man whose youth had preserved for him no affectionate solicitude; if he had gone out into life poorer than the son of the poor to whom his parents had bequeathed only poverty, poorer than the one to whom his father still bequeathed a blessing, his mother an admonition; helpless, forsaken, depressed because he had had no youth; oh, there is still no youth so God-forsaken that the crumbs when they are carefully gathered together so that nothing shall be wasted, may not become through the blessing of God an abundant compensation. And there is no youth, however brief it is, so God-forgotten that the memory of or the deep inward sorrow for it, would not be able to rejuvenate the one who never was young. For, spiritually speaking, the fulfilment is always in the wish, the soothing of the concern in the concern, just as God is already in the sorrow which is near Him. And spiritually he understood his need, and, spiritually speaking, he yearned for his youth. In another sense youth is only vanity, and the longing for it an even greater vanity : for "beauty is deceitful and favour is vain," and the flighty mind goes forth with short-lived hope, and the dance ends, and the jest is forgotten, and strength wanes, and youth is past, so that its place knows it no more. But the thought of youth about the Creator is a rosebud that does not wither, because it knows neither times nor seasons, and it is the child's most beautiful ornament, the bride's most glorious adornment, and the best raiment for the dying.

VI

THE EXPECTATION OF AN ETERNAL HAPPINESS

For our light affliction, which is but for a moment, worketh for us a far more exceeding and eternal weight of glory; while we look not at the things which are seen, but at the things which are not seen: for the things which are seen are temporal; but the things which are not seen are eternal. II Cor. 4:17, 18

Tell a man who your friends are, and he knows you; confide to him your wishes, and he understands you; for not only is your soul revealed in your wish, but he will also see through you in another way, since the wish cunningly betrays to him what you are in yourself. That is, while you are voicing your wish, he examines it to see if it can legitimately be wished. If this is not the case, then he knows not only your wish, but he draws an inference as to the confusion of your mind. In this connection someone has said that wishing is a foolish art, and we are tempted to compare one who has the habit of wishing with one who resorted to the beggar's staff through laziness: they both live on charity; they both are irresponsible; they both have nothing but importunities; they both are suspect in the eyes of justice.

However, wishing may also display a more attractive side. Who has forgotten that priceless diversion of childhood: wishing, which is enjoyed by all children, rich and poor alike! Who has forgotten those beautiful stories from a vanished age, in which things were as they are in childhood, where a wish is the meaning of life, and a blessed pastime. When in those stories a man or woman was granted the satisfaction of having three wishes, it was the custom, a sacred custom, that a man should first wish for himself eternal happiness. When he had assured that, then he might rightfully give himself up to the fun of wishing. Now of course the whole thing was only a jest; but let us never forget that in the midst of life's seriousness there is and ought truly to be time for jesting, and that this thought, too, is an edifying reflection. For whoever is rightly thankful and humbly understands the profundity of the thought that all his activity, divinely speaking, only proves the disparity between that activity and that which he must accept as a gift from life, he will also have time for the innocent jesting which is acceptable to God—he will also know how to wish. He will not spoil the beauty of the gift, or the certainty of the bestowing grace, by taking his own merit into account; he will not even become confused about it; he will simply learn from the excessiveness of the gift the quiet gladness that is not importunate in its unremitting activity, but is humble even in its gratitude. As the heathen offer long and superfluous prayers about what God already knows beforehand, so it is also a heathen fault always to be busy, always enslaved in earnest activity.

It is a merit of our age that in many ways we have known how to work the wish weary, and thus to divorce the soul from its habit of wishing. It is to its advantage, if it has thereby developed an honest seriousness, which for the sake of the good renounces the deceitfulness of wishing. We do not reproach the age because it has made the idea about the power of the wish into an epigram, if it thereby stimulates someone to work with his own hands instead of borrowing strength from the wish. But the wish for the happiness of heaven, is this also merely an epigram, as the wish for the assistance of heaven has become to the frivolous, who believe that one should rely upon God in the same way that one relies upon men, so that if one helps himself, then God does the rest? And if the wish about the happiness of heaven has become a proverbial expression, has one thereby tried to incite men to work the harder in order to acquire it? This seems by no means to be the case. Rather the eternal happiness seems to have become what the thought about it has become, a loose and idle word, sometimes almost forgotten, or impudently dropped from the language, or indifferently pushed to one side as an outmoded form of expression one no longer uses, but only retains because of its oddity. And whereas in the old days one acquired eternal happiness by the grace of God, now too often the eternal happiness seems to have become like an aged and infirm pensioner who sustains his life in the house of the rich on the wretched crust of poverty.

To whom then shall that man go who wishes to consider what consequences the expectation of an eternal happiness has for the earthly, anxious life; with whom shall he take counsel? Everyone in our time is very familiar with civic affairs, so let us for a moment speak about them; let us use them to illustrate the answer to that question. If someone in the state wishes to have one or another matter considered and acted upon, he does not summon strangers and aliens, who have no connection with the fortunes of the country whose welfare they must consider. Nor does he call together idle and irresponsible vagabonds, " who learned to be idle and to wander about from house to house, not only idlers but tattlers also and busybodies "; for decisions by such people will only raise more questions, instead of producing a decision. Finally, one does not call together robbers and evil-doers, in order to give them opportunity to consider at leisure how they may best devour the land. Therefore one chooses quite a different course; one assumes that a certain kind of interest is desirable, that one whose own welfare is as closely linked with that of the country as possible, is the best assurance that the opinion rendered will not come to be as homeless as the inventor of the opinion.

So, too, the consideration of the matter about which we are speaking calls for similar precautions. If anyone believes that this present life is not merely a life of labour but also of reward, not only a sowing but also a harvesting, then we must leave him to follow the precepts of a prudence which accords with his view of life. On the other hand, we should not care to ask advice from him, for he is an alien and a stranger, who has no acquaintance with and maintains no connection with that remote country about which we ask. If someone merely thoughtlessly and to pass the time allows his thoughts to wander about, curiously and unstably occupied with the future, then we must leave him to seek fellowship and co-operation among the like-minded, " whose idle speech eats as does a canker."

Finally, if someone, no matter for what reason, is in conflict with that future, so that he is not only as ignorant as the alien and the foreigner, not only as irresponsible as that romantic knight of thought, but who wishes with all his might to destroy it, then he would certainly be least fitted to take part in a deliberative council. So one chooses otherwise. One assumes that personal concern not only does not make a man biased, but that it is precisely this which makes him capable of reflection. One assumes that the fact that his welfare is intimately connected with that future, is just what makes him qualified to consider it. Therefore, the man who owns treasure in heaven and whose soul is bound up in this treasure; the man who here on earth acquired friends who are able to welcome him in the next world; the man whose thought has preceded him and precedes him to prepare a place for him; the man whose concern anticipates an explanation which life denies; the man whose longing holds the beloved fast, and does not release him in death; the man whose sorrow continues to follow the dead to the grave; the man whose feeling would revolt at the terrible thought of cancelling out the happiness of heaven, would rebel more than a citizen on earth if someone should wish to destroy his native land : every such man is a good citizen, a well-intentioned man, from whom the questioner may dare to expect guidance and assistance, an answer to his question.

But perhaps we have gone about the whole matter in the wrong way; perhaps eternal happiness is something which, to a certain degree, is a matter of course, so that it is foolishness to speak about something which follows of itself. Eternal happiness is a matter of course, nothing follows from it; let us therefore not waste time first by raising a doubt about that which goes without saying, and then by setting at rest the doubt through which we never attain the certainty we do when we accept it as a matter of course, and finally waste time on the consequences of the concern of doubt.

But whether it is a matter of course or not, this view still does not deny that the happiness of heaven is a good, and can only disapprove of the wish for it in so far as the wish expresses a kind of concern which is not needed, since eternal happiness comes of itself, whether one wishes it or not. And at bottom every man wishes, except that the individual does not call attention to the fact that he is wishing; for in the same way every man breathes, but just on that account it would be foolish if the individual wished to set himself apart and rejoice in the fact that he can breathe.

My hearer, let us for a moment speak foolishly, or rather let us for a moment continue to speak foolishly; for you have certainly already noticed that this speech is foolishness, almost through its very cleverness. Let us then foolishly assume that God in heaven is like a weak man who could never find it in his heart to deny anyone eternal happiness, whether he wanted it or not; so weak, in fact, that he, as it were, forced it upon everyone, whether he wished it or not. Such a weak character is sometimes seen in life. He owns one or another good, and in the smaller circle which constitutes the sphere of his activity, it is notorious that he distributes it to everyone. They all get this good—this they have in common; but the difference, in what does this consist? In this. Some of them harden their hearts in indifference, almost make fun of the weak man; unconcerned about him, they pursue their own affairs, excuse themselves from every antecedent concern as to whether they were worthy and had not accepted his goodness in vain; they absolve themselves from every subsequent concern as to whether their gratitude truly appreciates the giver and the gift.

Others, on the other hand, accept the good doubtfully in the form of a wish; and even if they think they do not deserve the gift, their heart and good will are yet favourably disposed toward that man through whose goodness they received it; and even if they regard that goodness as weakness, they conceal the thought from him and from themselves, believe themselves justified and under obligations to behave in this way, because gratitude is the only expression which indicates their relation to him; for a gift it is, and a gift it remains.

If this held true about the reception of eternal happiness, my hearer, how would you wish to accept it? Would you wish to accept it as that first man accepted the earthly gift? Even if you believed your eternal happiness was absolutely assured, you would still feel a deep sense of shame whenever you compared your life with theirs for whom concern about this matter filled many a moment, many an hour, whether it was the wish which engaged their attention, or the heart which was moved in gratitude, or the mind which they disciplined according to their best insight and with all their strength, to be well-pleasing to the Giver, and by means of which they prepared for the transition. For a sudden transition is a terrible hazard. We have sometimes imagined how terrible it must be for the intoxicated suddenly to awaken with all his thoughts in confusion; we have sometimes pictured the horror which must have seized upon the rich man when he awakened in hell; but if it were the case with eternal happiness, that the instant a man breathed out his last sigh he awakened to this bliss, a man whose thought had been as distant from it as the abyss is from heaven: it seems to me that this man must die again from shame, must wish himself away, because the bliss of heaven and his own unworthiness could not tolerate each other. It seems to me that this man must feel as unhappy as one who in a foreign land wishes only to leave it.

We have spoken foolishly, but even so it has certainly shown that a man would not dare to become indifferent to the thought about an eternal happiness. How then could eternal happiness become a matter of indifference to one for whom the speech did not need to venture out to the extreme limits of thoughtlessness, but whose soul was well disposed to listen to the earnest word of earnestness, that "God is not mocked"; whose soul is well-prepared to consider what would entirely overcome that confusion, that "no man can serve two masters, since he will hate the one and love the other"; whose soul is fully awakened from its sleep to understand what would certainly plunge the sleep-walker into the abyss, that "love for the world is enmity toward God"? Such a one has the spiritual sense to be disgusted with the idea that eternal happiness, in spite of its glory, might be nonsense; maturity of understanding enough to realize that eternal happiness is as little to be taken by violence as it is to be redeemed like a forfeit in a game. Such a one truly has time to consider the one thing needful, courage to desire eternal happiness; earnestness to reject the flattery of light-minded thinkers; fear and trembling in his soul to be terrified at the thought of breaking with heaven, or taking it in vain.

But then his thought about this eternal happiness will not be wasted, or his wish be in vain; his anxiety will not be an unfruitful trouble; his prayer not without blessing, like the inactivity of the lilies which do not spin, or the improvidence of the birds who do not gather into barns; his labour not without its reward, even if he does not deserve the happiness of heaven, but only becomes fitted to inherit it through the vigilance of expectation. And this occupation will also become a reward to him in this life, and the result of this expectation a blessing to him in time. For the expectation of an eternal happiness is able to do what ordinarily seems impossible, to be in two places at once: it works in heaven and on earth, it "seeks the kingdom of God and His righteousness, and these other things are added to it." If the expectation does not do this, then it is deceitful, a sick soul's craftiness that would sneak out of life, not a sound soul's frank presence in the temporal. Then it is not an expectation of the eternal, but a superstition about the future; then man does not rest in the trustworthiness of the eternal, but jests with the possibility of the future, which is merely intriguing, like the solving of a riddle. Then is the expectation an insidious craving which has not taken counsel with earnestness about the various decisions of fulfilment; for the more profoundly earnestness understands the fear of the separation—if this does not destroy the responsibility and force the soul, as it were, to surrender—the truer is the expectation.

The result of the expectation is, then, two-fold; but let us this time continue to reflect on the result as it concerns the present life; let us in our reflection always keep the words of the apostle, which we read at the beginning, before our eyes, while our thought lingers with that concerned and powerful witness of the future, the Apostle Paul, and so let us speak about

THE EXPECTATION OF AN ETERNAL HAPPINESS AND THE SIGNIFICANCE THIS EXPECTATION HAS FOR THE PRESENT LIFE.

The expectation of an eternal happiness will help a man to understand himself in the temporal existence. We often and with reason praise the tested look of experience because it is far better able to help one to the right way of life than is that of youth, which is at the service of the imagination, deluded by mental illusions, clear-sighted at a distance, while still its deceptive second sight cannot endure the inspection of an observer. In contrast to the precipitancy of youth, experience has the advantage of being strong in detailed reflection. Precisely because of this, therefore, it is important as a guide in life; for life in the temporal existence is seen only in part and as a dark saying, which is best understood when it is understood gradually. The advantage of experience is that it always has a standard by which it measures, a goal toward which it strives; and when it estimates the extent of the finite, it always knows how to gauge the individual; and when it progresses from the certain, it estimates the uncertain. It knows how to strike a trial balance, to determine the length of the way and the time. It has a standard for strength and endurance, for opposition, for dangers and difficulties, and, in proportion as life appears favourable or disturbing, it knows how to get along. It is not easily taken by surprise, and even if this happens, it soon collects itself and measures again. Perhaps many a human life is passed in this way, active in the service of the temporal existence, but also belonging absolutely to such existence.

If, on the contrary, a man's soul is expectant of an eternal happiness, then will this expectation certainly disturb him for a moment; it will cause him to despise experience, since its goal is too insignificant for him, its standard too low. But neither the impetuosity of youth nor the giant strides of the imagination will help him, and yet he cannot get along without a goal and a standard, for without these life is desolate and confused.

Still, he who has only the standard of the temporal existence goes down with the temporal, and perhaps does not even last as long. Even if one's life passes quietly and peacefully, events may still take place which his experience has not exhausted. If this happens to a man, he becomes the prey of despair. And, on the other hand, if he succeeds in slipping through life without any such dispensation of Providence upsetting his calculations, then, if he has learned nothing higher in life, he is still a child of the temporal existence, for whom the eternal does not exist. If, on the contrary, a man preserves that expectation in his soul, then he has a goal that is always valid, a standard which is always valid, and valid in itself; by means of this goal and this standard he may always understand himself in the temporal existence. As success and prosperity, the favour of men, victory and gain, will not trick him out of his goal, and give him the false goal of vanity in its place, teaching him wrongly to rejoice as one who has no hope, so neither shall sorrow nor the false goal of suffering teach him to sorrow in despair as one who has no hope.

" For our light affliction which is but for a moment, worketh for us a far more exceeding and eternal weight of glory." These are the apostle's words, which we read in the beginning. My hearer, if you had never heard Paul's name mentioned, if this name, so far from being what it has been to you from earliest childhood, a name revered and sacred, were unknown to you, imagine this, and then consider that these words are submitted to you with the request that from them you infer what the lot of the man must have been who could give life on earth and eternal happiness hereafter, such a testimony. Then you would doubtless scrutinize the words, you would compare them with the testimony of others about life's distress and eternity's glory; and then you would certainly conclude that this man must have lived a fairly quiet and undisturbed life in honourable obscurity, remote from the great decisions of life; not, indeed, absolutely unacquainted with the secret wisdom of suffering which exists for those initiated into its secret, but still not put to the extreme test in earthly distress, in peril of the soul's temptation. If you were asked to substitute a similar expression for this one, you might perhaps use a not unfamiliar verse, which we are not able to quote here because it is in a foreign language, but the beautiful meaning of the happily chosen words is about like this : that the earth is beautiful enough as a halting place for one who expects an eternity, but not beautiful enough to make a man forget that he is still only on the way. And this expression would no doubt satisfy you and others.

Imagine now that at the same moment a man entered who said : " These words are by the apostle Paul," and that he told you, what certainly no one needs to tell you, that Paul was halted on the way of offence, and hence was certainly tested in the perils of the soul; that he was carried up to the third heaven, and hence was indeed tempted to acquire a distaste for the earthly life; that he had borne witness with such passion that to his listeners he seemed mad; that for forty years he was tossed about in the world, with no certain dwelling-place; outlawed and abandoned, a stumbling block to the Jews and to the Greeks foolishness; rejected by the world; in peril of life, in hunger, in nakedness, in prison, and finally executed as a felon. Would not this amaze you? Would it not make you giddy, because your standard was not equal to such a scale!

Let youth try its hand at this! Aye, youth is swiftly stimulated to admiration, and its ideas are no less swift. When it gets a round number, then it quickly reaches the goal, and quickly adds it up. Even if it is inspired by the thought of Paul, oh, its enthusiasm does not understand him, and merely deludes itself.

Let experience spell its way forward; it would doubtless say: " Such a life is a perpetual affliction, not to be endured." A perpetual affliction—is this the clarifying interpretation of the words of our text : " our light afflictions, which are but for a moment "? And yet Paul was certainly not without a goal and not without a standard, for eternity was his goal, and its eternal happiness his measuring-stick.

When the thunder clouds of affliction began to gather and to threaten with their terror, when the soul would fail from fear and anxious expectation, then I think, if we dare to speak thus, that Paul took out his measuring-stick, measured with it, and lo, the affliction was brief and light. When the community went astray, when false doctrines and human instability drifted about it so that the way of truth became impassable, and there was no goal, then was heaven his goal. When he is sitting in prison, when error grows and flourishes while he can do nothing; when the goal of his activity is foolishness to experience, because it goes backward, then is heaven his goal. When the intensity of the suffering deprives his soul of its composure, then, I think, he takes out his measuring-stick, and lo, the suffering becomes brief and light, while it would have been unendurable if he had sought for guidance on the basis of human consolation. When the burdens of life rest heavily upon him, when thought adds the burden of past days to these, and he almost sinks beneath the weight; when experience has long lost courage and is willing to declare him " the most wretched of men "; when even the one ordinarily resigned to the will of God, has no other consolation than to wish " that all his calamity were laid in the balance," no other alleviation than the satisfaction of knowing how heavy the burden was : then Paul weighs it, and lo, it becomes light. For the bliss of heaven is above and beyond all measure a great and eternal weight of happiness, and only he was the most wretched who " had hope for this life only."

Experience indeed understands about weights and measures, but what can it do? It is scarcely able even to lift the apostolic sufferings and place them on the balance, but Paul understands that the blessedness of heaven has an eternal overweight. Experience indeed knows how to comfort in many ways, but only the blessedness of heaven knows how to comfort beyond all measure. Experience has long known how to bring gladness to the anxious, but a joy beyond all understanding it naturally does not know. Experience knows all the many inventions of the human heart, but a joy which does not originate in any human heart, it does not know. And yet the life which is without a goal and a standard is comfortless and confused; and yet the life whose experience did not end with verifying that experience is not enough, is only a race of the uncertain, which gets lost on the wrong way; a battle in the clouds, which the wind blows away; a writing in the sand, which is blotted out by the waves. He who has experienced this, will certainly search for a goal which is always valid, a standard which is always valid. And the expectation of an eternal happiness is a refuge in time of need, a fortress life cannot take by storm, an order that need and sufferings cannot cancel. And constant association with this idea nourishes a man better than the mother's milk the nursing babe, and from this concept he returns strengthened, and especially strengthened when the purpose of his striving is not to wean himself from this nourishment, but to accustom himself to it.

When the demands of life exceed the judgment of experience, then life becomes confused and comfortless, unless the expectation of an eternal happiness regulates and calms it. When it is demanded of the rich young man that he shall go away and sell all of his goods and give the money to the poor, then experience does not know how to help; for the demand was not for just a part of his wealth. And if there was someone of whom it was not required that he must sell everything in order to become perfect, since his possession was of such a quality that hardly any one would buy it from him, then what does experience know about it? And he who does not need first to go and bury the dead because they were buried long ago, but whose sorrow has only increased with the years, what support does experience have for him, if the thought does not comfort him that there are always more born than die? And if there is a solitary pain, which indeed gnaws deepest, the experience of another will not comfort the sufferer, for he does not hear the shriek of anguish, and even if he heard it, he could not judge the intensity of the pain by the shriek; his own experience will not help him, for that is why the shriek was stifled, because the pain could not be understood. And he whose mouth was bound as not even the mouths of the oxen were bound that threshed out the grain for others; and he whose soul was anxious, even when he made others glad; and the one, the door of whose lips was locked, even if he knew that his words would attract the attention of the curious, but scarcely gain him sympathy in the pain—how will experience be able to comfort him? But the expectation of an eternal happiness consoles beyond all measure.

There is a covenant of tears with God, and this covenant is not seen, is not heard except by the One who sees in secret and understands from afar; but he is in a covenant of eternal happiness with the God who will dry all tears. And there is a fellowship of suffering with God, whose secret is the assurance of an eternal happiness in confidence with God.—An eternal happiness hereafter? Do you ask, my hearer, what this is and what it will bring? Is it not enough for you that it is even here able to make the affliction brief and light, that it is able to join your anxious soul to the inward joy, inseparable, like everything which God has joined together, fruitfully, like the covenant God Himself has blessed?

The expectation of an eternal happiness will reconcile every man with his neighbour, with his friend, and with his enemy in understanding of the essential. The child wants everything it sees, and the youth is not much better; he wants everything to accommodate itself to him, and the whole world to humour his wishes. But experience knows how to shift and divide; it makes a difference between mine and thine; it gives to the king what belongs to the king, to his neighbour what belongs to him, to his enemy his due, and retains its own. For this reason we praise experience, that it has thus arranged life which in the realm of temporal existence passes in sheer reciprocity. Perhaps many a human life is thus tirelessly engaged until it is finished with temporal existence. But if it is passed in this way, then is such a life merely wretched, however much it is bedizened; petty, whether it occupies itself with millions or with pennies; pitiful as a childish game, if it ought to be earnest. It indicates that if human life wishes to pass in this way, then it is fortunate if distress and danger interrupt this monotonous security, in which the nobler and better qualities of a man sink down in lethargy, as if under a spell.

When the common danger stands at every man's door alike, when a common misfortune teaches men to co-operate, and impresses upon them the need of compromise, then it is indeed seen how they are reconciled by an understanding of the common danger, and how this reconciliation benefits them collectively and individually. But when the danger is past and the misfortune blows over, then they return only too soon to the old mode of living, and the compromise forced upon them through necessity sometimes bears within itself the germ of a more profound disunity than that which had been thrust aside. And even if that reconciliation casts a beautifying radiance over a period of the individual's life, it still does not really belong to him but to the one who reflects upon it, and to the observer who succeeds to the reflection, until the story about it is also forgotten.

Even if it is attractive to look at, such a life still belongs to the temporal existence, is the fruit of the temporal existence, but is also the prey of the temporal existence, and the most one can say of it is that it was a beautiful moment. But this beautiful moment of the temporal existence is still, in comparison with the eternal, only like the brief, silvery gleam of counterfeit metal. On the contrary, he whose soul expects an eternal happiness, has always present in himself that which is valid in itself, and against which all the petty appears as the petty. He is constantly influenced by an aspiration which does not bring him into conflict with anyone, or with anything earthly, whose possession does not exclude anyone else. That is, he can lose the earthly, and if he loses it in the right way, then its loss will make the difficult easier, so that a camel can go through the eye of a needle; and he will not wish to exclude anyone, if he himself is anxious in the right way.

"While we look not at the things seen, but at the things not seen, for the things seen are temporal, but the things not seen are eternal." These are the apostle's words we read at the beginning of this discourse, and so we may well go on. While ordinarily one leaves the happiness of heaven for a later consideration as to what it may sometime be, it would doubtless be better to do this in the case of the earthly and temporal things, to let them pass for what they are, and not consider them. For he who regards the temporal will gradually become incapable of considering the eternal, and he in whose sight the earthly becomes too important, will gradually lose the ability to prize the heavenly. But the things seen are temporal; and the temporal is not only perishable, but it is at variance with itself, and therefore it must be dissolved and cannot endure. This is why his treasure causes pain to the miser even while he is gathering it; pain while he possesses it; pain when he must abandon it. This is why the prodigal scatters without pleasure what the stingy hoards without joy; this is why the new wine bursts the old containers; this is why forgetfulness wipes out the vain achievements, as well as the great toil and sorrow through which a man believes that he attains importance; this is why time consumes the earthly affection and even the hate, which, powerless as it is, would brave its way into eternity. But he who turns away from the temporal to the eternal, and is concerned for his own eternal happiness, he is reconciled with himself, and reconciled with everyone. For the eternal is always in harmony with itself, and its harmony excludes only that which excludes itself.

Still " concerned for his own eternal happiness "—is this expectation not a new burden one assumes, instead of being the eternal medicine which heals all sickness, even when it is unto death? Sometimes men have chosen another kind of certainty than that of concern. They employed a particular criterion, drew up conditions, and through the help of these they were assured of eternal happiness, in the same way that one is assured that what he holds in his hand exists. They did not notice that this temporal assurance was only an illusion; they did not notice that they " hung eternity in a cobweb "; they did not notice that it was a bird in the hand they had caught, a bird which wanted to fly. But while, because of this great certainty, they forfeited more and more the eternal happiness, they won—the right to let the determinations be decisive for others, the right to exclude others. Let them retain this right; it would still be, in truth, the most distressing misunderstanding, if a man in his zeal to exclude others is so soothed by the idea that he does not even dream that he is himself excluded. What wonder, then, that the temporal existence again delighted in its rights, that hate and wrath and earthly partiality and worldly considerations again intruded on the eternal to set it at odds with itself and make it contentious! Who is not terrified by such perversity? For my part, I have always tried in vain to understand it.

But, still, let us earnestly consider this matter; for the bliss of heaven is and continues to be the decision which decides everything. Moreover, even if the concern did not procure for a man the humble entrance into heaven, it would still be worth while to strive after it, so that there may still be an inwardness, a holy of holies in the soul, where consciousness draws back, abandons the world, shuts itself into itself, becomes reconciled with itself and thereby with the inequalities of life; an enclosure where finite thoughts, in so far as they presumptuously wish to push themselves in, are found overthrown (like the statue of Dagon before the ark of the covenant) before the sublimity of the concern which is solely concerned about it in its validity, as the expectation is not, which would triumphantly enter heaven, and wishes that its festal entrance shall be decisive for others.

In so far as that distressing misunderstanding, "which became a prey to worldly wisdom," was due to the fact that it joined the bliss of heaven to finite conditions, it might perhaps again seem, through a misunderstanding, that the thoughtlessness, the careless foolhardiness which is not troubled by any condition, might be preferable. However, this is very far from being the case, and we are agreed that everyone who is without concern, is once and for all excluded from considering a matter for whose consideration concern affords the only approach. That misunderstanding, then, did not lie in the fact that one accepted the conditions, but in the fact that the concern for discovering these conditions was so quickly satisfied that the individual even gained time and opportunity and purpose to decide the question for others concerned. And yet, as soon as the concern ceases, the individual to whom this happens is excluded from the reflection. On the other hand, the one who is truly concerned understands very well that there must be a condition, but finitely he will never be able to fathom this; for the concern prevents a finite understanding. Even when he has considered it most intensively, he must still confess that from a finite standpoint he cannot decide what the conditions are; for it is precisely the finite which the anxiety takes from him. In everything he finds out there will always be a residuum of uncertainty, and this uncertainty nourishes the concern, and the concern nourishes the uncertainty. This uncertainty may be expressed in this way—that he expects eternal happiness by the grace of God. But, again, he expects God's grace, not by virtue of some finite condition; for then it is not grace, and then, too, the concern will soon transform itself into earthly confidence. If he is now constantly concerned in this way, but also constantly saved through grace; if he constantly perceives that it would be a distressing sign if the concern should cease, how could he ever get enough vain assurance to decide this question for another?

Still, suppose, too, that there were certain conditions which one could accurately state in words, and by means of which the observant thought might test what the condition of the individual was, how could he, if he was again concerned (and if he were not, then everything would be vanity), how could he ever with finite certainty decide whether these conditions were present within him? These conditions being then acts, definite conceptions, moods, who knows himself so intimately that on his own responsibility he would dare to vouch that these conditions were present in himself just as they ought to be, not bastard children of doubtful parentage! Who could do this if he were truly concerned, and who must not be truly concerned if he would consider the question seriously! But if an uncertainty constantly remains behind in his soul, on account of which he must take refuge in grace, how could it then occur to him to wish to decide this question for others? For before one begins on others, one must first be absolutely certain himself. But whoever through grace is absolutely certain, something we indeed wish for the individual, he is, humanly speaking, absolutely uncertain.

Let us for a moment speak metaphorically, and through the imperfection of the metaphor direct attention to that eternal validity of which we speak. There is sometimes found in an army a little selected group which is called the band of the immortals, and in time of war it is regarded as a great honour to be selected to belong to it. Suppose now there were a man (we know very well that this is an unhappy aberration which never happened, and I hope nothing similar ever will happen) whom the thought of being chosen for this group occupied as much as the thought of inheriting the eternal happiness of heaven ought to concern everyone. The conditions for eligibility were familiar to everyone : there was required prowess in battle, but in addition there were certain external conditions—a stipulated height, physique, and so on. He must then prove whether he satisfies all these requirements, not in general, not in a slip-shod manner, for he was too concerned for that, and he knew that if he lacked the slightest of these requirements, he would be rejected. And the question as to whether something was lacking, or whether everything was present in the right proportion, would be decided by the commander of the army on his own judgment. On his own judgment; for all the conditions might be separately present, but not united in that vital harmony which determined the choice. I think this judgment might well become to him the unrest of concern. Suppose, however, that he felt perfectly confident, but we still do not forget that he was as much concerned about this selection as a man ought to be about the eternal happiness of heaven. One difficulty would still remain. The choice was not to be made immediately; he must wait several days. What might not happen during these days ! And even if these passed without any bad luck, yet suppose at the moment he entered the palace of the commander he should happen to stumble! I wonder if such a man would have the time or the opportunity or the disposition to go around and observe the other candidates in order to see whether they might fitly be chosen for this band. I wonder if in his deep concern he would understand that to have been almost selected was still a rejection. Would he not with deep concern realize this, if he was as much concerned about being selected for this group as every man ought to be about inheriting the eternal happiness of heaven?

Still, even if a man knew the conditions to the last letter, and understood that he fulfilled them unequivocally (let us assume this)—still would he have time and opportunity and serenity of mind enough to wish to decide the question for others? How? Is not the happiness of heaven so great a good that it needs no augmentation through any external circumstance? He who possesses eternal happiness can neither wish to become happier through some irrelevant thought, nor to be disturbed in his happiness by any irrelevant thought. So if a man who believes that his own eternal happiness is assured, nevertheless considers some such thing, it indubitably proves that he is not considering eternal happiness. And, just as the consciousness of having done a good deed may cause one to lose the reward, so this irrelevant thought may well cause a man to lose his eternal happiness. One who was himself concerned would scarcely wish to exclude anyone; but would he, perhaps, as is sometimes suggested, be sympathetic enough to wish another chosen? Oh, spare your sympathy for a better cause, and if you can do anything for a man, then do it, modestly as is becoming to you, for we are all unprofitable servants, and even our benefactions are only human inventions, frail and very ambiguous.

However every man acquires the eternal happiness of heaven only through God's mercy and grace, and this is equally near every man, so near, that it is a matter between God and himself. And let no third party who has himself received grace mar this by unwarranted meddling.

Even if there were a man (something I truly have not experienced) who embittered my life for me early and late, and made me think evil of everything, should it disturb my eternal happiness if he, too, were saved? Or should I be vain enough to wish to assist him by my sympathy! Oh, the concern about an eternal happiness! It turns the thoughts away from all unseasonable considerations! Even if there was someone who had borne the heat and toil of the day, and if I were not called until the eleventh hour, and our wage proved to be the same, I wonder if it would disturb him, when he considered that the compensation was eternal salvation! He indeed had richly and in abundance, nor would he get more by my being excluded. And if there was a righteous man who from his youth up had kept the commandments, and throughout a long life had expected the eternal happiness of heaven (which truly is a rarely honourable distinction), and I were a robber who "yet to-day," hence at that very instant, had come as far as he : I wonder if that would be able to disturb him. Certainly, if I were to believe that it was because of my worthiness, then it might indeed offend him, and offend heaven itself, so that I should again be thrust out. But if I am now willing, with the observance of all the forms and without any mental reservations, to confess that it was through grace, I wonder if that righteous man would continue to be so unfair, not to me, for I had certainly been admitted—but to himself through retaining his anger. And if there were, not what one in the more exact sense calls so, but what in the plain daily speech one rightly calls a simple man, and you, on the contrary, my hearer, were a wise man who profoundly asked, "What is truth," and restlessly meditated upon the question with ability and success—I wonder if it could disturb you that he became equally as happy as you, and that the infinite happiness of heaven made you both equal.

Certainly, when you come to die, then there will be a difference; then it will be said, and said with reason, that learning sorrows, and its votaries deplore the loss. And your funeral will be different, for it is a beautiful custom that men clothe the dead in his best apparel; but still the question is whether death will not reclothe him. And if it should be what we call a husband, a man who had lived happily with his wife and had begotten children by her in contentment, who had let his heart rejoice with other men, but had seldom been stirred by thoughts which have made you oblivious to everything by day, and which have kept sleep from your eyes at night: I wonder if it would disturb you if he became as happy as you. "Oh, if God held all truth in His right hand, and in His left the eternal striving"—no, if God held in His right hand eternal happiness, and in His left also the concern which had become your life's content, would not you yourself choose the left, even if you still became like one who chose the right? There must still be an equality, and what is indeed more disheartening than the equality to which men sometimes flee, the equality of death, which makes all equally poor; and what is more blessed than the equality which makes all equally happy?

Is this not so, my hearer? And because of this you said to God in your heart: "Father in heaven, when I consider the matter of my eternal happiness, then I do not bring out the reckoning; for I know, indeed, that I cannot answer one to a thousand, and I also know that Peter stood more securely upon the waves of the sea, than does the one who stands on his own righteousness against Thee. And I will not build my eternal happiness on any deed I may have done, not even the best, for only Thou dost know whether it was a good deed; and not upon the best that I might do, for only Thou dost know whether it might become a good deed. Preserve, then, my soul from the pettiness that would disparage Thee and Thy gift, disparage myself by making myself greater than others. Preserve my soul from the reflection which would penetrate what is not given me to understand. Tear out from my soul the sophistry which cunningly takes the best and leaves me the poorer. What as a child I did easily and naturally, in that I believed without understanding; what I have done later, have done, I know, have believed a man against reason; what I shall continue to do, even if being clever is commended more highly than believing; what I shall strive to do with all my might, so that the glory of the intellect shall not deceive me and injure my soul: should I not be willing to do it for Thee; should I not, since I can still do nothing of myself, wish for concern and confidence and sincerity in believing Thee, and in this faith expect Thy eternal happiness!"

VII

MAN'S NEED OF GOD CONSTITUTES HIS HIGHEST PERFECTION

"Man wants but little here below, nor wants that little long" is a high-minded saying, well worthy of acceptance, and worthy also of being accepted as it desires to be accepted. For it is too earnest in its intent to wish to be admired merely as a beautiful sentiment or a neat bit of phrasing. As such it is indeed sometimes present in our speech. We quote it for the benefit of some needy person, perhaps for the sake of offering him some degree of consolation in passing, perhaps merely for the sake of saying something. We say it to ourselves in the heyday of our prosperity; for the human heart is deceitful and only too prone to take even high-mindedness in vain, proud of needing little—while using much. We say it to ourselves in the day of our need; and we immediately hasten ahead in order to receive ourselves at the goal—when we shall have realized the lofty task. But in this we serve ourselves as little as we honour the saying.

Indeed, our need is not for long. But as it sometimes happens that "when the day begins to lengthen, the cold begins to strengthen," so it is always the case that the winter of our deprivation and discontent can make the day seem long, even though life and time be short.

How much then is the little that a man needs? It is quite impossible to answer this question in general terms. Even one who has had the experience, if not of needing little then at least of having to make a little suffice, cannot in general terms determine how much that little is. Just as time often brings new consolation to the sorrowing, new restoration of vigour to the abject, new gains to those who had experienced great losses, so even when it persists in taking away it nevertheless deals solicitously with the sufferer. It rarely takes everything all at once, but only little by little, thus gradually accustoming him to do without; until at length the sufferer perceives with astonishment that he needs even less than what he once regarded as the absolute minimum. He sees that his wants are now so small that he can remember how he once shrank back in terror from the thought of needing so little; though in this he did not think very clearly, since it is certainly not the smallness of the want that is the truly terrifying thing. He remembers how he once excited and heated his spirit by reflecting upon the contradiction involved in needing so little merely in order to go on needing so little; though in this he did not fully understand himself, since the contradiction could surely not be removed merely by needing more.

How much then is the little that a man needs? Let life itself answer the question; and let this discourse do what the sorrows and tribulations of life sometimes effect, namely the stripping a man of his possessions in order to discover how little he needs. And do you also lend your aid, my hearer, in the degree to which your special circumstances make you able and willing to participate. For the discourse does not wish to overwhelm you with sudden fear, seeing that it is engaged in trying to find consolation. Nor does it wish to deceive you, as " when the ice and snow of despair create the delusive mountain stream that lures the caravan from the way, and leads it into the desert to its destruction." Indeed, it cannot terrify you if you have made trial of the process it is about to describe, and if you have thus found the consolation. And if you have not made the trial, the discourse which confronts you with it can terrify you only if your strength lies in the view that such things happen but seldom. But who then is the more unfortunate? Is it the man who has made trial of the experience? Or is it not the soft and cowardly fool who can not perceive that his consolation is an illusion, since when misfortune really comes it helps him little that the occurrence was a rare one.

Let us then take it away from him : wealth and power and influence, and the deceitful service of false friendship, and the obedient subjection of his pleasures to the whim of his desires, and the triumphs of his vanity over the admiration of his worshippers, and the flattering attention of the throngs, and the envied magnificence of his entire presence. Now he has lost it, and is content with less. Just as the world cannot recognize him on account of the great alteration in his circumstances, so he finds it hard to recognize himself—so changed is he : that he who once needed so much now needs so little. In truth, it is far easier to understand and much more cheerful to contemplate how this latter change can make him unrecognizable to himself, than how that other change, the change in his circumstances, can make him unrecognizable to other men. For what folly there is in the notion that a human being should be known solely by his clothes, so that men do not recognize him when he is unclothed; and is it not a melancholy thing that our admiration is reserved for the clothes and not centred upon the man! A more godly view of life, however, readily perceives that the man is about to be clothed upon, and to be clad in festal garments; for the earthly wedding-garment and the heavenly are very different.

But a little with contentment is great gain. Let us then take that too away from him—not the contentment, but the little he has left. He does not suffer want, he is not compelled to go hungry to bed. But he does not know from whence his needs are to be supplied, either in the evening when he falls asleep from his anxiety, or in the morning when he wakes to live with it. Nevertheless, his wants are somehow supplied, the little that he needs in order to live. He is a poor man; and this phrase which it is so hard to hear, he must hear applied to himself. He feels the burden of his poverty doubly, since it is not self-chosen. He is not like a man who renounced his wealth in order to try an experiment, and who perhaps therefore finds himself more easily in his self-chosen poverty, though not necessarily more excellently, if perchance he merely renounced one form of vanity in order to acquire another and a greater. " Man wants but little," says the proverb. But to know that one's wants are few, without in any moment knowing with certainty that these few wants will be supplied—whoever is able to carry this burden needs but little. He does not even need that which nevertheless is something, namely to have the satisfaction of his few wants assured to him. A man needs no more if it is true that he needs only a little—in order to live; for when the time comes he will doubtless find for himself a grave, and in the grave all men need equally little. Whether he owns the grave in which he lies, or has a leasehold for a hundred years (strange contradiction this !) or has had to force his way in among others, has had to struggle even in death to find for himself a little place : all have the same amount, all need equally little, and all need it only for a little while.

But the short time before, of which the saying speaks, may perhaps seem long. For even if the way that leads to the grave is short, even if you never had occasion to see him wearily walk the path to the grave in order to make conquest with his eye of the little country he intends after death to make his own, might not the way in another sense be very long indeed? And if he sometimes lost his courage, and failed to understand at times that man wants but little here below, had you nothing else to say to him than merely to repeat in his ear this one saying? Or did you perhaps have something else to say, something that came so naturally and so easily to your lips that you found yourself perhaps not fully trusting the consolation you offered him, namely the familiar phrase, " Then you will have to be content with the grace of God."

Let us pause here a moment, lest everything be thrown into confusion : the thought, our discourse, and the human language itself. Confused, namely, in that the roles are reversed though the relationship remains the same, so that it is the other who has the consolation while you lack it, the other who is rich while you are needy; though the very opposite seemed to be the case until you heard the little magic word that changed all. Perhaps the word did not even win your attention; for we often use many a word in this manner, as the child uses the significant word without becoming aware of the spear-point of the thought, which wounds unto death in order to save the life. To let the grace of God suffice us! The grace of God is surely the greatest of all good gifts, on this point we do not propose to raise a controversy; this belief is at bottom the most earnest and blessed conviction of every human being. But we so rarely evoke the thought; and if we wish to be honest with ourselves we must admit that in the last analysis, although without fully becoming aware of what we do, we quietly apply to this conception the old adage that "too much and too little spoils everything." For if a man were really to think this thought in its eternal validity it would at once nullify all his worldly thinking, imagining and desiring, and turn everything upside down. And this is something that a man cannot long endure. Hence he falls back to the lower level of earthly things, to his customary speech and habits of thought. And the older he is in years the harder it is for him to learn a new language, especially one so markedly different. Now and then this comes to his attention, and he senses that there is something wrong about the use which he makes of the word, intermingled as it is with all sorts of worldly speech. He thus acquires a bad conscience with respect to it, and is not happy in its employment. And yet, it really is the truth that the grace of God is the most precious of all good gifts.

If a man had what is less precious indeed than the grace of God, namely, the entire sum of all the treasures in the world, and you were to be so bold as to admonish him to rest content with this, he would doubtless smile at you. If, on the other hand, he were himself to say: "Now I shall try to be content with what I have," such speech would doubtless seem repugnant; for what more could he ask to possess? And how great the insolence of "trying to be content" when one has everything. Whatever we are engaged in trying to make suffice, must surely be something that is little; and to strive to be content with the most precious of all possessions seems indulgence in a strange mode of speech.

And further, this consolation is offered to the other by a man who does not himself appear to understand it. This is as strange as if someone were to offer a needy person the gift of a coin, admonishing him to be content with the gift, although the fact was that this coin was one which made its possessor the owner of the entire world.

How strange that the giver could appraise his gift so modestly as to match it with the advice to be content! Is it not as if a man were going to a banquet, invited by some great personage, and met on his way a humble person who was not invited; and for the sake of consoling him after a fashion, said to him: "You will have to rest content with the privilege of sitting at table in the kingdom of heaven." Or if the humble man himself said: "Alas, I am not invited by the great man, nor could I accept the invitation even if I were; for I have a previous engagement, and must content myself with sitting at meat in the kingdom of heaven"—would it not be a strange form of speech?

The more one thinks about it, the stranger does the earthly life and the human language become. Intermingled with all of life's earthly and worldly differences, which are already quite sufficiently insistent upon being taken at their own evaluation, we thoughtlessly permit the distinction of the divine also to make its appearance, and in such a manner as to show that it is at bottom really excluded. When a man comes to us in the name of the king, this authorization opens every door. But it is a last desperate recourse for a man to come to us in God's name, and whoever is compelled to be content with such an authorization must be content with little. If someone came to a great man's door, and the servant failed to make out on what errand he came, and the great man himself came to the door in impatience, and saw standing there a humble man who presented himself as coming in God's name—would not the door in all probability be shut in his face?

But the discourse does not wish to startle you, my hearer, nor to shock you out of your continuity with yourself. When we speak of being content with the grace of God, the reason doubtless is that the grace of God does not express itself in our experience as a human being would like, or finds it easy to understand, but speaks instead a more difficult language. When the grace of God grants to a man what he likes and desires, he is not merely content, but happy and grateful; under such circumstances he deems himself fully capable of understanding that God is good and gracious. That this is a misunderstanding, to the refutation of which, however, no one need leap too promptly and eagerly, is certain enough. One need not on that account omit to train oneself in the truer and more difficult interpretation while there is still time and opportunity. If it is possible for a human being to persuade himself of the grace of God without the intermediation of any temporal testimony, or without leaning upon that interpretation of God's providence which makes it profitable for him according to his own ideas of what is profitable, then indeed it is quite certain that for him the grace of God is the highest good. And he will then strive to rejoice in God's grace so as not merely to rest content with it; and he will give thanks for it so as not merely to find it barely sufficient. He will not grieve over what God has denied to him; he will not be overmuch concerned with the difference in mode of expression which formerly existed between God's everlasting faithfulness and his own childish littleness of faith. For now this difference in language no longer exists, in that " his heart is strengthened by grace and not by meat."

If someone suffering from some deprivation, enjoyed the

friendship of a great man, but this powerful friend could do nothing to alleviate his suffering (which is comparable to the grace of God being without external confirmation), the mere fact of his friendship with the great man would nevertheless mean much to him. But here perhaps we touch the difficulty. The sufferer might readily persuade himself that the great man really was unable to do anything for him; but how could any man in any finite sense be persuaded that Almighty God could do nothing for him! Hence it results that our thoughts in their impatience steadily insist that God can surely do for us what we wish Him to do; and it is because of man's impatience that the language speaks of trying to rest content with the grace of God. In the beginning, when this impatience was at its height, and cried out most loudly to be satisfied, it could scarcely be made to understand that the contentment of which we speak could be praiseworthy. But as the impatience subsided, and the sufferer found rest and peace in the serene incorruptibility of the inner man, he began to understand this more and more, until at last his heart was moved, and he came to behold a vision, even if only intermittently, of the divine glory—the divine glory which had taken upon itself so humble a form. And if this glorious vision vanishes, so that he again becomes a sufferer, as in truth he was even while he beheld the vision; if it again seems to him that it requires a contented spirit to find the grace of God sufficient for his needs; he nevertheless sometimes admits to himself with shame that the grace of God is something that one may well find worthy of one's contentment; aye, that it is of all things most worthy to be desired; aye, that it is of all things most blessed to possess.

So then it happens, little by little, for the grace of God can never be seized by force, that the human heart becomes in a very beautiful sense more and more discontented, more and more burning with desire, more and more filled with longing, for the assurance of the grace of God. And behold, now all things have become new, everything is changed. In the case of the earthly goods of life the principle obtains that man needs but little, and in proportion as he needs less and less he becomes more and more perfect. A pagan who knew only how to speak of earthly things, has said that God was happy because He needed nothing at all, and next to Him in happiness was the wise man, because he needed little. But in the relation between a human being and God this principle is reversed: the more a man needs God the more perfect he is.

The word which speaks of letting the grace of God suffice us is by no means intent merely upon offering us consolation, and upon re-affirming this consolation whenever earthly want and deprivation makes it seem necessary. For when a human being has fully awakened to its import it calls him aside, to a place where he no longer hears the earthly mother-tongue of the worldly mind, nor the customary speech of men, nor the alarums of the actors on the stage of life. But he stands now where the word is glorified, and confides to him the secret of perfection, namely, that to be in need of God is no shameful embarrassment, but precisely the perfection of human life, and that it would be the saddest of all tragedies if a man passed through life without discovering that he needed God.

Let us then strive to interpret to ourselves more clearly this edifying thought:

MAN'S NEED OF GOD CONSTITUTES HIS HIGHEST PERFECTION.

The truth of this principle, that standing in need of God constitutes a perfection, would seem to be attested by a familiar circumstance, one which may serve at least as a passing reminder. In the churches of the various countries it is customary, after the sermon, to pray for the ruler and the members of the ruling house. That prayers are also offered for the sick and the sorrowing cannot prove that being in need of God constitutes a perfection, since these are sufferers. But the ruler is a great man, the most powerful in the land; and yet intercession is made especially for him, while it is only in general terms that the sick and the sorrowing are mentioned, though the church hopes and trusts that God in His heaven will understand the petition in a quite particular manner, so that though the church does not specify any particular person, God nevertheless thinks of each individual separately. And if God's understanding is of a different sort, if His cares and responsibilities for the government of the world permit him too to concern Himself with individuals only in a general way—aye, then may God help us! Ah, this is still the last resort of every human being in his misery. Even when he cannot endure this last thought, that God's providence for individuals should be merely general in its character, even then he says: God help me endure this thought; and thus gets God, in spite of all, to concern Himself particularly with him.

But why is prayer offered especially for the ruler? Is it because he has earthly power, and holds the fate of many in his hands? Is it because his well-being determines that of countless others? Is it because every shadow of misfortune that passes over the ruler's house also darkens the homes of all the people? Is it because his illness interferes with the functions of the state, and his death disturbs its life? Wholly worldly as such a concern is, it may nevertheless not unbecomingly enlist the thoughts of many. But such a concern will scarcely prompt anyone to pray or at any rate not prompt anyone to pray, except with the reservation necessary whenever we pray for earthly goods; for from this point of view a ruler constitutes just such an earthly good. When understood in this manner the prayer would become more and more earnest and personally pressing, the more closely the petitioner's own life was tied to the life of the ruler, until at last the prayer ceased to be intercession, just as the wife's prayer for her husband can scarcely be called intercessory. But the church cannot pray in this manner, precisely because it makes intercession; and it makes intercession for the ruler, doubtless, because it is convinced that the higher a man stands the more he needs God.

Nevertheless, even if such intercessory prayer is offered in all churches, it does not follow that the ruler on whose behalf it is offered has himself an understanding of the truth that his need of God constitutes man's highest perfection. And even if the individual church-goer tacitly consents to the intercession, and if, alas, the many who do not go to church have no objection to this prayer being offered, it does not follow that all these understand it in a godly manner; in the sense, namely, that the higher one rises in the scale of earthly power and greatness the nearer one merely comes to the need of intercession. It is only too easy for the great to take such prayer in vain; and it lies only too near at hand for those who pray, to utter such prayer in vain. On the other hand, if a man rightly and earnestly understands this thought, his life inevitably tends to become more difficult : this we do not deny. And one who tried to produce this consciousness experimentally, on his own responsibility and initiative, not leaving it to God to teach him, does not yet understand it earnestly enough. It is God Himself who best knows how to utilize a man's own anxieties for the purpose of extirpating all his self-confidence; and when he is about to sink down into his own nothingness, it is again God Himself who can best keep him from continuing to maintain a diver's underwater connection with his earthly self. Let us then admit that this thought renders life more difficult, without on that account becoming dispirited or cowardly, wishing to receive in our sleep what others have had to earn by labour and exertion. When the believer says enthusiastically that his suffering is light and brief and the yoke of self-denial easy, let us not take this profession in vain. On the other hand let us not doubt that the yoke of self-denial really is profitable, or that the cross of suffering is pre-eminently ennobling. And yet us hope to God that the time may come when we too may venture to speak enthusiastically. But let us not too soon demand this degree of advancement for ourselves, lest the enthusiastic words of the believer should make us downcast, when we discover that we do not at once succeed. It frequently happens that a man imprints upon his memory one or another strong word or phrase. Then when suffering comes to him he remembers the word, and thinks to conquer at once in the joy of the word. But even an apostle does not always use strong expressions; he too is sometimes weak, he too is filled with anxiety. Thus he gives us to understand that the strong expression is dearly bought, and that it can never be possessed except so as to give one occasion again and again to be reminded of how dearly it was bought.

But though this understanding makes life more difficult, not only for the thoughtlessness of the fortunate man and for the many who yearn to be like him, but also for the unfortunate, since the understanding in question does not by any means exercise a magic potency, or affect life in any outwardly decisive manner—should we on this account recommend it doubtingly, or desire it double-mindedly? Nevertheless it must give us pause to note that what is offered to us as a consolation, begins by making life more difficult, in order finally, aye, finally in truth, to make it easier. Each miracle of truth is like the wonder at the wedding-feast in Cana : Truth pours out the poor wine first and keeps the best to the last, while the deceitful world pours out its best wine first. Because a man became unhappy, even " infinitely unhappy," as he perhaps says of himself, it by no means follows that the understanding of life which constitutes a condition for the acceptance of the consolation, the understanding that he can do nothing of himself, has come to full growth and maturity within him. If he believes that it is only the means that are lacking to him, then he still believes in himself. If he believes that he could help himself if given power, or the admiration of men, or the attainment of his wish; if he thinks that his complaining constitutes a just claim upon anything temporal, a claim that becomes increasingly valid in proportion as his complaint becomes increasingly loud, then he still has a bitter cup to drink, humanly speaking, before the consolation can come to him.

Hence it is always a matter of considerable difficulty for anyone to offer another a consolation of this nature. For if a troubled soul were to make an appeal to a man for help, and he were to reply: "Indeed, I know where consolation may be had, an indescribable comfort; and what is more, this consolation gradually transforms itself within your soul into the highest of human joys," the anxious individual would no doubt be willing to listen attentively. But when the speaker goes on to say: "Before this consolation can be yours, you must learn to understand that you are absolutely nothing in yourself. You must cut down the bridge of probabilities which seeks to connect the wish, the impatience, the desire, the expectation, with that which is wished, desired and expected; you must renounce the intercourse which the worldly mind has with the future; you must retire into your self, not as into a fastness that still bids defiance to the world, while the individual keeps his most dangerous enemy with him in the fortress, aye, while it was perhaps precisely on the advice of this enemy that he shut himself in—but a man must retire into himself so as to sink down into his own nothingness, making an absolute and unconditional surrender," there would doubtless be one or another who would go home sorrowful, like the rich young man of the many possessions, though himself having few possessions, and yet resembling the rich youth of the many possessions so much that it would have been quite impossible to tell them apart. Or if some anxious soul had run riot in overmuch deliberation, and had become the prisoner of his many thoughts, so that he could not act because it seemed to him that the considerations on either side balanced each other exactly; and another were to counsel him in these terms: "I know a way out of your difficulty which will give you full assurance of victory. Yield your wish and act; act in the conviction that even if the opposite of what you wish results from your action, you will nevertheless have conquered," there would doubtless be one or another who would turn his face away in impatience, because it seemed to him that such a victory was not to be distinguished from a defeat, and because such a way out seemed harder to endure than the doubting soul's multifarious unrest.

What then is man? Is he but another jewel in the great chain of being? Or has he no power, can he himself do nothing? And what is this power? What is the highest he can will? What will be the answer to this question, when the daring of youth and the power of manhood combine to ask, when this glorious union of courage and strength holds itself ready to sacrifice everything in order to realize the great ambition, and speaks of its purpose in terms of burning zeal : " If no one else in all the world has achieved it, I am nevertheless resolved to achieve it. If millions of men fell by the wayside and forgot the task, I will nevertheless persist in striving—but what is the highest of human tasks?" For our part we do not propose to cheat the highest aim of its true cost, nor do we intend to conceal the fact that it is seldom attained. For the highest of human tasks is for a man to allow himself to be completely persuaded that he can of himself do nothing, absolutely nothing.

This is indeed a rare kind of greatness. It is not rare in the sense that only an exceptional individual is born to the purple, for everyone is born to it. It is indeed a rare kind of wisdom; but it is not rare in the sense that it is offered only to a few, since it is offered to all. Wonderful rarity, which is not debased through being offered to all, or in being shared by all ! When a man turns his mind to outward things it may seem to him as if he could accomplish what exceeds the measure of human astonishment, could achieve what would satisfy him as nothing else would, could realize what would concentrate upon itself the jubilant admiration of men. But the rare and lofty greatness of which we here speak is not well suited to be admired. It cannot tempt the sensuous man. On the contrary, it condemns as a fool every would-be admirer, who does not understand what it is that he admires. It bids him go home; or it judges him to be a deceitful soul, and bids him retire into himself.

To a merely external contemplation man is indeed the jewel of creation. But all his glory is, as such, but external, existing in and for and by outward things. Does not the eye aim its arrows outward every time passion or desire stretches the bowstring? Does not the hand seek to grasp some external thing, is not his arm outstretched? Is not his mind attuned to a hymn of conquest? But if he is unwilling to be the weapon in the service of unclarified cravings, aye, in the world's service, because the world upon which he fixes his desire itself awakens this desire; if he is unwilling to be a stringed instrument played upon by unclarified moods, or rather, played upon by the world, because the movements of his soul are determined by the manner in which the world plucks the strings; if he does not wish to be a mirror that reflects the world or in which the world reflects itself; if he is unwilling to play this passive role, but desires first to control the eye before it marks out something that it desires to conquer, in order that the eye may belong to him and not he to the eye; if he wills to lay hold of the hand before it is outstretched to seize some outward thing, in order that the hand may belong to him and not he to the hand; and if he wills this with such earnestness that he does not hesitate if necessary to pluck out the eye, to cut off the hand, to close the windows of sense—then all is changed; the power is taken away from him and the glory. He no longer strives with the world, but with himself.

Behold him now. His powerful figure is held in a close embrace by another equally powerful figure. They enfold one another so fast, they press upon one another with such equal suppleness and strength, that the wrestling cannot even begin; for it is as if the other figure would instantly overwhelm him. But this other figure is himself. Thus he can do absolutely nothing, and even the weakest of men, untried in this struggle, can do far more than he. This struggle is not only exceedingly strenuous, but it is at the same time fearful; unless indeed he has plunged himself into the struggle of his own accord, following the dictates of his fancy, in which case it is not the struggle of which we here speak. When life under the providence of God forces a man out of the shelter and security of its routine and elects him to be strengthened in this annihilation, the experience is one which knows no illusion and permits no evasion. It is impossible to say that the individual might have more power under other circumstances; for when the individual strives with himself, circumstances cannot decide the outcome.

This is man's annihilation, and this annihilation is his truth. This knowledge he will find it impossible to evade; for he is his own witness, his own accuser, his own judge. He is himself the only one who could bring consolation to bear, since he understands the need of the annihilation, and he is also the only one who cannot bring consolation to bear, for he is himself the sole instrument of his annihilation. To achieve an understanding of this annihilation is the highest task for every human being. To brood over this understanding, as over a treasure entrusted to his keeping, entrusted to him by God Himself as the secret of the truth, is man's highest and most difficult achievement. For the deceptive and falsifying interpretation of life is easy enough, so that a man becomes something at the expense of the truth. This is the highest and most difficult task that a human being can perform—but what do I say, not even this is in his power. Man can at the most will to understand that this fire only burns until the fire of the divine love lights the flames in that which the first fire could not consume.

In this way man becomes a helpless creature. For every other understanding of life, in terms of which he understands that he can help himself, is a misunderstanding; though the acceptance of such an interpretation may make him seem bold in the eyes of the world, bold through having the courage to remain in a misunderstanding, that is, by not having the courage to understand the truth.

But in the heavens above, my hearer, dwells the God who can do all things; or rather, He dwells everywhere, though men fail to perceive His presence. " O Lord, if Thou wert an impotent and lifeless body, like a fading flower; if Thou wert like a brook that runneth past; if Thou wert like a building that suffers decay with the passing of time—then would men take note of Thee, then wouldst Thou be a suitable object to engage our low and brutish thoughts!" But now it is not so; and it is precisely Thy greatness which makes Thee invisible. For Thou art too far removed from the thoughts of men in Thy wisdom that they should see Thee; and Thou art too near men in Thy omnipresence to permit them to see Thee. Thou dost conceal Thyself from man in Thy goodness, and Thy omnipotence causes him not to see Thee, for then he would himself become as nothing! But God in heaven can do all things, and man can do absolutely nothing.

Does it not seem to you, my hearer, that these two, God and man, are well suited to one another? But if they are so suited to one another, the only remaining question is whether you will consent to be glad over this wonderful piece of good fortune, namely that you two are so well suited to one another. Or would you rather be as one who is not at all suited to God, or as one who can himself do something, and hence is not altogether suited to God? For you can neither change God nor could you wish to change Him, so that He should not be able to do all things. It may perhaps seem hard to become as nothing; but even in human affairs we nevertheless speak otherwise. For if misfortune came and taught two human beings that they were suited to one another either in friendship or in love, how slight does not the distress that misfortune brought them seem to be in comparison with the joy that the same misfortune also brought them, namely, the discovery that they were suited to one another! And if two human beings in the very hour of death made the discovery that they were suited to one another for all eternity, what importance could they possibly attach to the brief if bitter moment of separation which is called death, in comparison with an eternal understanding!

It is in this sense that man is great; and he arrives at the highest pitch of perfection when he becomes suited to God through becoming absolutely nothing in himself. But let us beware lest we admire this greatness frivolously, or take our admiration of it in vain. Did not Moses as the Lord's messenger address himself to a degenerate people for the sake of emancipating them from themselves, from their slavish minds, and from their slavery under a tyrant's yoke? What are even the greatest of heroic achievements over against what we call the works of Moses; for what is it to level mountains and to fill up rivers in comparison with letting a darkness fall upon the whole face of Egypt! But these were only so-called the works of Moses; he could do absolutely nothing of himself, and the deeds were the Lord's. The difference is worth noting. Moses does not form resolutions or outline plans, while the wise men in council listen to him attentively, because they recognize this leader as the wisest among them; Moses can do nothing. If the people were to say to him: "Go to Pharaoh, for your word is strong, your voice is triumphant in persuasion, your eloquence irresistible," would not Moses have to answer: "Ye fools! I can do nothing at all, I cannot even sacrifice my life for your sakes, unless the Lord so wills it. I can only refer everything to God." He makes his appearance before Pharaoh, but what is his weapon? It is the weapon of the impotent : prayer; and he does not know what will happen even at the moment when his last words have already reached heaven. He merely believes that whatever happens will be for the best. He returns to his people; but if they make as if to praise him and offer him their gratitude, he will doubtless reply : "I can do nothing at all." Or when the people are overcome by thirst in the desert, and appeal to Moses for help, saying, "Take your staff and bid the rock give forth water to drink," Moses will doubtless answer : "What is my staff other than a stick?" And if the people continue to press, saying: "But in your hand this staff is a mighty instrument," then Moses will doubtless say: "I really cannot do anything; but since the people so desire it, and since I cannot myself endure the sight of their misery when they languish from thirst, I will smite the rock, though I have no faith that the water will gush forth"— and the rock gave no water. So Moses does not know beforehand whether the staff he holds in his hand is to be the finger of the Almighty, or merely a stick of wood; of this he is ignorant even in the very moment that he brings it down upon the rock. He knows it only afterwards, just as he always sees merely the back of the Lord. Humanly speaking, the weakest individual in all Israel has more power than Moses; for the weakest person in the land still thinks that there is something that he can do, while Moses knows that he can do absolutely nothing. In one moment to be as if stronger than the strongest, stronger than all others, stronger than the whole world, inasmuch as the wonder is performed through him; in the next, or rather the same moment, to be weaker than the weakest, in so far as even the weakest person still clings to the belief that there is at least something that he can do—such greatness will not tempt the ambition of the vain soul, provided it takes the time to understand wherein the greatness consists; for in the absence of such an understanding it would doubtless be prompt, in nauseous cowardice, to wish itself in Moses' place.

But if this view of life, namely, that being in need of God constitutes man's highest perfection, makes it more difficult to live, it does so only in so far as it considers man from the point of view of his perfection, and seeks to stimulate men to view themselves in this light; for through this view of life *a man learns to know himself*. And the life of each human being who does not know himself, is in a deeper sense mere delusion. The failure to discover whatever talents have been entrusted to him, the consequent mission to seek their development to the greatest possible extent in accord with the circumstances of his life, so that the roots of his life may penetrate ever deeper into the fibres of existence—such self-delusion is doubtless seldom encountered. Men rarely fail in this. They avoid dealing frivolously with themselves and their powers; they are not like a happily gifted child who does not know how much is entrusted to it, or a thoughtless youth of great wealth who does not understand the significance of riches. What we call a man's self has a value like the value of money. Whoever knows himself knows how much he is worth to the last penny, and understands how to invest himself so as to yield the maximum return. If he does not know how to do this, then he does not know himself and is deceived, as the worldly wise will doubtless tell him, and persist in telling him step by step as his life unfolds itself. They will tell him that he does not extract the joy of life from the spring-time of youth; that he does not value himself truly, in accordance with what riches are really his; that he fails to see that men will take him at his own valuation; that he has not known how to make himself significant, and thus to make life significant for himself. Ah, but even if a man knew himself ever so well after this fashion, if he thoroughly understood how to put himself out at interest—could he on this account be said really to know himself? But if he does not know himself his life is in a deeper sense delusion. And in this worldly-wise age of ours, is it really so very rare a thing for a man to involve himself in such delusion?

The prudential self-knowledge we have just described—what is its nature? Is it not a knowledge of a man's self in its relation to something else? But is it a knowledge of a man's self in its relation to himself? This means that in spite of its seeming trustworthiness such self-knowledge is ultimately a very dubious thing, lacking in any solid foundation, since it concerns only a relation between a doubtful self and a doubtful other. This other could suffer alteration, so that someone else became stronger, richer, more beautiful; and his own self could suffer alteration, so that he became poor, ugly, impotent; and such a change might take place at any instant. If this other, in relation to which he calculates his wealth, is taken away he is deceived. And if it is something that can be taken from him, he is deceived even if it is not actually taken from him, because the entire meaning of his life was based upon a something of this precarious nature. There is no deception when that which can disappoint us does disappoint us, but rather must we say that there is a deception when it does not.

Such self-knowledge is thus very imperfect, and is far from regarding man from the point of view of his perfection. For it would surely be a strange sort of perfection of which one must finally, after having praised it in perhaps the strongest possible terms, say that it is at the same time a delusion. Along this road one cannot reach a point of view which has regard to man's perfection; and in order even to begin to consider man from the point of view of his perfection one must emancipate oneself from all such considerations. This is difficult enough, just as it is difficult to rouse onself from a dream without continuing the dream, dreaming that one is now awake. In a certain sense it is also a complicated task, because a man's real self seems so distant from him that the entire world appears to him to be nearer than his self. And it is also a terrifying occupation, because the deeper self-knowledge begins with that which one who refuses to understand it must call an anxiety-breeding deception. For instead of the entire world he gets merely himself; instead of being master of his fate he becomes a needy petitioner; instead of being able to do everything he can do nothing at all. Ah, how difficult here again not to fall into dreams, dreaming that one does all this of himself.

When man turns about, so as to confront himself in order to acquire an understanding of himself, it is as if he blocked the way for that first self of which we have been speaking. He interferes with its movement outwards, with its yearning for the surrounding world which is its object, and with its pursuit of it; he calls the first self away from external things. For the purpose of inducing the first self to acquiesce in this recall, the deeper self makes the surrounding world reveal itself as it really is, namely as uncertain and precarious. It is indeed the truth that the world about us is unstable, every moment admitting of a change to its very opposite. The man has never lived who by the exercise of his power or by the magic of his wish could hold this variableness within the bonds of restraint. The deeper self thus proceeds to picture the outer world, with its elusiveness and its mutability, in such terms that it no longer seems desirable to the first self. Either the first self must contrive to slay the deeper self, to plunge it into oblivion, when all is lost; or it must admit that the deeper self is right. For to assert stability of that which constantly changes is a contradiction. As soon as it is admitted that it is of the nature of the outer world to change, it follows that it may change at any moment. However much the first self may shrink from this acknowledgment, there has never lived so clever a phrase-maker or so subtle a sophist that he can refute the eternal insistence on this point of the deeper self. There is only one way out, and that is to silence the deeper self by letting its voice be drowned in the roar of the world's changes.

What has now happened? The first self has been brought to a standstill; it cannot move. The environment may actually be quite favourable, ah, so favourable, it may seem so palpably reliable, so evidently steadfast, that almost anyone would be willing to forecast a favourable outcome, provided only a beginning be made : it boots nothing. Whoever witnesses this struggle in his own soul, must acknowledge that the deeper self is in the right; this very minute everything may be changed, and whoever does not discover this truth is always engaged in basing his life upon what is uncertain. Never in all the world has there been so nimble a tongue that it could beguile the deeper self, provided the deeper self is permitted to give itself expression. This is indeed a painful state : the first self sits there and gazes at the alluring fruits displayed all about it, and it is so clear that it needs only to grasp the means at hand to achieve a complete success, as everyone must admit. But the deeper self sits there thoughtful and serious, like a physician at the bedside of the sick. But it also wears an air of translucent gentleness, because it knows that this sickness is not unto death but unto life.

The first self has, let us say, a specific wish. It knows that it is in possession of the conditions necessary for the realization of its ambition; the surrounding world, as it understands it, is as favourable as possible. It is as if these two, the fortunate self and the favours of fortune, were merely waiting for one another—oh, what a merry life! But the deeper self refuses to retreat; it does not bargain, it makes no compact, it withholds its assent. It merely says that even in this moment everything may be changed. Other men come to the assistance of the first self with suggested explanations. They call upon him to seize the means. They explain to him that such is the law of life, that some men are the favourites of fortune, that they ought to enjoy life, and that he is one of them. Then his heart beats fast within him, and he longs to make a start.

That a child whose father is strict must remain at home, is something that cannot be helped, since the father is the stronger. But he is no child, and the deeper self is merely his own self, and yet it seems stricter than the strictest father. It is quite impossible to ingratiate oneself with the deeper self; it either speaks quite unreservedly or not at all. Then there is danger in the offing; they are both aware of it, both the first self and the deeper one. The latter sits there anxiously concerned, like the experienced pilot, while a secret council is being held to determine whether it were not better to throw the pilot overboard, since he brings contrary winds. But this does not yet happen; what follows? It follows that the first self cannot move a single step forward. And yet, yet it is clear that the moment of happiness hastens to depart, that fortune is already in flight. For so men say, namely, that if one does not seize the moment while it is there it will soon be too late. And whose fault will that be, if not the fault of the deeper self? But this cry again is of no avail.

What sort of unnatural state is this, what does it all mean? When something of this kind takes place in a man's soul, does it not mean that this mind is beginning to give way? Ah no, it means something quite different, it means that the child is about to be weaned. For it is quite possible for a man to be thirty years old and more, fully forty years, and still be only a child; aye, it is even possible to die as a child of advanced years. But it is so enchanting, so beautiful, to be a child! And so the child lies at the breast of time in the cradle of the finite, and a figure called probability sits at the side of the cradle and sings a lullaby to the child. If the wish fails of fulfilment, and the child becomes restless, probability hushes it and says: Now just lie still and sleep, while I go out to buy something for you; next time you may be sure that it will be your turn. So the child falls asleep, and the pain is forgotten, and its cheeks redden again with the glow of new wishes, though it once seemed as if it would be impossible ever to forget the pain. To be sure, had he not been a child the man could not have forgotten the pain so easily; and it would have appeared that it was not probability that sat at the side of the cradle, but the deeper self sitting at his deathbed, in the death hour of self-denial, when this self arose to an eternal life.

When the first self thus yields to the deeper self they are reconciled, and become companions on the way. Then perhaps the deeper self will say: "Let me see, I had almost forgotten it over our long struggle, what it was namely that you wished so intensely. At the present moment I believe that there is nothing to prevent the fulfilment of your desire, provided you do not forget the little secret that we two share with one another. So now you can be well content." Perhaps the first self will then reply: "But now I do not care so much about it; I feel that I shall never be happy as I was before, oh, as I was when my soul was filled with yearning. To tell the truth, I do not believe that you understand me." "Neither do I believe so: do you really think it would be desirable if I understood you in such fashion that I desired this thing as much as you? But have you lost anything by no longer caring so much about it? Consider on the other hand what might have happened if the world had deceived you, and you know it might have done so. This was what I impressed upon you; I said only that it was possible, and thereby implied indeed that what you regarded as a certainty was really only a possibility—what then? In that case would you not have been the prey of despair? And then you would not have had me to rely upon, for you will recollect that the ship's council was almost on the point of deciding to throw me overboard. Are you not better off through having lost something of your burning desire, and through having gained instead the assurance that life cannot deceive you? To lose in that manner, is it not to gain?"

"The little secret that we two share with one another." Thus spoke the deeper self. What is this secret, my hearer? What else than the truth, that in relation to external things a man can do absolutely nothing? If he moves immediately to grasp the external it may change in that very instant, leaving him deceived. He may on the other hand accept it, with the consciousness that it is subject to alteration, and he will not be deceived even if it changes, for he has the consent of the deeper self. If he proposes to act immediately in relation to outer things, and in this fashion to accomplish something, everything may in an instant come to naught. But if he acts, not immediately but in the light of this consciousness, he will not be deceived even if it all comes to naught, for he has the consent of the deeper self.

Nevertheless, when the first self and the deeper self thus become reconciled, and their common mind is turned away from outer things, there has as yet been realized only the first condition necessary for self-knowledge. In order that a man may really know himself, new dangers must be met and new conflicts must be won. Only let not the aspiring soul be deterred or terrified, as if it were an imperfection to be in need, when the need in question is a need of God. Let it not entertain the thought that its need is a shameful secret it were better to hide, when the need is a need of God; nor let it consider it a sad necessity which one seeks to put a better face upon by avowal, when the need is a need of God. A more profound self-knowledge teaches one precisely that one needs God. But the first and superficial sense of depression evoked by this thought would deter a man from beginning, unless his attention was directed in time to the thought that this need constitutes his perfection, and unless his enthusiasm was stirred by meditation upon it. For it is a far more imperfect thing not to need God; and when it seems to a man that he does not need God, he is in truth merely mistaken.

Even if a man had realized the greatest and most glorious of feats, if he still thought it had all been done in his own strength; if by curbing his spirit he had become greater than one that conquers a city, and yet believed that he had done this in his own strength, then his perfection would virtually be merely a misunderstanding. But such a perfection would be little praiseworthy. On the other hand, whoever perceives that he cannot do even the least thing without God, that he cannot even rejoice in the happiest eventuality without God, is nearer to perfection. And whoever understands himself thus, and finds nothing at all painful in the awareness, but only a superabundance of happiness; whose heart hides no secret wish or preference for a happiness which should be a happiness on its own responsibility; whose mind feels no shame in letting other people see that he can do nothing of himself; who seeks no special compact with God, not even stipulating that his impotence should be concealed from the eyes of men; but in whose heart joy always conquers because he jubilantly, as it were, throws himself into the arms of God in unspeakable wonder over God who can do all things —aye, such a man is indeed the perfect man, whom the apostle Paul describes better and more briefly as one who "glories in his weakness," and who has not even had so many and so dubious experiences that he has learned to express himself more voluminously.

Men say indeed that not to know oneself is to be deluded and imperfect; but they often refuse to understand that he who truly knows himself, knows precisely that he can do nothing of himself.

Thus in relation to outward things, man can do nothing. But inwardly, can he do nothing here? In order that a power should really be a power it must have opposition; if it has no opposition it is either omnipotence or an illusion. But if a man is to have opposition, from whence is it to come? Inwardly, the opposition can come only from himself. So then a man strives with himself in inward conflict, but not now as before, when the deeper self strove with the first self to prevent it from concerning itself overmuch with outward things. The man who fails to discover the existence of this inward struggle is involved in a misunderstanding, and his life is consequently imperfect. But if he does discover this struggle, he will here again be made to understand that he can do nothing of himself.

It may seem strange that this is what a man must learn from a study of himself; why then praise self-knowledge? And yet it is so; and if the entire outer world conspired to teach him, he cannot learn from the world that he can do absolutely nothing. Even if the entire world united to crush and annihilate the weakest of human beings, he could still preserve in his mind a feeble notion that he might have been able to do something under other circumstances, when the power opposed to him was not so overwhelmingly superior. That he can do nothing at all is something he can discover only by himself. Whether he conquers the world, or stumbles over a wisp of straw, he can in either case know in himself that he can do absolutely, nothing. If someone wishes to propose a different explanation, let him remember that he has to do solely with himself and not with others; then every evasion will at once be detected. Men think it a difficult thing to learn to know oneself, especially when one has many talents and is equipped with a multitude of capacities and dispositions, and must acquire an adequate understanding of all this. The self-knowledge of which we speak is not so complicated; every time a man grasps this brief and pithy truth, that he can of himself do nothing, he understands himself.

But can a man not overcome himself in his own strength? This is indeed sometimes asserted. But has one who says this proved himself or understood himself in what he asserts? For how can I be stronger than myself? I may be stronger than the weakest; and perhaps there lives or has lived a man of whom one might say that he surpasses all others in strength; but no man was ever stronger than himself. When we speak of a man's overcoming himself by himself we usually think of something different, or something merely external, where the combatants are not equal. Thus when it happens that a man who was once tempted by the lure of the world's honours overcomes himself, so that he no longer stretches out his hand to seize them; when a man who feared the dangers of life, so far drives out his fears that he no longer flees the dangers; when a man who had lost his courage and confidence overcomes himself to the extent of standing fast, not absenting himself from the arena of decision : then we do not speak in depreciation of such a man, but rather praise him. But if he wishes to save his soul from a new form of vanity, and to safeguard himself against driving out devils with the help of the devil, he will promptly confess that he cannot overcome himself inwardly. By this he does not mean that evil has once for all achieved a power over him. No, but inwardly he can only reach the point, and that by his utmost endeavour, of withstanding himself; and this is not the same thing as overcoming himself. Inwardly he creates in his mind the temptations of glory and fear and despondency, and those of pride and pleasure and defiance, greater than the temptations that meet him outwardly. It is because he thus creates his temptations for himself, that he is engaged in a struggle with himself. If he does not strive in this manner, then he merely strives with an accidental degree of temptation, and his victory proves nothing with respect to what he could do in a greater temptation. If he conquers the temptation which his environment presents to him, this does not prove that he would conquer if the temptation came in the most terrible form that his mind can conceive. But only when it presents itself to him in this magnitude does he really learn to know himself. In this manner it is present to his inner self; and hence he knows in himself, what he has perhaps failed to learn from the world, that he can be absolutely nothing.

My hearer, surely you are not one of those who think that these are merely the dark and sombre thoughts of a melancholy temperament, and you surely do not wish to thank God because you have never been visited by such melancholy? If it really were the case that such thoughts are a symptom of melancholy, is this the fashion in which we ought to love God and men? To offer God thanks for an imagined preferential love is to deceive Him, and to give Him to understand that if the heavier burden had been laid upon your shoulders, you might not have been able to believe in His love; for when this is admitted it becomes a very different matter to thank God that one has escaped being tried in the more difficult struggle. To flee from the sight and consciousness of the individual you are pleased to call melancholy, is to wish to ignore the fact that he too is a human being. And since you dare not call him an evil-doer you must admit that he is an unfortunate being, as such precisely needing your sympathy, which you show him by asking him to take up his habitation among the tombs like a leper, while you dare not acknowledge him as a fellow human being—is this to love God and man? But if it is regarded as an evidence of melancholy to speak as we have done about understanding oneself, then it must also be regarded as a folly inseparable from such melancholy to consider this view of life as one that conceives man from the standpoint of his perfec-

tion; and it must be deemed a still greater folly to rejoice
in this perfection. And yet, why should not such a man be
glad? The perfect is always a source of joy. And this joy
of which we here speak is not based upon God's imaginary
preference for some particular person, nor does it flee
from the sight of the sorrowing. On the contrary, in this
joy a human being loves everyone who is beset by sorrow.
And so it is in very truth. You will not wish to stamp such
a person as melancholy, my hearer, when the truth is that
he is the only one who is really glad. For whoever is
happy in God, and over God, rejoices, and again I say,
he rejoices. Why does the apostle Paul, when he gives us
this beautiful admonition : "Rejoice, and again I say unto
you, rejoice," why does he pause a moment and cease to
speak, before again for the second time he bids the believer rejoice? Because he has in the intervening moment,
as it were, taken time to listen to all the terrible things
that may be said in contradiction. That is to say, he summons the terrifying thought that a man can do absolutely
nothing, in order to allow his joy to gain a perfect victory :
" and again I say unto you, rejoice!"

The view of life which holds that man's need of God
constitutes his highest perfection, does indeed make life
more difficult. But at the same time it views human life
according to its perfection; and in this understanding,
through that gradual joining of experience to experience
which constitutes a good understanding with God, man
learns to *know God*.

In so far as a man does not know himself, nor understand that he can of himself do nothing, he does not really
become aware, in any deeper sense, that God exists.
Though he may at times use the name of God, and occa-
sionally invoke Him, in the great crises of his life perhaps
thinking to see Him, and be moved by the vision, as it is
impossible to catch even a glimpse of God without being
moved—nevertheless, he is in a manner piously deceived
if he deems himself on this account clearly conscious of

God's existence, or thinks that God's existence ought not to make itself manifest in this earthly life with a very different emphasis—in this life whose meaning is always confused unless God's presence is continually implied. We call such self-deception well-meaning, we use as beautiful a name for it as possible, we do not intend to break out into heated condemnation. But nevertheless we wish for every man that God's existence may become clear to him with a certainty of a very different order, and with a decisiveness that leaves no room for vagueness.

Whoever can do nothing of himself, cannot undertake the least enterprise without God's help, or without coming to notice that there is a God. We sometimes speak of learning to know God from history; we bring out the chronicles, and read and read. This method may perhaps succeed; but how much time is not required, and how precarious often is not the result, how near to the misunderstanding which is the sensuous man's wonder over what is ingenious! But whoever knows in himself that he can do nothing, has each day and each moment the desired and indubitable occasion to experience the living God. And if he does not have this experience often enough, he knows very well the reason. The reason is that he has become involved in a misunderstanding, and thinks that he can do something of himself.

When he goes to the house of the Lord, he knows that God is not there. But he also knows that he can of himself do nothing, that he cannot even put himself in a spirit of devotion; so that God must be there if he is really moved to devotion. Alas, there are many who live in all other respects without a concern for God, but who nevertheless do not omit to go to church. What a strange contradiction! They gather in the house of prayer, they say to one another: "God is not here, He does not live in a house built with hands." Then they go home; but at home God does not exist for them at all. But whoever knows himself in the manner described above, knows indeed that God does not dwell in temples made with hands. But he also knows that God is with him in the night, when he is refreshed by sleep, and when he wakes in anxious dreams; in the day of need, when he vainly looks about him for comfort; in the tumultuous chaos of his thoughts, when he listens in vain for a word that might save him; when in danger of his life, and without help from the world; in anxiety when he fears himself; in the crisis of his despair, when he works out his salvation with fear and trembling. He knows that God is with him when anxiety seeks to overwhelm him, its suddenness like a flash of lightning, when it is as if it were already too late, and there is no time to go to the house of the Lord. Then God is with him, coming more quickly than the light that penetrates the darkness, swifter than the thought that dispels the fog; present as promptly as only He can be, who was already there. And if it were not so, where could be found the messenger who could move quickly enough to fetch the Lord for the troubled mind! And before He could come, some time must still elapse! But this is not the case; only he believes it who thinks that he can do something of himself.

It is possible indeed to come to know God in precisely the same way on the day of gladness, provided we also understand that we can do absolutely nothing. But it is just as difficult to hold fast to this thought on the day of gladness as it is to hold fast to it in the hour of sorrow. When a man is at the height of his happiness the thought suddenly tempts him : would it not be still more glorious if he could do it all himself? Then his joy acquires a false bias; it does not swing upward to God but swerves away from Him; and this is a sign that new exercises are needed. When everything again becomes uncertain, when the thoughts seethe in a welter of confusion, when memory threatens to give notice and refuses any longer to serve, when the past comes before the mind only in the form of fearful anguish, when even the most sincere purpose is through the treason of anxiety transformed into insincerity toward oneself—then one understands again that a man can do absolutely nothing of himself. But in and with this understanding God is immediately present, commands the confusion, and remembers everything that has been confided to Him. For the tried individual has doubtless confided in God. In the chaos of his anguish and temptation, when the outcome threatened to be more terrible than death, he hastily entrusted to God what lay upon his mind, things which, if he himself forgot them, and God in His heaven also forgot them, would annihilate him forever, and transform the entire content of his life into a terrible delusion. These things he has entrusted to God, until with God's help he again fights his way through the terrors in his breast, achieving patience and winning peace of mind through trust in God.

If a man whose life had been involved in some critical difficulty has a friend, and if in some later moment he finds that he cannot hold fast the meaning of his past, when anxiety creates confusion, and the accusing thoughts rise up in all their strength against him—then, as he strives to win back to his former understanding of himself, he will doubtless go to this friend and say: " My soul is sick, and nothing is clear to me; but I confided everything to you. You remember it; explain the past to me." But if a man has no such friend he will doubtless have recourse to God —if he has ever confided anything to Him, if God has been his witness in the critical hour of decision, when no one else understood him. He who had recourse to a friend was perhaps not understood; and what is still harder to bear, perhaps he became an object of disgust to himself when he learned that his confidant had not understood his need though he listened to him, had not suspected the reason of his anguish, but had merely listened out of curiosity to the story of his remarkable collision with life. But such a thing could never happen with God. Who would dare to think of God in such manner; although because he does not dare to think such things of God, he may be cowardly enough to forget God altogether—until he stands before the judge who condemns him. But this could never happen to one who has taken God as his witness; for where God is the judge, there is no judge when God is the witness.

But it does not by any means follow that life becomes easy for a man who thus learns to know God. On the contrary, it may become very hard; and it will certainly become more difficult than the sensuous man's contemptible life of ease. But in and through this difficulty his life constantly gains deeper and deeper significance. Or shall we perhaps say that it has no significance for him that God is always present in his thoughts, that while of himself he can do nothing he can with God's help do more and more —that he can gain a victory over himself; for with God's help he can indeed do this! Shall we say that it has no significance for him that he learns more and more to die away from the world, learns to cling less and less to external things, to that which life brings and takes away, to that which it is given him outwardly to accomplish—but learns also to care more and more for the things of the inner man, for the understanding with God, for the privilege of remaining in this understanding, and for the learning to know God as the power that makes all things work together for good when he loves God? Shall we say even that it is without significance for him that it makes the adversities of life easier, since it is always true that a man who has something else to think of and is thereby prevented from dwelling on his sorrows, finds these easier? Shall we finally say that it is without significance for him, his blessed reward, that he comes to understand that God is love, and that His goodness passeth all understanding; and that he does not need to depend on the testimony of others in this respect, or on a contemplation of history or of the order of nature? To understand these things is certainly far greater; but the problem is to understand them in such a way as in truth to profit from the understanding.

We do not wish to be understood as saying that a knowledge of God which consists of an absorption in dreamy wonder and enthusiastic contemplation of Him is alone of the highest worth; for God cannot thus be taken in vain. Just as the self-knowledge which reveals one's own nothingness is the necessary condition for knowing God, so the knowledge of God is the condition for the sanctification of each human being in accordance with his specific end. Wherever God exists in truth there He is always creative. It is not His will that men should bask in the contemplation of His glory in spiritual sloth; but He wishes, through coming to be known of man, to create in him a new man.

If it were so, let us assume it to be so, that a man without knowing God, could by himself be ennobled and developed to the same degree, I nevertheless ask you, my hearer, whether knowing God does not have in itself the highest significance? And if a choice were conceivable, so that a man could progress equally far either by himself or by knowing God, which would you choose? Even in the minor human relationships you would choose the latter. For if it were possible that you could be developed in solitude as much as by learning to know some other human being, to whom you were drawn with your whole soul, the fact that you learned to know him would have in itself the most beautiful significance for you. The most beautiful significance—ah, no, you are well aware that at least when we speak of God, it is quite otherwise. For the knowledge of God is the most decisive factor in every human life, and without this knowledge, a man would become absolutely nothing. Without God he would perhaps scarcely be able to grasp the most elementary secret of the truth, that he is of himself absolutely nothing; even less would he be able to understand that it is his need of God that constitutes his highest perfection.

VIII

LOVE CONQUERS ALL

(ON THE OCCASION OF A WEDDING)

Unclarified moods rest in the depths of the soul, secure in love's beautiful assurance; the organ tones have ceased to sound, and only their echoes again move the soul, desiring to translate the beautiful assurance into sacred feelings; now is the time for speech! The voice of an individual will be heard. How poor the words from his lips must seem in comparison with the wealth of feeling in the beautiful and sacred emotion! May not the spoken word be disturbing, the well-meant word inopportune, and the word of guidance portentous! And yet it must be spoken, and it must be spoken with decisiveness. The indeterminate wealth of feeling must be expressed, the word must be named; clarity without in the least wishing to disturb, must extract from the word its utmost significance.

What a change, what commensurability in this incommensurability! For what is so clear and precise and definite as a man's duty is and ought to be, and what is so mysterious as the impulse of love! And yet, love must here become duty. And what is more transparent and intent upon the future than a sacred promise, and what is less concerned with the future than the presence of love in the lovers! And yet love here demands a promise. And what is so terrible to mention as a curse, and what is so remote from this as the pure joy of the lovers! And yet this word must be mentioned in connection with love!

But it is a free matter, and just as the lovers become free by being bound to one another, so is this step a resolve of the free will. We are glad with those who to-day rejoice, whom love has made free in their union, but it must not be spoken with veiled words or disparagingly about the marriage pledge, as if it were something less significant because it is a free act, since, on the contrary, it is the one thing needful in connection with the most beautiful form of human happiness.

And so now these two, whom life has joined together in the happiness of love, are at this moment resolved, and a pact is to be instituted between them. A pact forever. Forever—is not this word by its very strength almost portentous, since it is as if death came between, and it is upon the grave one lays the garland of everlastings? Oh, far from it, for this ominous word is a beautiful announcement. The marriage pledge is indeed like a garland of everlastings, but love weaves it, and duty says it must be woven, and it is love's happiness to weave it, and duty says it must be woven—each day from the blossoms of the moment. Eternity is not here through with time, but the pact of love is eternity's beginning in time. The eternal resolution and the duty must forever remain with the wedded pair throughout time in the union of their love; and each anniversary shall be a solemn holiday, with power in its remembrance and hope in its promise.

The spoken word must be definite, and it must also be uttered with authority. And the speech shall be addressed to you, respected bridegroom; it does not offer congratulations, but the speaker asks you an earnest question, and he has authority to demand an earnest answer. He does not ask you about your happiness, but whether you have consulted God and your conscience. The question is not intended to dissipate your happiness, nor is it indifferent to it. The question desires only to make your happiness secure, if you answer deliberately, and it is asked in earnestness for your own sake, lest you answer frivolously. And though it seems to you so wholly natural, so completely in harmony with the order of things, that you should be bound to one whom the early wishes of parents and relatives had selected, to one with whom you felt yourself united in an anticipation that finally passed over into certainty, to one to whom you felt yourself drawn in so many ways, until love revealed itself as the ultimate ground, and took over the preparation into its glorious possession : nevertheless though our earnest question need by no means give pause to a hectic and surprised resolution, which often enough gives rise to late regrets, it would make you pause with a sense of the responsibility of duty, to lay the emphasis of choice upon the quiet experience.

And next the speech shall be directed to you, respected bride; it will not disturb you with its question or trouble you by arousing difficult thoughts, but it will ask you with the same earnestness as the equality of the pact requires, whether you have consulted with God and your conscience. Oh, the question will not make your happiness precarious, it will not make you weak, it will make you, in the freedom of earnestness, equally strong with the husband to whom as a wife you are to be submissive. And though you feel with a joyous confidence and perfect trust that happiness could not have come for you in any other way, that it could not be otherwise than that you should be united with him whom long association and the close relationship, and participation in so many things, and mutual sympathy bound to you until love came and explained all that went before as a beautiful preface, a dowry of security, a wealth of happiness : nevertheless, though the earnest question is far from wishing to interrupt the many thoughts, it would still imbue you with the sense of the responsibility of duty to lay the emphasis of choice upon the almost imperceptible transition of this quiet experience.

And then there is required a promise, and the speaker has the authority to require it. But the requirement is in all its earnestness a challenge to the lovers. It will give the worthy a solemn opportunity to announce freely and in the sight of God that which it is hard for the lovers to keep silent about, that which it is sweet to communicate to a confidant, that which, when here expressed, receives its consecration.

When this has been done, the officiating authority will unite the happy pair and make earnestness of what is already earnest. For the act itself has its own earnestness, and when this is not found in the wedded, the act is desecrated, for marriage is not merely a temporal event. But when the earnestness exists, the officiating authority gives to the act the stamp of earnestness, and the pact is concluded.

On the other hand, the unauthorized discourse has no lovers to unite. But still, my hearer, you can give it your attention. For as was said above, the act has its own seriousness, and this does not consist in external happenings, that some curious people have come as witnesses, that two persons have effected an outward change in the circumstances of their lives. And that earnestness the authorised speaker presupposes in the wedded pair, and that it is thus mature. If it came into being only in that moment of the ceremony, who would dare to answer the question which asks about something past, though this past is also the present? Or, if the speaker in that moment must develop this earnestness in the lovers, then must he speak quite otherwise; he must say much which it is risky to say now at the last moment, difficult to say to just these two, though it would have been profitable for them to have considered it. Hence there is given a reflection which in earnestness of thought already stands before the altar. To such a thoughtful consideration, then, my hearer, I invite you, and with the marriage ceremony in mind, I shall consider the theme

LOVE CONQUERS ALL,

viewed as the resolution that constitutes marriage.

And you, my hearer, will you also hold that solemn moment fast before your thought, and not concern yourself with the deliberation in any other manner than as if it concerned yourself; it may be that for you the marriage pact is something in the future or something past; for it is something irrelevant only to a fool. And surely here we are in agreement, that a discourse about godly matters should never be contentious or discordant with anything except that which is ungodly. When therefore the poor man, or one who in a humble situation works for his bread, without on that account being excluded from the happiness of love, when he must gather in toilsome care and take many a weary step in order to get the necessities together, while the master or overseer only too well understands, perhaps, that the duties of the service must first and foremost be attended to, when there is left only the scanty opportunity, the sparingly measured time, for the godly consideration of the heart's concerns, upon which the privileged, perhaps wisely, perhaps foolishly, spend so much time—when these two lovers finally also stand before the altar and in all brevity are declared wedded: Oh, my hearer, we are surely agreed that God, who is present when the pact is made, not only as a witness but to grant His blessing upon it, does not in His blessing make a distinction like that in the speech of men. Because He alone is rich, He has but one blessing, and at one and the same price for all; be the believer great or humble, wise or simple, clothed in gold or in linsey, rich in thoughts or poor in spirit. But if anyone, man or woman, attacked by an aristocratic distemper, be inhuman enough to find the sacred observances too simple, if anyone wished to invent new rites, then are we agreed, my hearer, that this is the miracle of the godly ordinance, that the simple finds everything therein, and the wise more than he can fathom, when he earnestly thinks himself in relation thereto, and thinks earnestly about himself.

An old adage says that love is older than everything else; and many a beautiful and profound thought has been linked with this word, in order by the aid of the adage to explain existence. But just as the adage is valid in relation to great things, so it is also valid wherever love is present: it is older than all other things. So in the life of an individual; when love awakens it is older than everything, for when it is, it is as if it had been there a long time, it presupposes itself far back in the distant past, until all search for its origin ends in the inexplicable. While one generally says about all beginning that it is difficult, this does not hold true of love. Its happy awakening knows no labour, and no preparation precedes. If love does indeed sometimes generate pain, it is not itself born with pain: lightly and jubilantly it breaks forth in its mysterious becoming. Miraculous beginning!—But the life of freedom requires a beginning, and a beginning is here a resolution, and the resolution has its own labour and pain, the beginning its difficulty. The individual conceiving a resolution cannot be finished, for then would he already have experienced that of which the resolution is the beginning; but if no resolution is taken, then such a man will doubtless share the experience that sometimes comes to a speaker, that only after he is finished and has already spoken, does he know how he ought to have spoken: only after he has lived, does he know how he ought to have lived (sorry profit from life's experiences!), and how he ought to have made the beginning with the good resolution, bitter wisdom, now that there lies an entire life between the beginning and the dying man!

So the word says that love conquers all, and therefore the marriage ceremony, which is not a festive congratulation but a godly challenge, does not greet the lovers as victors, but invites them to a struggle, encloses them in the arena of a state well-pleasing unto God, encourages them to fight the good fight, strengthens their striving by means of the marriage pact, promises them victory as it also takes a promise from them, gives them a blessing for the long journey—but also informs them that the struggle is there: a struggle to be fought through, trouble to be endured, danger to be experienced, a curse if it is not borne in harmony as a blessing. And yet, is it the right place here to evoke such sorry considerations, that come soon enough with the dark thoughts and the sad experiences : in the moment of joy to call to mind the days that have no pleasure in them? But is it then sad that this high-minded word actually means something, that it is not sounding brass, not a jubilation over an imaginary victory which is badly won, or still bad if it is supposed already won, but the announcement of an actual victory which shall be gloriously won! And is the place so unsuitable— the holy place? Is it so inopportune for joy to think about the danger; is there perhaps no time for this—in the urge of danger there is surely less time! Alas, time comes and time goes, it takes little by little; it takes from a man one good whose loss he feels, and his pain is great; alas, he does not discover that it has already long since taken away from him the thing of greatest importance : the ability to form a resolution, and that he has become so familiar with this condition that there is no dismay over its loss, the last thing which might help him to gain new strength for a renewed resolution.

No, in earnest the saying means very much, indeed it means everything to the truly wedded pair. But it desires to be understood in earnest; it does not wish to visit the wedded couple as an unexpected guest, gracing the wedding day with his high presence; but it desires to make its home with them, to meet the test of the years, to answer for everything. It is thus it would be understood, and only thus can it be said : it must be said by a beginner, but only by one who begins with the good resolution. For he who became old in the faithful service of love, tested as gold is tested and found true—for the noble poet says of the maiden, a little in love, that her young soul was tested gold, but the years and the dangers are the test—hence the venerable figure who in the course of years won the rich and incorruptible beauty of faithfulness, loyal to his pledge as his own conscience required, faithful with a man's courage and with a woman's tenderness, with a man's intrepidity and with a woman's sympathy, with the sober reflection of the understanding in the inwardness of the heart, he will doubtless say with the mild, friendly, unassuming admonition of age: " My little children, love conquers all." And he moves youth, and almost deceives it, for when he says it, then it seems so easy, and it is so pleasant to hear him say it again. But if youth accepts the saying vain-mindedly, and would frivolously weave a bridal-wreath from it, then the experience that comes in life's struggle, intervenes between youth and venerable age, saying: " Step aside, learn respect for the venerable, but learn first what the difficulties are," and then he points to him with this word, " See, here, that love has conquered all!" Oh, how beautiful to be old, how illusory is not all eloquence beside such a witness! Has conquered all! This is the last word, and is indeed somewhat different from the first. Stay your course, O wanderer, pause to consider this difference; when you grasp it, you will doubtless be a man of resolve! *Has* conquered; so says experience engaged in the struggle of life, respectfully, about the veteran in the service, whom the marriage pact called to the good fight, whose life leaves no irregularity behind, since he became no man's debtor, because he loved much. In civil life, it is often the case that if anyone would travel to a foreign country, and he owes someone a debt, the creditor will refer the matter to the civil authority, and the journey will be prohibited. Oh, if the obligation of a sacred pledge is left unfulfilled, or but poorly fulfilled, is it not like an objection that makes the last journey the flight of a defaulter—but, no, how does it help to flee? The justice which watches over existence cannot be evaded.

So much for *has* conquered all. But our theme says: Love conquers all. And so it ought to sound in the beginning, and so it is rightly said by the resolving individual. But no one can be said to be resolved who is ignorant of the danger, who excludes the danger from his thoughts, instead of including in his resolution a real conception of it, whose courage has therefore lost its victory, just as good deeds lose their reward, because the victory anticipated it. Nor is he resolved who runs as if uncertainly, and who certainly misses the goal when he believes he has attained it. Nor is he resolved who, improvidently trusting in some mysterious power, dares to begin the journey without including in the resolution a real conception of God's assistance, of its necessity, and of its sufficiency. Nor is the resolution of which we speak, a common resolution because in such a moment the two are of like mind, and both without a resolve.

Does life give evidence of only one kind of unhappy love in marriage, when death separates them and only the sorrowing one remains behind? Oh, death does not have this power to make unhappy; if nothing else separates them, they are nevertheless united. Yet perhaps someone says, "I know very well what you mean and what the discourse hints at, but such things happen only to those who were never in love; whoever really loves, conquers all." And it is impossible to deny that he who really loves, does as the word says; but does it follow that the speaker has even as much as a clear conception of what it means really to love, and about life, and about the others? A clear conception of the change which takes place in the lover when he is called upon really to conquer all, and when this all is something real. What a difference between youthfully desiring to change the whole world and then discovering that it is one's self that is to be changed, and that the requirement is to do it with enthusiasm; or that the task is to preserve himself unchanged, alas, while everything changes! What a difference between the novel surprise of being the first inventor of everything, and then when trouble comes, the discovering that it is the monotonous repetition of what has been experienced by others thousands and thousands of times! What a difference between youthfully wishing to fight, and the explanation that he must suffer, and that it is this which he must do with enthusiasm! To desire victory; well, one may yield to a superior force but with the consciousness of being the stronger in comparison with the individual—and now the explanation that it is his own weakness he must fight against, and the requirement neither sympathizing nor regretful, but cruelly uncompromising : that one must be enthusiastic in the struggle. When then the great requirement of the imaginary task does not give imaginary strength, but it is in reality the small and despised task that is to be done; when one does not defy a world which cheated one's expectation, but sits there abandoned by the great expectation concerning oneself, deprived of every evasion; when no broad prospect tempts one to dare the venture, but one sits inactive, despondent before the humble task of patience, which becomes even more humble because time is wasted in dreaming youth's dream over again; aye, then there is opportunity to show that one really loves, or rather that the occasion has waited too long, that it should not have been permitted to become what it is; and had the beginning been made with a resolution, then one might have understood in time that things could come to such a pass.

Consider one who resembles a lover, an enthusiast. Does life show only a single case of half-finished labour, of interrupted plans, of a sorry and miserable outcome of a brilliant beginning? Is this the only case where the striving individual was prevented by death from finishing the work, from perfecting the plan, from attaining the goal? O Death, thou art powerless; dost thou presume to mock an enthusiast ! No, the brief misfortune of the moment of death is soon overcome, and he truly dies with honour, aye, with the glorious accomplishment of his task who dares say with truth, " It was death that prevented me !" " But," says perhaps an enthusiastic youth, and thus every enthusiastic youth, " I know what you refer to; you need not even name it. I will not be disturbed or delayed or made despondent—but such things do not happen to the really enthusiastic." And this is undeniable; but does it follow that the speaker even has a clear conception of what it is to be really enthusiastic? What he will say when it is no longer his task to spring forward like a lion, but to remain in the same place and, in spite of all exertion, not to be able to move; when the task is not to traverse the world in easy flight, but to endure in a dead calm in which the enthusiasm threatens to expire; when the task is to feel the weakness, and yet not let go the enthusiasm, to hope against hope; when it is the task to endure in the long toilsome drudgery which is inseparable from every enthusiastic enterprise; when abandoned, one must even defend oneself against a sympathy which is the ruin of enthusiasm, although it seems so soothing, and be misunderstood because one does it; when it is of no avail to rush forward in wild abandon, but it is required that one assume a strait-jacket, and be enthusiastic in it; aye, there is the opportunity to show that one is really enthusiastic. And if one has begun with a resolution, it will indeed appear with what profit this was done, since it was not the drawing in of a youth's refreshing breath of air, but a self-questioning which from a distance apprehends the danger.

The first condition for a resolution is to have, that is to will to have, a real conception of life and of oneself. What is here sown in tears is reaped with songs of joy, and the grief is overcome; for the first loss is the best loss, and the first pain the saving pain, and the strict upbringing the profitable one, and the early discipline the strengthening discipline, and the shudder of the resolution gives courage, and its chastisement awakens the attention, and the final victory is the essential victory, and the last honour the only true one!

Oh, death has no power to place saddening signs upon the path of marriage through life. And yet the signs are there. What significance do they have then? There is in the folk-life many a curious custom connected with a wedding, many a mocking jest, which still has its significance, many a teasing roguery which is not without beauty, but might it not be an acceptable custom if the bridal couple before they go to the house of feasting should go to the house of mourning, that is, to the serious contemplation from which one does not fetch the bridal veil, but the resolution? Let the bride appear before the altar in all her charm, let the myrtle-crown grace the beloved; it is the humility of the resolution which alone makes her acceptable in the eyes of God, and the real conception of the resolution makes her strong in holy weakness—strong to conquer all.

It is not the purpose of the discourse, even if it could do so, to terrify by means of harrowing descriptions, to evoke horror, to which only the serious speaker, when he speaks with authority, can give the sure effect of earnestness and prevent the intrusion of despondency and low spirits, aye, even of disgust, into the impression. Oh, but are those married people alone separated between whom a divorce was effected, between whom the uniting wedding pact became a curse; are they alone unworthy of the marriage state who made a wretched beginning by regarding the pact as a worldly agreement for earthly gain, and ended as they began; or for whom the wedding union became not a salvation but a snare that stimulated the craving of the senses; is he only a bad husband who in cowardice and lack of manliness courted adoringly a woman's beauty, who then slavishly ruled in a cowardly spirit over a slave, to whose beauty he was himself a slave in jealousy, until he ended with the ingratitude of a dastard, because the years had taken youth and beauty away from her to whom he was wedded?

Oh, no, it is here as it is with death in life. Not only are they the prey of death who lie upon a sickbed, and whom the physician has given up. Many a one whom death has marked goes about among us. And so there is many a marriage that divorce has marked. No separation has come between the married couple, but an aloof indifference divides them and makes them alien to one another—and yet, for this is why we speak about it, and yet, perhaps the old feelings are not wholly dead. There is no strife between them, no hostile difference, but feeling seems to have withdrawn itself far from the daily intercourse; and yet, perhaps they love one another, but they await an event which will tense the bowstring of resolution and lure the feeling forth to expression, for the daily events are too insignificant. They feel almost ashamed before each other because of this boredom with the insignificant events. They long perhaps for an understanding, but they cannot rightly get to speak with one another, precisely because there is an opportunity every day, and consequently the opportunity goes unused because it is more difficult to reveal themselves to one another. They were once so happy, oh, so happy, and this consciousness which ought to strengthen them, which at least ought always to be clear, now weakens them. They lose the zest and the courage to venture, and this vanished happiness acquires a sickly, exaggerated glamour for the two lonely people. Time passes so slowly, a whole life lies there before them, they fear to make, one to the other, the first admission which could unite them in a vigorous resolution, boredom takes the place of harmony, and yet they abhor divorce as a sin. But life is so long—and then the thought of death steals in, for death looses all bonds; they scarcely dare admit it to themselves, and yet so it is. They wish themselves dead, as if that were not unfaithfulness—and yet perhaps they still love one another, and death would perhaps make them realize it. And then one seeks to find the fault in the other, and, instead of a candid discussion of the trouble, misunderstanding conducts its sorry business and estranges them from one another in suspicion and distrust, through uncharitableness and precipitancy, with reconciliation flaring up and nourishing the disease, while they still love one another.

Was it always poverty and straitened circumstances and the troubles of life which produced these consequences? Oh, a marriage of wealth and abundance is sometimes carried out, after the brief honeymoon is over, as if on bread and water, in the midst of superfluity. Was it always sorrow over incorrigible children which at last brought estrangement between the parents? Oh, it is often evident that a rare good fortune in this respect did not help the parents. Was it always the years which led to this sorry condition? Oh, how short a time is sometimes needed before this change takes place. Was it always an original disparity in age, in culture, in social position, which soon or late must generate misunderstanding? Oh, sometimes the two are so well suited to one another that they only lack gratitude in order to be happy. Was it always environment and family relations and connections that ruined the well-begun marriage? Alas, what boots it to place the responsibility on others? The weed of evil has the peculiar property that all weeds have—it sows itself. The good seed requires care and labour; if that is lacking the good seed dies—and then the weeds come up of themselves.

Now let the observer who takes himself into account, who in a decisive moment evokes this thought, let him ask himself this question : " Dare I say that all these wedded couples did not begin with what one calls a real love for one another, so that they felt the sweetness of surprise when love awakened, felt the unrest of longing, found time to vanish when they were together, and found it so long when they were separated, found themselves glowing at the thought of being everything to one another?" Let him ask himself the question : " Dare I deny that the sad outcome may also have its explanation in the fact that in the time of youth and hope and surprise and precipitancy one lacked guidance and earnestness to renounce the softness and allure of the moment and the illusions of the imagination in order to subject oneself to the discipline of the resolve?"

For what does the resolution, which is the rebirth of love, desire? Will it stifle the joy because it wishes to save it; is its care a false friendship because it is not immediately understood? Is it nothing but pain because its beginning is not without pain; is it an eternal imprisonment because it in earnest and eternally binds the two lovers together? But its beginning is not without pain, and not

without a shudder. Consider an enthusiast. Filled with
a highminded purpose, he would accomplish so much, but
lo, under the labour of the resolution, the conception of
life and of his own weakness so overwhelms him that he
sinks in impotence, and only the conception of his duty
holds him in continued effort to win the resolve. What a
change! Now he fights bravely under the strict surveillance
of duty, he does the little assigned for each day, but to a
T as duty bids; and so he is still enthusiastic, since he
understands that whether it is little or much, when duty
bids it is always much. And lo, he succeeds, and the
resolution is won, and the work is begun on a real scale,
and lo, it is successful, and the work goes forward, and
lo, it is successful, and lo, it succeeds beyond expectation,
and the first enthusiasm awakens to a new and stronger
life. And now his enthusiasm is not a precipitate purpose
or a continued impetuosity; nor is it glowing hot in youth,
drowsy in manhood, and as smoking flax in the evening of
life. No, that first enthusiasm went out as in the night,
when resolution came into being, and then he gained a
new enthusiasm and the blessed surprise of wonder from
year to year, even to the evening of life. And so will the
wedding ceremony in the strict discipline of the resolution
take away fancies and disappointments, and love will
secure its sure refuge within the impregnable fortress of
duty, and will give the resolving individual new enthusiasm, and, as time goes on, a daily wonder over his happiness.

But perhaps someone says : " It is insulting to speak thus
to the lovers; instead of admiring and eulogizing, aye, of
considering with respect the lovers' rare good fortune,
thus enviously and pessimistically to make their good fortune suspect." Now, to show respect for a rare good fortune, even if it were ever so rare, would seem frivolous in
an edifying discourse which is not even attuned to find
edification in the variances of fortune in life. And could
not that objection really be an outbreak of love's seduc-

tive persuasiveness, that dangerous power which generates impulsiveness in the hearer? We show respect for the rare gift of the poet, if he uses it well; but I wonder if that love which inspires the poet to song is found thus in everyday life and in every couple who are united by the marriage pact? The poet himself says that it is rare, and the poet's happy gift is also rare, just as is that love : the best wish of a perfect existence, yet no, the most beautiful dream of an imperfect view of life. Therefore the poet explains nothing; he seeks in sadness of song this remembered rarity, he seeks it burning in the craving of desire, he touches the strings powerfully in its honour, as if it were found. He sits weak in the whisper of longing, he creates by the power of his imagination the sought-for thought. We praise him, and a people is proud in the right place when it is proud of a distinguished poet! But the poet cannot help us ordinary folk, for he cannot tell us how we should conduct ourselves to become the rare individual he seeks. There is the poet's sadness. For the poet is no proud and haughty person, but his soul extends into the infinite. And when he must say to an individual, or of an individual, " No, it is not he," or " It was not she," then he has no wish to offend. Himself distressed, he seeks the consolation of song. Therefore we must not be angry with the poet; he loves existence and perhaps feels the most pain that this or that individual was not the rare example. " And yet," says the poet, " no one can make himself this rare thing. He is a paragon, and thereby the miracle."

Now, if this paragon existed, and one should talk with him about what this address is concerned with, he simply would not understand it, nor would he answer as that objector answered, for no speech can disturb so rare a genius. But an illusory echo from poets' songs, a delusive repetition of poetic works, this he finds disturbing. On the other hand, he who feels that he is not himself this gifted individual, is concerned, and he is not disturbed by a speech reminding him of his concern, but rather he seeks edification in religious reflection. Further than this the address does not wish to go in meeting such an objection, but, my hearer, consider now the marriage ceremony itself. Who performs it? Is it a poet? No, it is a man of authority. And the rite lays everyone under sin, and the man of authority makes it earnest with the individual, and lays each one under sin who is pledged by this rite. Should it be offensive, then, if the address calls attention to the significance of the resolve, and that only the resolved individual dares to say at the beginning that love conquers all? To me it seems offensive to assume about anyone that he had not considered this. Even the happiest earthly love needs the rebirth of the resolve, the strict words of the marriage rite, its strengthening influence in the struggle, its blessing upon the way.

In seeking to make clear the sacred resolution of marriage, the address has thus reminded you, my hearer, of what you yourself have often considered, for the speech is far from being instructive. You are then in agreement with it, and yet perhaps you say: " The address is right, but much earnestness is required for the speech to produce the right impression, lest it foster impatience and disorder the spirit." And in this you are quite right—that there is much earnestness required; verily to be a good reader or a good listener is just as great an art as to be a good speaker, and that is very great when, as here, the address is imperfect and without authority. Was not this your meaning? For you surely would not intend by this criticism to place the blame upon the speaker, as if you gained something by accusing him? Let us consider this a little more closely. Just as there is needed for making a resolution an actual conception of life, so there is also needed, as was said at the same time, an actual conception of oneself. There was perhaps one who sent his spying thoughts out to get a manifold impression of life, but who could not take himself back, who gave himself out—alas, and lost himself. But whoever binds another human being to himself by the marriage pact, by that pact enters into an obligation which no time can dissolve, and which every day requires fulfilment; from him is required a resolution, and in this resolution an actual conception of himself. And this real conception of himself, and this inwardness, this is earnestness. Now, as it is doubtless true that as this love, which the poet sings, is a longing in every human heart, so there is also in everyone a longing, a wish that desires what we might call a teacher and a guide in life, a tried man upon whom one can rely, a wise man who knows how to advise, a noble man who encourages by his example, a gifted man who has the gift of eloquence and the emphasis of persuasiveness, the serious man who guarantees the appropriation.

As a child everything is easy, one is free from the difficulty of choosing; aye, even if a father was not as he should be, the respect the child has, his unconditional obedience, helps it sometimes to learn the good even from such a father. But then comes the period of youth and of freedom, and the time when with the beloved he seeks such a guide. Then it is important that this freedom and this choice do not become a snare. This guide which the longing seeks is a rare individual. Sometimes he is not found in every generation, and even if you are contemporaneous with such a highly worthy one, to whom you are wholly willing to yield yourself, he may not perhaps be in the same place as you, or he was there but had to leave, or you had to leave—and so, aye, so must you be content with less, that is you must try to help yourself. In life there is confusion enough; the most varied things are proclaimed and praised and despised and repeated; the most varied patterns show themselves, and disappoint, and show themselves again; the most varied guidance is proffered, and always there is companionship on the way; consolation and evasions and appeals, and warnings and songs of victory and cries of complaint are heard in wildest confusion. Ah, love and marriage are things in which everyone is experienced, and about which everyone has an opinion, and can in truth have if he earnestly wishes it. Every human being, even if unmarried, should have an abiding place, and yet there is perhaps many a marriage which does not have it, but is blown about by every puff of wind.

Now the young man thinks, misled by an accidental experience, that when the external circumstances of prosperity and happy relations of life favour love, then it is secure, and he does not perhaps consider that the liberty of action which the mental state thus attains may generate difficulties. Now one has an exaggerated conception of the depth of sorrow in loving, and cannot settle down to the simple labour of making a living; now another gives himself up too much to a bubbling over of the feelings and distaste follows; now one of the parties has a little sober-mindedness and wishes to use it, but the other misunderstands it and believes it is coldness and indifference; now one party wishes to plan carefully and economize, and the other one does not understand it, and ascribes it to a lack of sensitiveness for anything higher. Now one becomes despondent because the repetition about him makes him bored with his own; now another's first happiness makes him impatient; now he compares, now he remembers, now he loses—who could ever finish recounting all this; no address can do it, and this makes little difference, but no human being can do it, and that is what is terrifying. Only one power is capable of doing it; that is resolution, taking heed in time.

Where is earnestness to be learned? In life. Quite true, and the state of marriage acceptable to God offers an exceptional opportunity. Thus is earnestness learned—provided one joins the resolution with an actual conception of oneself. The resolution itself is earnestness. And in order to learn earnestness from what we call the earnestness of life, earnestness is already presupposed. For earnestness of life is not like a schoolmaster in relation to a pupil, but rather in the position of an indifferent power in relation to that one who must himself be something of a schoolmaster in relation to himself as pupil. Otherwise one might even learn from the earnestness of life indifference to everything. We wish for guidance, and yet it holds true even in relation to this, that we must have earnestness in order to be helped by it. Or is it not evident even in relation to this exceptional guide, when he stood among us, that one hit upon many things to weaken the impression he produced, as if one were not himself the loser by this, as if it were the wisdom of the years to become more and more fastidious, more and more inclined to reject, instead of becoming more and more judicious.

And when there is none such, what then? Aye, the world never has a lack of guides. Behold, here is a man who would guide everybody, and cannot help himself. Now one is proclaimed as wise, and admiration recognizes him as such because he cannot even understand what the common man understands. Now someone has a power of eloquence and leads astray, having the powerful works of untruth. Now what we learned in childhood has become old-fashioned, and we must learn it all over again. Now someone would tear a husband from his wife's side, make him important through participation in great enterprises, and teach him to think slightingly about the sacred vocation of marriage. Now one would tempt the wife, and teach her to sigh under the heavy yoke of matrimony. Now one dangles before the husband and wife a community fellowship that makes the marriage relation unimportant. Now one would teach the married couple to enjoy life, taking the children and therewith the cares of life away from them, so that the parents can live for higher things. And then our expectations are tensed by something extraordinary, a new order of things to come, and we all, both married and unmarried, get a vacation, like children because the schoolmaster is moving, and we are free until he gets settled. But we are no longer school-children, and everyone shall give an account of himself before God, and the sacred obligation shall give every day its task and its responsibility. Where then do we find guidance if we do not work out our own soul's salvation

with fear and trembling, for thus we become really earnest?
Otherwise it will soon appear that one guide cannot be
followed because, although he means well, he is weak; and
another not, for, though there is force and unction in what
he says, they say he does not really mean it; or one is too
old to satisfy the times, and another is too young. Aye,
how could an address even come to an end if it tried to
describe this confusion in life?

But what do you think, my hearer, of one who had the
show of earnestness in rejecting everything, but not a trace
of its power in possessing the least thing? What would
you think of such a man if he were married, and had been
married without forming a resolution, and then lived un-
troubled about the most sacred pledge, that is to say without seriously troubling himself about it? Had not separation already marked such a marriage, where the married
couple belonged to one another, but not in earnest?

Nay, earnestness is within a man, and only a fool runs
after it, and only a coward buys the indulgence of medi-
ocrity by being like the majority, and striving after this;
and only the fearful man is disturbed in a more noble
striving by paying attention to the judgment of others. If
there is no guide in life, the earnest man still does not
walk blindly. Oh, and even if the appointed guide in the
place where you live, my hearer, were perhaps incompetent, well, if you will, you may be the good auditor who
still profits from the incompetent address. And if he who
here speaks is too young, or if he perhaps does not express himself clearly, or if his thought is perhaps confused, well then, my hearer, lay the address aside, or, if
you will, do the great thing, be the reader who profits even
from an unfortunate address. Verily, as there may be a
power of speech which can almost perform wonders, so
there is also a power in the listener which can work wonders if he will. In such a listener there is earnestness; he
says, " I wish to be edified," and lo, he is edified. But the
earnestness lies in a resolution. If someone fears this,

E.D.   G what wonder then that he seeks consolation in the fact that others are caught in the same difficulty, and look to right and left; if anyone thinks that resolution is a fragile thing, and that the resolved individual skates on thin ice, ah, what wonder then that he must always have many about him to get courage to live? But you, my hearer, believe that the resolution offers the highest happiness, that even if love's richest happiness could be secured to you in some other way for your entire life, you would still choose the life of resolution and the wedded companionship in danger. For the resolution works the miracle with marriage, as with the wedding in Cana : it first pours the poorer wine, and keeps the best for the last. And love is the best adornment for the beloved, but resolution is a power in the heart of him who is imperfect. So the resolution of marriage is that love conquers all. Aye, it conquers all; but verily it goes out in adversity, if no resolution holds it fast; it perishes in prosperity, if no resolution holds it fast; it degenerates in the daily round, if no resolution heartens it; it is smothered in conceit, if no resolution humbles it. Love abides, but the resolution is its abiding place wherein it rests; love is the refreshing essence, but resolution is the flask in which it is preserved. Love abides; it guides through life when the resolution accompanies it, but it loses its way when the resolution does not guide; it gives life significance when resolution interprets it day by day; it suffices for the whole of life, when resolution exercises its restraint; it lays hold of the eternal if the resolution has made a place for it there; it conquers everything when the resolution is present in the day of battle—and the final honour is the only honour.

Is this kind of talk envious? Is it envious to say to the happy, "I know where you can keep your happiness secure"? A little coquettish sadness, which precisely is envy, might perhaps stir the senses of a happy man. Is this sort of speech insulting? Is it insulting to say to anyone, "I am convinced that you yourself know and have considered this, for which reason I merely remind you"? Is the speaker intrusive who stands aside and speaks half softly to himself?

And then there is required for the resolution of marriage a real conception of life and of oneself; but herein there is already contained the second great requirement, which is like the first: a real conception of God. The one corresponds to the other; for no one can have a real conception of God without having a corresponding one about life and himself, nor can he have a real conception of himself without a similar one about God, and no real conception about life without a similar one about himself. A poetically creative imagination or a conception at the distance of an indifferent contemplation, is no real conception. Nor does the conception of God come as an accidental supplement to the conception of life and of oneself; on the contrary it comes and crowns the whole, interpenetrating everything, and it was present before it became manifest.

The lovers are happy, and on the day of happiness, one is surely nearest to God. But there is required a real conception of God, there is required an understanding between God and the happy individual, and thus there is required a language in which they can speak with one another. This language is resolution, the only language in which God wills to have intercourse with man. For if the happy individual were ever so enthusiastic in expressions of gratitude for his happiness (and where is the happy individual who does not feel this need of being grateful!) and if he even used God's name, it does not follow that he really spoke with God, had a real conception of Him, entered into an understanding with Him, and profited by the understanding. For the thanksgiving for the happiness, were it ever so remarkable, were the expression ever so filled with pathos, the soul ever so burning with zeal, God will not understand—only the resolution which takes over the happiness. And if the name of God be mentioned at the beginning and end, it does not therefore follow that one speaks with God, when the conception in which the worshipper offers his thanksgiving, is not of God, but of happiness, fortune, great profit, and other things; or about a mysterious power over whose intervention one stands amazed—and worships.

The resolution should not make the happy individual ungrateful, on the contrary it should make him worthy, and only in the resolution does gratitude become earnest. Therefore the gratitude of the resolution knows that this happiness is a task, and that the grateful individual now stands at the beginning. Hence the thanksgiving of resolution is sober-minded; it understands that God has in this happiness spoken to the resolved individual, but also understands that this is the beginning of the conversation. Is this to think deprecatingly of happiness? Is it not rather to think worthily about God? If someone talked with a wise man, and immediately upon the first words of the wise man, he interrupted him with his thanks, because he now needed no more help : what would this show other than that he did not talk with a wise man, but with a wise man whom he himself transformed into a fool? A wise man is a human being, and so something external, and in so far someone may say with truth, even if he talked foolishly, that he had talked with a wise man; but God exists only inwardly. Whoever speaks with Him therefore, as this man did with the wise man, does not really speak with God. Just as there is an immature love that says, "True love conquers all," without having any conception of the struggle; just as there is an immature enthusiasm that says the same thing with a similar rashness : so there is also an immature gratitude that would thank God, and yet only deceives itself into thinking that it thanks God, and defrauds God of the thanksgiving. The thankfulness of resolution is earnest, and therefore acceptable unto God; its thankfulness is also the good beginning by which the task is half done; and with God's help the resolution will certainly conquer all. It does not give thanks once for all, nor with earthly and deceptive self-conceit or folly; nay, the resolution is the beginning, and the thanksgiving of the resolution is the beginning of thankfulness, the beginning of the solemnity which will keep many an unnecessary danger at a distance, strengthen the soul in real danger, echo in pæans of praise on the day of victory; it is the beginning of the vigilance which will find the wedded pair preserving it in the evening of life, expectant after the wedding as the wise virgins were before the wedding, the watchfulness which will make the last thanksgiving the most beautiful, make the last response to God's voice, whose beginning was this happiness, into an acceptable and true thanksgiving.

If anyone thinks that this is nevertheless disturbing, if without really understanding himself, he ventures in confusion of mind to think slightingly of God, if he thinks that happiness loses by becoming earnest, that the happiness was made less by being the beginning of happiness : would it then be more beautiful, would it be wiser, would it better stand the test of life, if the beginning were without resolution? Would it be more beautiful if the happiness, so to speak, immediately separated the two who were united : would it be more beautiful if a vain woman's heart listened with pleasure to the praise of an adorer who thought that he owed her all, in that, though grateful for his happiness, but confused in his thought, he knew no one else to thank for it? Or that the proud head voluptuously bent its ear to listen to the adoration of the weak, who glad in her happiness, humbled in gratitude, knew no one else to go to but to him, him to whom she owed everything and her happiness—him who defrauded her of the best life? Would it be more beautiful, would it be wiser? Would it better stand the test—even then, when the yoke must be thrown off and the struggle begin; or if this did not take place, then when the wretch never became a man, but without manly spirit went all his life tied to a woman's apron-strings? Or when the pitifully faithful woman slaved through life, not as a wife, but without frankness loved her master, and that master was her husband? Or is idolatry at first more beautiful, its foundations wiser, its progress in life more trustworthy, than a rational worship of God?

If anyone thinks that the conception of God which the resolution brings, is a check from which the happiness would rather be free: would it then be more beautiful, would it be wiser, would it better stand the test of life, if the two without a resolution were unchecked in passing the brief moment in sentimental dreaming with one another, if they danced away the health and vigour of love on their wedding day? Was it more beautiful, was it wiser, did it better hold on to the best in life—then, when they stood weary at the beginning of the way, and lo, the jest was over, and it was not earnestness that remained, but distaste and boredom, and a confused awakening to a long life from a confused dream of youth? Should the brief lust of a pair of sensualists be more beautiful and wiser and more trustworthy in life, than the humble beginning of a true marriage?

Is there anyone who thinks that the resolution can come later when it is really needed? So it is not needed then, not on the wedding day, when the eternal pledge is entered into? But then, later? Can he mean that there was no thought of leaving one another, but of enjoying the first gladness of their union—and so united, of finding support in the resolution? Then when toil and trouble come, and need, be it physical or spiritual, stands at the door, then the time is there? Aye, indeed, the time is there—the time for the resolved individual to muster up his resolution; but not just the time to form a resolution. It is true that distress and failure may help a man to seek God in a resolution, but the question is whether the conception is always the right one, whether it is joyful, whether it does not have a certain wretchedness, a secret wish that it were not necessary, whether it may not be out of humour, envious, melancholy, and so no ennobling reflection of the trials of life. There is in the state a loan-association to which the indigent may apply. The poor man is helped, but I wonder if that poor man has a pleasant conception of the loan-association. And so there may also be a marriage which first sought God when in difficulty, alas, sought Him as a loan-association; and everyone who first seeks God for the first time when in difficulties, always runs this danger. Is then such a late resolution, which even if it were a worthy one, was not without shame and not without great danger, bought at the last moment, is that more beautiful, and wiser than the resolution at the beginning of marriage?

But perhaps no distress and difficulty come in life, so that the resolution is not needed. Far be it from this address to terrify childish people, and still farther from it, to praise resolution as a means of serving something lower. Well, then, O childish one, who knows not the peril of the spirit, suppose the marriage is fortunate, that here is a marriage that life coddles, and fortune smiles upon continuously—what then? Then this childish marriage has lost the best, for the resolution itself is the best. It is not a wretched invention against the misery of life, but the garment of salvation, and the resolved individual arrayed therein, worthily bears prosperity, and is strongly armoured thereby to conquer in the evil day, and yet the garment is the same.

Alas, the life of marriage and the circumstances of marriage are so very different in the world, and yet there is one resolution that is, or may be common to every marriage : that love conquers all. This resolution is the beginning, and in this resolution there is contained a real conception of life and of oneself, and thereby also of God—so that the end may well be as the beginning, that love has conquered all. But imagine two marriages, my hearer. The one must wearily pursue its narrow way through many difficulties, the other is borne as on the hands of fortune through life; now they have both come to the end of life, and love has conquered all. Of the first marriage it must be said that the wedded pair learned much in the strict school of life, but when it must also be said that in the evening of life they were not essentially different in their earnestness than when in the beginning they gained earnestness in the strict discipline of the resolution: was this not most beautiful? And if of the other couple it must be said that in the evening of life they were not essentially different in their earnestness, but had also through a long life, been essentially as earnest as when on their day of happiness, resolution had made them mature in earnestness: was not this most beautiful? For the youthful earnestness of the resolution is not formed piecemeal, but with God's help it is formed of a conception of life, and of one's self, and of God, and is therefore an eternal soundness, and perhaps never gained later in this way.

IX

THE JOY IN THE THOUGHT THAT IT IS NOT THE WAY WHICH IS NARROW, BUT THE NARROWNESS WHICH IS THE WAY

There is a commonly accepted figure of speech, used by everyone, which compares life to a way. The simile can certainly be used to advantage in many ways, but the necessary unlikeness implied in the figure is no less worth attention. In the material sense the way is an external reality, indifferent as to whether anyone travels on it or not, indifferent as to how the individual travels it, the way is the way. In the spiritual sense, on the contrary, the way naturally cannot be physically pointed out. It does in a certain sense indeed exist, whether anyone travels it or not; and yet in another sense it only really becomes a way, or it becomes a way for each individual who travels it; the way is: *how* it is travelled. A man cannot point and say: "There runs the way of virtue"; he can only tell how to travel on the way of virtue; and if anyone does not wish to travel precisely this way, then he, in fact, goes another way. On the other hand, it would indeed be an absurd way of speaking, to define a highway by *how* it is travelled. Whether it is the youth who, with a confident spirit and head erect, walks easily and lightly, or it is one enfeebled by years, who with bowed head toils slowly forward; whether it is the fortunate man who hastens forward toward the goal of his desire, or the anxious individual who has turned his back on the wish, and goes slowly forward; whether it is the poor foot-sore wayfarer, or the rich man in his comfortable carriage: the way is the same for all, the way is and remains the same, the same highway.

The dissimilarity in the figure appears most clearly when there is at the same time talk about a way in the material sense, and a way in the spiritual sense. Thus when we read in the holy Gospel about the Good Samaritan, then the way in question is the one between Jericho and Jerusalem. We are told about at least three, and indeed really about five men, that they went " on the same way," whereas, in the spiritual sense, we may still say that each one went his own way—alas, the highway makes no difference; it is the spiritual which makes the difference and the difference of the way. The first was a peaceable traveller who went on the way from Jericho to Jerusalem, perhaps on an errand, perhaps on a devout mission, in any case, a peaceable traveller on a lawful way. The second was a robber who travelled " on the same way "—and yet on an unlawful way. Then there came a priest " on the same way "; he saw the unfortunate man who had been attacked by the robber; he was perhaps moved momentarily, but nevertheless he continued his walk with his usual thoughtlessness, swiftly moved by an impulse, but without depth. Then came a Levite " on the same way "; he saw the unfortunate man, he passed by unmoved, proceeding on his way—alas, the highway really belonged to none of the travellers, and yet the Levite walked " on the same way," his way, on the way of selfishness and hardness of heart. Last of all there came a Samaritan " on the same way "; he found the unfortunate man on the way of mercy, he knew by his example how one walks on the way of mercy, he knew that, spiritually understood, the way is precisely this : how one goes. Therefore the Gospel says to the learner : " Go thou, and do likewise," that is, when you walk thus on the way, like that Samaritan, then you walk on the way of mercy, for the way between Jericho and Jerusalem has no advantage with respect to practising mercy. All of this happened " on the same way," and yet once it was the law-abiding way, the second time the way of lawlessness, the third time of thoughtlessness, the fourth time of hard-heartedness, the fifth time of mercy. There were five travellers who, according to the evangelist, went " on the same way," and yet each went his own way.

Consequently, the spiritual fact, how one travels on the way of life, make the difference and the difference of the way. That is, in so far as life, in the common understanding of it, the fact of living, is compared with a way, the metaphor expresses only the commonplace, that which all the living have in common through the fact of living; to that extent they all travel on the same way, they are all on the way of life. But when the matter of living becomes earnest, then the question becomes how a man is to walk, in order to walk the right way on the way of life. The wayfarer asks about it, not as one usually asks about where the way goes, but how one walks on that way, and how one is supposed to walk. Still, merely in order to ask this rightly, some power of reflection is required, for impatience will readily be deceived, and, spiritually understood, merely asking where the way is, is as if everything would then be decided, in the same sense as when the wayfarer has found the highway. And worldly wisdom is very willing to deceive by repeatedly answering the question of where the way is, while the difficulty is ignored, that, spiritually understood, the way is : *how* it is travelled. Sometimes worldly wisdom wishes to teach that the way goes over Gerizim, sometimes over Moriah, sometimes that it leads through one or another science, sometimes that it consists in certain maxims, sometimes certain external acts. A man is not willing to admit to himself that all this is deception, because the way is : how it is travelled. For it is indeed true, as the Scriptures say : two men may be sleeping in one bed, the one is saved, the other lost; two men can go up to the same temple, the one goes home saved, the other lost; two men can recite perfectly the same confession of faith, the one may be saved, the other lost. How does this happen, unless just because, in the spiritual sense, it is a deception to know where the way goes, since the way is : how it is travelled?

But even the one who has learned to ask correctly how

one must go, still asks about one thing: whither the way leads. Any commendation regarding the perfection of the way can still mean nothing if the way does not lead to perfection—alas, the more perfect the way is, if it nevertheless leads to perdition, the more distressing it is. And on the other hand, however hard and toilsome the way which is to be followed, if it still is the way of perfection, it is nevertheless joyful.

How now does one walk on the way of perfection? For on the way of pleasure one moves easily, as in a dance. On the way of honour one walks proudly, crowned with garlands. On the accommodating way of fortune one walks humoured in all his wishes. But how does one walk on the way of perfection? The one who asks earnestly, the one who stands on the way and asks about the old accustomed paths, he will also receive an earnest answer: that the way is narrow, that on the way of perfection a man walks in tribulations. Whether you consult the Old Testament covenants or the New, concerning this there is only one opinion; there are many answers, but they all say the same thing, the answer is constantly the same, only the voice is different, so that the answer by the help of this difference may win the different. So definite and decided is this single opinion of the Scriptures, that the way of perfection is in afflictions, that perhaps concerning nothing else are there found so many scriptural passages which all say the same thing: that " he who wishes to serve God must dispose his soul to temptations " (Sirach 2 : 1); that " we must enter into the kingdom of God through much tribulation " (Acts 14 : 22); that we " are appointed to tribulation " (I Thess. 3 : 3), and so on.

Therefore we shall not cite any particular Biblical passage, but rather rely upon the complete and perfect impression of the common teaching of the Scriptures, that on the way of perfection one walks in tribulations; and therefore we shall for the edification of a sufferer (for these discourses are indeed the Gospel of Suffering), consider the joy in the thought

THAT IT IS NOT THE WAY WHICH IS NARROW, BUT THE
NARROWNESS WHICH IS THE WAY.

Consequently, the way of perfection leads through tribulations; and the subject of this discourse is, the joy for a sufferer in this thought. Hence the discourse is not this time the admonishing one of how one must walk on the way of affliction, but the joyful one for the sufferer, that the affliction is the how which indicates the way of perfection. In the spiritual sense the way is : how it is travelled. Which is then the way of perfection, that is, how does one walk on the way of perfection? One walks in afflictions. This is the first how; the second is, how one is to walk on the way of affliction. That this second must never be forgotten, either first or last, is certain enough, but neither must it be forgotten, on the contrary it must be remembered, moreover, the sufferer will be exactly strengthened for that purpose, when he has really found for himself the joy in the thought that the way of perfection is through afflictions—he who through being a sufferer is exactly in affliction.

When affliction is the way, then is this the joy : *that it is hence* IMMEDIATELY *clear to the sufferer, and that he* IMMEDIATELY *knows definitely what the task is, so he does not need to use any time, or waste his strength, in reflecting whether the task should not be different.*

What is it that makes a child, even if for comparison one uses a vigorous man, able to do what the vigorous man is hardly able to do; what is it which helps by giving the child a start? Manifestly this, that the child has no difficulty at all in learning definitely what the task is, what it has to do—for the child has only to obey. The task is a matter for the thought and consideration of the parents and superiors. As soon as the child is told what it is to do, then this is the task. How far it is right or wrong does not concern the child at all; it not only must not, but it dare not, spend even a single moment on that kind of reflection; on the contrary, it must obey *at once*. The child is then indeed weak in comparison with a powerful man, but it is also the weak who has a very essential advantage, the weak who unconditionally comes to apply his whole strength in perfecting the task, and so effectively that there is not a single moment wasted in doubting about the task, not the least bit of strength lost in irresolution about the task. The task is set with the emphasis and reliability of authority, this is the start; but then one still gives the child headway by adding: "Do it at once"—so the child does the amazing, aye, truly, then a child can do, what even an energetic adult is rarely enough able to do. Who has not frequently looked with amazement at this amazing thing: what a child is able to do! If the father or mother, or merely the nursemaid, says with authority: "Now go to sleep at once"—then the child sleeps. There are current worldly stories about many amazing accomplishments of men, and yet there is only one, he who was called *der Einzige* (the only one), of whom it is said that he was able to sleep when he would. For otherwise, take an adult, even a very strong one; he is in the same situation as the child, who, in the opinion of its parents, needs to sleep; he says to himself: "You might as well go to sleep." I wonder too if he can, like the child who goes to sleep at once! Alas, when he is ready to lay his head on the pillow, then the opposite happens: the unruly thoughts at once awaken. Then perhaps all his thoughts become promiscuously confused; when he sometimes doubts whether it is right to sleep, whether his work will not be neglected, and what then is to be feared; when he again wishes to fall asleep, but is not able to. At last he becomes impatient; he says: "What good does it do to lie here if I cannot sleep?" He gets up again, yet not to work, for now he can neither work nor sleep. For if it is true that one rises up so refreshed from the rest of sleep that it is sometimes almost tempting to stay in bed and not get up, then truly, after a vain attempt to sleep, it is in another sense difficult to get up; truly, after a vain attempt to sleep, one gets up even more tired.

The difficulty for the older person, which doubtless is also the advantage of authority and maturity, is that he has a two-fold task : he must work to find the task and to get it definitely established, and then he must work to discharge the task. And that which makes it difficult consists exactly in getting the task clearly in mind, or in establishing what the task really is. Perhaps men are after all not so unwilling to spend time and industry, nor are they incapable—if only it could become indubitably clear to them what their task is. But the trouble is that the communication of this cannot in any decisive sense fall to one's lot from without; it must come through the person concerned himself. The adult is indeed authoritative, he is to be his own master. But it is the Lord and Master who will assign the task, as the parents and superiors do with respect to the child; hence the adult is at one and the same time master and servant; the one who is to command and the one who must obey are one and the same. That the one commanding and the one obeying are one and the same is undeniably a difficult relationship; it can so easily happen that the servant intrudes in the consideration of the task and, conversely, that the master pays too much attention to the complaint of the servant over the hardships involved in performing his task. Alas, then confusion enters, so a man, instead of being his own master, becomes unstable, doubtful, fickle; he runs from one thing to the other, he tears down and builds up and begins from the beginning, he is tossed about by every gust, yet without moving from his place; moreover, the relationship at last becomes so preposterous that his whole strength is exhausted in hitting upon ever newer innovations in the task —like a plant which runs to seed, so he runs wild in fussy reflections or in unfruitful desires. In a certain sense he expends much time, much industry, much energy, and it is all as if wasted, because the task is not established, because there is no master, for he should indeed be his own master.

When a team of horses must pull a heavy load, what

can the driver do for them? Of course, he cannot himself pull it, and the mediocre driver can whip them, as can anyone, but the competent driver, what can he do for them? He can help them to get headway in pulling the wagon by concentrating their whole strength in a *single* moment and in a *single* start. If in the contrary, the driver causes a misunderstanding, if he curbs them so that the horses think that they should merely be ready to pull together at a given signal—but the driver meant that they should pull now; or if he pulls on the reins unevenly, so that one horse thinks that it is to pull, the other, that the driver is merely holding it in so that they will start together : aye, then the wagon does not move, even if the horses have plenty of strength. But as one, not without a certain distress, sees this sight, sees that there is strength enough, but that the one who is master, the driver, wastes it : so one sees, not without distress, when a man behaves in a similar way. He does not lack strength, and a man never really does, but he wastes it; he who should be master (and that is certainly himself), demoralizes his energy—such a man works with scarcely one-third of his strength expended in the right place, and with more than two-thirds applied in the wrong place, or against himself. Now he stops the work in order to begin reflecting on it from the beginning, now he works instead of reflecting, now he foolishly pulls on the reins, now he wishes to do both things at once—and in spite of all this he never moves from the place; in spite of all this, life comes, as it were, to a standstill; he cannot get the task so firmly fixed that it is established, while he may break away from this labour and have his strength ready to perfect the task. The task does not become a burden, but he has plenty to do with the burdensome : bungling through the task in order if possible to get it established. If this is the case, then naturally he never comes to bear the burden; he cannot even once get it established; at the moment, so to speak, he will turn his back in order to take up the burden, it is as if the burden fell off, and he must again pile it up.

Alas, when one observes human life, one must frequently say with sadness : " They do not themselves know what energies they have; they more or less prevent themselves from learning, because with their many energies they work against themselves."

Let us then consider more carefully the subject of this discourse. The sufferer is in affliction : now for it. If he can only get the task established, then he will surely succeed in holding out; if he immediately knows definitely what the task is, then much is already gained. But doubt will if possible prevent this; it wishes slyly to draw all his strength away from him, and to let it serve in the wrong place, in discovering what the task is, or in a thousand inventions with respect to what it might be. If this happens, if doubt triumphs, if it fools him into striving where he should not strive, then must he succumb to affliction.

Is it not then a joyful thought that it is true that affliction is the way? For then it is indeed immediately clear what the task is. Doubt wishes to make the sufferer wonder if it might not still be possible for the affliction to be taken away, and he still continue to walk on the same way—without affliction. But if affliction is the way, then it is indeed impossible for it to be taken away, and the way still remain the same. Doubt wishes to make the sufferer wonder if it were not possible that he had mistaken the way, that the fact that there is affliction might not mean that he is on the wrong road. But when the affliction is the way, the fact that there is affliction on the way cannot possibly signify that he has gone wrong; on the contrary, this is the sign that he is on the right way. Doubt wishes to make him wonder if it would not be possible to go another way. But when affliction is the way, then it is indeed impossible to walk on some other way. Consequently, there can be no doubt as to what the task is; not one single moment, not the least bit of strength, is to be used in additional reflection; this, that affliction is the way, establishes the task, makes it certain what the task is. And truly, however hard the affliction may be, no affliction is still so hard as this affliction of restless thoughts in a doubt-ful and irresolute soul.

The sufferer then holds out; he goes forward in afflic-tion on the way of perfection—but the affliction becomes harder and harder. Now that is as it should be. But if only the task is established, then much is already gained; and far be it from us to help to circulate the lying reports, that little by little it becomes easier on the narrow way, that it is only the beginning that is narrow. The relation is precisely reversed, it becomes harder and harder. We can easily make sure of this, if we only pay attention to men and *wish* to see. There is perhaps very rarely found a man who has not at some time made a beginning in will-ing the good, but most men fall away just when it appears that the way is becoming harder instead of easier. If a man has advanced so far that all illusions about wishing the good to a certain degree, about the good to a certain degree having a worldly reward, disappear; if he really becomes earnest in wishing the good, only then does the way really become hard, and from now on harder and harder. One is always correct in saying this, lest one de-ceive men by fabulous stories, entice them one moment in order in the next moment to make them even more im-patient. But that which contains no deceit, the everlasting certainty is : that affliction is the way. So there must not be one single moment, not one bit of strength used in further reflection : the task is established, affliction is the way.

If anyone then wishes to make the sufferer believe that others walk the same way so easily, so carefree, without afflictions, while he walks in tribulation, then the task is again established; the sufferer has but one answer : the affliction is the way. Far be it from us, too, this hypo-critical talk about things being so different in life, so that some travel on the same way without tribulation, others in tribulation. For it is indeed possible that some walk with-out affliction, but truly, he does not walk on the same way without affliction as the one who walks in affliction, for

the affliction is the way. There is a certain worldly prudence which does not like to break absolutely with the
good, but also dislikes exceedingly to renounce absolutely
the good days and worldly advantage of effeminacy; this
prudence is really very resourceful in the kind of invention, that it is so different—not in life, for in that there is
no untruth, that it is so different on the way of perfection.
Let us recall what was explained at the beginning of this
discourse, that in the spiritual sense the way is this : how it
is travelled. Lo, when a poor wayfarer, whose feet are
possibly sore, wincing at every step, almost drags himself
forward on the way : then there is, even if it is never right
for him to be envious, nevertheless, much good sense in the
thought of envying the rich who ride by him in comfortable carriages. For the highway is completely indifferent
to the distinction of how one travels it, and too it is undeniably pleasanter to drive in a comfortable carriage than
to walk so oppressed. But in the spiritual sense the way is :
how it is travelled; and then it would certainly be a strange
thing if on the way of affliction there was the difference
that there were some who walked on the way of affliction
without afflictions. Thus the task is again established; the
sufferer at once knows definitely what the task is, for the
affliction is the way. If someone travels without afflictions,
then so be it; then he merely goes on another road, which
is his own affair. But doubt cannot lay hold on the sufferer
and make him doubtful by the thought that others walk
on the same way without afflictions.

If what the proverb says is true, that well begun is half
done, then it is also true that establishing what the task is,
is half the labour, aye, more than half. But since the affliction is the way, the task is also established; not even Satan
himself is able to smuggle in a doubt as to what the task
is. If doubt is to secure full scope, then the affliction must
be brought into an accidental relation to the way. Thus if
a wayfarer is speaking about a road and says : " This way
is hard," then something accidental may be expressed by
that, perhaps that there is another way which is easy, and

which nevertheless leads to the same destination. Or the way may perhaps be easy at other times, but just at this time it is difficult. On the other hand, when affliction is the way, then every doubt about affliction being the task, is an attempt to go—on the wrong way, since there is only one single way, the way of affliction which the sufferer is on. The doubt concerning the task has its stronghold constantly in the idea that there might be other ways, or that the way might be changed so that the affliction would be taken away. But when affliction is the way, then the affliction cannot be taken away without taking away the way, and there cannot be *other ways*, but only a *wrong way*.

Is this then not a joyful thought, joyful for the sufferer, who is on the way of affliction, joyful because it does not need even the slightest reflection as to whether the way is the right one, joyful because he can immediately begin on the task, begin with the concentration which has all its strength collected and ready to endure the affliction. For when affliction is the way, then it is surely not in a disconsolate sense the unavoidable, by no means; he could not indeed wish to avoid it, since it is the way. With this thought the sufferer is at once under full headway to' endure the affliction; he cannot so much as waste a moment or spare a glance to look about him; no, he is in affliction with all his might, joyful in affliction, rejoicing in the thought that the affliction is the way. That is, it is not really the task which gives strength, for the task is indeed that which is prescribed, for whose accomplishment the one to whom the task is assigned must use his strength; and yet we may say that the task gives strength. If the parents know how to set a task with authority, if a driver knows from experience how to set the task, then it helps indescribably. And so too for adults, when the task is fixed with the authority of eternity, then it helps indescribably in performing the task. If a child is so unfortunate as to have a father who does not know how to command, or a horse is so unfortunate as to have a mediocre driver : then it looks as if the child and the horse do not have half the strength they actually possess. Alas, and when the adult, who is a sufferer, gives his own soul into the power of the fickle and inconstant : then he is actually weaker than a child. But then it is also joyful that the affliction is the way, for then it is immediately established, and established immovably, what the task is.

The affliction is the way—and this constitutes the joy : *that it is consequently not a characteristic of the way, that it is hard, but a characteristic of the affliction, that it is the way, so the affliction must consequently lead to something, it must be something practicable and appreciable, not superhuman.* Each of these thoughts contains a more closely edifying determination of this joy, and therefore we shall pause to consider each separately.

It is not a distinguishing quality of the way that it is hard, but a distinguishing quality of the affliction that it is the way. The more closely the affliction and the way are connected with each other, the more firmly established also is the task. When it is said : the way is hard, then the latter is a closer determination of the way; there are two thoughts : the way—and the fact that it is hard. Then we say : " It is indeed true, the way is actually hard." But then there are still two thoughts, so it is as if the doubt were granted a little concession, as if it might here squeeze itself in between the way and the fact that it is hard; as if the doubt might still have something for itself, when it wishes to make the sufferer wonder whether it might not be possible that there could be a way without its being hard, or without being as hard as it presumably is; for doubt whispers : " The question must be solved thus, the way, and after that : it is hard." But if the affliction is the way, then must doubt expire, then it cannot possibly recover. One determination is not then superior to the other; the whole assertion does not split itself, for the apprehension, into a noun and an adjective, no, they are one and the same : the affliction is the way, and the way is the affliction; they belong together so exactly that doubt cannot even draw its breath between them, for they are one thought; they belong together so exactly that the relationship between the affliction and the way is one of inseparability. A closer relationship can never exist. Take the affliction away and you take the way away; take the way away, then you take the affliction away. So exactly do they belong together, so firmly is the task established.

The affliction must lead to something. That is, one cannot draw an inference in this way : a way is hard, consequently it must lead to something. In so far as a way is a way, the inference is valid, that it must lead to something, for as soon as it does not lead to something, it also ceases to be a way. The inference is valid in so far as the way is a way, but not because it is hard; this adjective makes it, for one who is not yet strong in the faith, almost, as it were, more doubtful whether the way can also lead to something. If, on the contrary, the affliction itself is the way, then the conclusion follows : it must lead to something. For here the inference is not drawn from the fact that it is hard, but from the fact that it is the way.

These are the Master's own words : " Narrow is the way which leadeth unto life "; and when He has said that, it is everlastingly established. Truly, we do not commend the fact that someone has gone astray in a multiplicity of thoughts; oh, but if that were the case, then will we gladly assist him with a more imperfect expression of the same thing, more imperfect, because it is only understood by one who was not unacquainted with doubt, and therefore is also only temporarily serviceable to him, until he again learns the more perfect expression : to hold solely to the words of the Master. Certainly, the fact that the Master has said these words is still the most assured defence against doubt; for to believe it, in the sense of obedience, is still far more certain than the certain : that, in the sense of thought, it is impossible for the thought to doubt it. Alas, because it is impossible for thought, it does not follow from that that it is impossible for the thinking man; he can, for all that, despondently or defiantly, will to doubt. However, if it is not the Master's own word, that the affliction is the way, it is nevertheless His teaching, for does He not teach that affliction is profitable? So it is He, nevertheless, who vouches for the words. For this a man can do; he can clearly and with clear thoughts explain what the thought implies, but he cannot vouch for the thought—only the authority can do that; and only He, who is the sole authority, can vouch for all authority.

When it is said : "Narrow is the way which leads to eternal life," then the thought is this : well, it is true that the way is narrow, the affliction an obstacle, a hindrance on the way; one must go through, but then it also leads to eternal happiness. Consequently, affliction is a *barrier, a hindrance on the way,* yet one must go through. But if the affliction itself is the way, what wonder then that one must go through, what wonder then that the affliction leads to something ! Doubt will gladly deprive the sufferer of confidence, will let him stick in affliction, perish in the despondent, aye, the presumptuous thought, that he is forsaken of God, as if he had fallen into a way which could only circumscribe him, as if it were in a despondent sense that the Apostle said : "We are all appointed to afflictions" (I Thess. 3 :3), as if there were no purpose in the affliction, but we were merely destined to affliction. If, on the contrary, the purpose of the affliction is to be the way, then there is immediately a breath of air, then the sufferer breathes, then it must lead to something; for then the affliction itself is indeed preferment. It is not a difficulty *on* the way, which, if I may speak in this way, makes a new relay necessary, but the affliction itself is a relay, the best relay; if one but lets it advise, then it helps one forward, for the affliction is the way.

Is this not joyful ! How confidently the sufferer can breathe in this thought ! He not only commits himself into the hands of God and goes to meet the affliction; no, he says : "The affliction itself is a sign to me that I am well advised, the affliction is my helper—for the affliction is the way." As long as the child still has a timid fear of the teacher, it can no doubt learn much; but when confidence has driven out the fear, and fearlessness has triumphed, then the higher instruction begins. And thus, too, when the sufferer, assured that the affliction is the way, has overcome the affliction; for is not this in the higher sense overcoming affliction, to be willing to believe that the affliction is the way, is the helper! The Apostle Paul says somewhere, "Faith is our victory," and in another place, "Yea, we are more than conquerors." But can one do more than conquer? Yes, if before the strife begins he has transformed the enemy into a friend. That is what it means to conquer in affliction, to overcome affliction, as one overcomes an enemy, assuming that the affliction is one's enemy. But it is more than conquering to believe that the affliction is one's friend, that it is not an obstacle on the way, but the way, not the hindering but the improving, not the discouraging but the ennobling.

The affliction must be something appreciable, practicable. What is it that can appear on a road and block it, so it becomes impassable? It is affliction. But when the affliction is the way, then is this way unconditionally passable. The sufferer can, if he so will, imagine the affliction increasingly terrible; this makes no difference one way or the other—it is everlastingly certain that the affliction is the way, and so it becomes impossible to imagine an affliction that can obstruct this way. Also one may see from this that the affliction may lead to something. For what could prevent a way from leading to something, what other than affliction. But if this cannot come as an obstruction on this way, then this way must eternally lead to something.

Wonderful! The way of affliction is the only one where there is no hindrance, for the affliction itself prepares the way instead of blocking it. But is not this good news! For what is more distressing than when a wayfarer must say: "Here there is no longer a path." And hence what is more joyful than that a wayfarer constantly dares say : " Here there is always a way !"

The affliction is not superhuman. No, if it were so, then would the way be blocked, and affliction would not be the way. The Apostle Paul says : " No temptations have befallen you except the human; but God will make both the temptation and the escape such that you may be able to bear it." But has God not made the temptation bearable when from eternity He has arranged it so that the affliction itself is the way? Then the affliction is made endurable once for all. And how can it be better assured that there is always a good way out of temptation, than when the affliction is itself the way? For then the affliction is always a way out, and a good way out of the affliction.

The superhuman temptation will tower high above a man; like the precipitous mountain which leads the wayfarer to despair, so the superhuman temptation will frighten the sufferer, transform him into a creeping thing, compared with the magnitude of the temptation. As a natural force belittles human effort, so will the superhuman temptation, strutting haughtily, proudly mock the poor sufferer. But, thank heaven, there are no superhuman temptations, there is only a lying fable, invented by a timorous or a cunning individual, who wishes to shift the guilt from his own shoulders, to diminish his own guilt by magnifying the temptation, to justify himself by making the temptation superhuman. The Scriptures say exactly the opposite; they not only say that there is no superhuman temptation, but they say in another place, where the discourse concerns the horror, in expectation of which men's hearts shall fail them from fear, they say to the believer : " When this happens, then lift up your heads." Consequently, the temptation has no superhuman magnitude; on the contrary, when the affliction is most terrible, the believer is taller by a head, a head taller, aye, he is indeed a head taller, as he rises above the affliction. And when the affliction is the way, then is the believer also above the affliction; for the way *on which* a man goes certainly does not go over his head; no, when he walks on it, then he plants his foot on it.

Thus there is a perpetual joy contained in the thought that the affliction is the way. The sufferer immediately knows definitely what the task is; he can immediately begin on it with all his might; no doubt can come sneaking in between the way and the affliction, for they are eternally inseparable; and therefore it is eternally certain that this way must lead to something, for here no affliction can obstruct the way, which is always passable, as the affliction is never superhuman.

It must certainly never be forgotten, it must again be said here in conclusion, that the second point still remains : how the sufferer is to walk on the way of affliction. Oh, but if it is true that it will be of little use to a man with a cold heart to cling to a dead understanding : truly the understanding which keeps a man happy and warm in affliction will also strengthen him for the next step : to walk rightly on the way of affliction. And that with a sure spirit, without doubt in the belief that the affliction in which a man finds himself is the way; is it not also the way to walk rightly on the way of affliction!

X

THE GLORY OF OUR COMMON HUMANITY

If it is true that the sorrow of concern, especially the longer and the more deeply it penetrates into the soul, or the longer it penetrates profoundly into the soul, also establishes itself more firmly : then it is indeed profitable to consider some diversion for the troubled soul, although not in the sense that the world frequently and foolishly enough recommends—the wild restlessness or the noisy stupefaction of vain diversions. If then the concerned one feels himself forsaken and yet, through a self-contradiction in his sorrow, does not desire sympathy, because this confining and restricting presses too closely upon him, so that he winces almost as much from the sympathy as from the pain : then if one leads him out into an environment where there is nothing to remind him of his sorrow—not even sympathy, where sympathy is, as it were, and yet is not; an environment which has the touching nearness of sympathy, in so far as it is sympathy, and also the soothing remoteness of sympathy, in so far as it is not sympathy.

This is the way the Gospel read leads the concerned individual out into the field, into surroundings which will include him in the great common life, which will gain for him the great fellowship of existence. But since the concern has now established itself firmly within him, it is evident that something must be done to get his eyes and mind diverted from it.

For this there are two exercises which the Gospel recommends. For if the concerned " beholds the lily " at his feet, then he looks *down* at it; and when he looks down at the lily, he does not see his concern. It is of course possible that in his sorrow he usually walked with bowed head, looked down and saw his concern; but if he looks down in order to see the lily, then he looks away from his concern. And if, according to the account in the Gospel, he looks at the bird in the air, then he looks *up* at it, and if he looks up at the bird, then he does not see his own concern. Of course it is possible that in his sorrow he also sometimes looked up when he sent a concerned sigh up to God, and followed it with a glance of concern; but if he looks up in order to see the bird in the air, then he is looking away from his concern.

How can one better describe the fact of the concern having established itself in a man's soul, than by saying that it is as when the eye *stares*? When the eye stares then it looks fixedly before it, it constantly sees one thing, and yet it does not really see that, because, as science explains, it sees only its own seeing. But then the physician says: "Move your eye." And so the Gospel says: "Divert your mind, look down at the lily and refrain from staring at your concern; look up at the bird and stop staring at your concern." If, then, the tears stop while the eye is looking down at the lily, is it not as if it were the lily that dried the tears! When the wind dries the tears from the eyes that are following the bird, is it not then as if it were the bird that dried the tears! Even if the loved one sits by and wipes away the tears, if the concerned one still continues to weep, is this then really to dry the tears? But the one who causes the concerned to stop weeping, he dries the tears.

This is what we venture to call a *godly diversion,* not as the vain and worldly diversion excites impatience and fosters the concern, but as the diversion which diverts, soothes and persuades, the more devoutly the concerned yields himself to its influence. Human ingenuity has invented a great many things to amuse and divert the mind, and yet the law for this kind of invention mocks the fruitless striving by the self-contradiction of the diversion. The art itself is at the service of impatience; more and more impatiently it learns to compress the multitude of diversions into a short-lived moment: the more this ingenuity increases the more it works against itself, since it appears that as the ingenuity increases, the diversion constantly lasts for a shorter and shorter time. Let us take an example, where the vain and worldly diversion shows itself as slight and self-contradictory as it is. Fireworks indeed delight the eye and divert the mind when the elaborate, blazing ephemerality is lighted in the darkness of the night. And yet, if it lasts merely one hour the spectator grows weary; if but one brief moment intervenes before each new ignition, then the spectator grows weary. The task of ingenuity is therefore to speed it up faster and faster; the highest, the most perfect performance consists in burning the whole display in a very few minutes. But if the purpose of the diversion is to while away the time, then the contradiction appears clearly, that the diversion, when it represents the most perfect art, may only while away a few moments—the more fearfully it becomes precisely evident how long the time is. One pays money then for admittance to a tension of impatience in having to await the beginning of the entertainment, and in the same moment it is over. As those antic flames blaze and immediately vanish into nothing, so must the soul be of him who knows only such diversions: in the moment of diversion he despairs over the length of time it takes.

Ah, how different are the godly diversions! For have you ever seen the starlit heavens, and have you ever found any more authentic spectacle! It costs nothing, so there is no prompting of impatience; it does not say, "Tonight, not later than ten o'clock sharp." Oh, no, the heavens wait for you, even if in another sense they do not wait for you—as the twinkling stars shine in the night, so have they shone unchanged for thousands of years. As God makes Himself invisible, alas, because of that there are many who perhaps have never really noticed Him: so the starry heaven makes itself, as it were, insignificant; alas, perhaps that is the reason why there are so many who have never really seen it. The divine Majesty dis-

dains the visible, the false obviousness; the solemnity of
the starlit heavens is more than unostentatious. Oh, but if
you stand quietly, if you perhaps went out there without
any particular motive, where year out and year in, unap-
preciated, it is visible; if accidentally you were to pause
and turn your glance upward—you would still find it true
that its persuasiveness increases with every moment; more
and more movingly it draws you away from the temporal;
what is to be forgotten sinks into deeper and deeper
oblivion with every moment you continue to observe the
starry heavens. O godly diversion! You do not disloyally
and treacherously call yourself a diversion, while with
empty noise and driving impatience you are still in a
covenant with boredom, into which you plunge men deeper
and deeper—through the diversion; no, you are in a covenant with the eternal, and therefore only the beginning is
difficult; when it is made, then the quiet of the diversion
increases and in it the persuasiveness.

Thus it is with everything in nature; it seems insignificant, and yet it is so infinitely right. If therefore you are
going hastily on an important errand, and your way leads
you along the sea shore—then take advantage of it! It is
indeed true that no one calls to you, you hear no invitation,
there is neither the voice of approval nor the thunder of
cannon, as in human recreations; and yet, take advantage
of it! Hasten, lest by pausing a moment you perhaps discover the persuasiveness in the uniformity of the swelling
billows. And so, too, with the lily of the field and the bird
in the air. If you are hurrying "to your fields, to your
trade, to your wife"—and a bird flies past you, then do
not watch its flight, for if your eye follows it, then you
perhaps would pause too long watching the bird. If it is
during working hours, when one must give attention to his
work, if the harvest-hand whets his scythe briskly and
swings it against the grain, then let him not look at the
lily at his feet, lest it persuade him, so that both the lily
and the harvest-hand remain standing.

But the concerned, he is not admonished; on the contrary, the Gospel prompts him to go out into the field, and then to stand still, in order to observe the lily and the bird, so that the godly diversion may cause the staring eye to move, may divert the mind within which the concern has established itself. Consider the lily, see how it stands in loveliness at your feet; do not despise it; indeed it still waits for you that you may enjoy its beauty! See how it sways back and forth, shakes everything from it so that it may continue to be lovely! See how it sports with the wind, quivers with every movement, so that quiet again it may rejoice in its happy existence! See how gentle it is, always willing to jest and play, while by yielding it still triumphs over the most violent storm, and weathers it! Behold the bird in the air, see where it flies; perhaps it comes from far away, from far, far happier scenes—but then those indeed still exist; perhaps it flies away, far away, to far more distant regions—then let it take your concern with it! And it does it without noticing the burden, if only you continue to look after it. See where it now soars, it rests —in infinite space; hence it rests where no rest seems possible! See how it finds its way; and what way through all the adversities and afflictions of a human life is yet so difficult as the "mysterious way of a bird through the air"! Hence there is a way and a way to find, where no way seems possible.

However, as all diversion is intended not only to pass the time but also chiefly to give the concerned individual something else to think of, we shall now consider how the concerned, who looks at the lily and the bird, dispels the mists by the aid of the godly diversion, gets something else to think of besides his own concern, and by forgetting his concern in the diversion he is led to consider

HOW GLORIOUS IT IS TO BE HUMAN.

"*If then God so clothed the grass of the field . . . should he not much more clothe you, O ye of little faith!*" Consequently God clothes the grass, or the grass is clothed; the beautifully formed sheaths of the stalks, the fine veining of the blades, the lovely shades of blended colours, the whole wealth, if we may speak in this way, of ribbons and bows and pageantry—all this is part of the clothing of the lily, and it is God who clothes it in this way. "Should He not much more clothe you, O ye of little faith?" "*Ye of little faith!*" This is the mild approach of the admonition; thus it is said to the one who was in the wrong, when love does not have the heart to speak severely: with uplifted finger it reproachfully says to him, "You of little faith," but it says it so gently that the reproach does not wound, does not grieve, does not dishearten, but rather uplifts and gives confidence. If a child aggrieved came to its parents and begged for something which the child had already and had had for a long time, but had not been aware of having, and therefore believed that it must beg in order to get it, instead of being thankful for having it: I wonder if the mother, mildly reproachful, would not say, "O my dear child, you will get enough to-morrow, you of little faith! That is, if you once come to understand better, then you will appreciate that you have it, that you have always had it, and that therefore it was a kind of ingratitude, although forgivable, moreover, suitable for a child, that you asked for what you had."

But if this is the meaning of the words, then the Gospel says not only that man is clothed like the grass of the field, but that he is clothed far more gloriously. By the aid of the added reproof (ye of little faith) it is really said: Should not God much more *have* clothed you? So the discourse is not about the new coat one wishes to have for Sunday, or about the new coat one so greatly needs, but about the ingratitude of being willing to forget how gloriously man is clothed from the hand of God. Would there not be an incongruity in the discourse if the first statement was that the lily was more gloriously clad than Solomon, and the last, "Should not God much more clothe you?" Would it not be incongruous if the latter was to be understood as referring to some articles of clothing a man may need?

Let us, however, rightly consider this question. It is

said that the lily is arrayed, but this is not to be understood in such a way that the lily's existence is one thing
and the fact of having raiment something different; no, its
raiment is the fact of being lily. Understood in this sense,
should not the human be far more gloriously clad? Or
should he be permitted, out of concern for articles of
clothing, absolutely to forget the first clothing. O ye of
little faith! O ye ungrateful, with your imagined need!
O ye concerned, even if your need is great, that you are
absolutely willing to forget how God has clothed you.
Learn from the ant how to be wise, but learn from the lily
how glorious it is to be human, how gloriously you are
clad, ye of little faith!

In the petty disquiet of the comparisons, the worldly
concern always seeks to lead a man away from the elevated
calm of simple thoughts. Being clothed means then being
human—and so to be well clothed. Worldly concern
occupies itself with clothes and with the distinctions of
dress: is it not then like the child who aggrieved comes
and begs for what it has, and to whom the mother, mildly
reproachful, says: "You will get enough in the morning,
you of little faith!" The Gospel wishes first to remind
even an indigent one that he must not completely forget
how gloriously he is clothed by God. And next, we are
indeed very far from needy, not all in the more earnest and
stricter sense, but, on the other hand, we are all perhaps
only too inclined to be concerned about clothes, and un-
gratefully forget those first thoughts—and the first clothing. But by considering the lily, the concerned individual
is reminded to compare his clothing with that of the lily
—even if poverty has dressed him in rags.

Ought not then the invitation to learn from the lilies to
be as acceptable to everyone, as the admonition is profitable to him! Ah, in the busy worldly life of the comparisons, those great elevating, simple first thoughts are perhaps forgotten more and more. One man compares himself with another; one generation compares itself with
another; and thus the accumulated multitude of compari-

sons really grows above a man's head. As everywhere ingenuity and busyness increase, there come to be in every generation more and more men who toilsomely labour throughout their whole life far down in the deep subterranean regions; aye, like miners, who never see the light of day, so these unfortunates never come to see the light : those elevating, simple, primary thoughts about how glorious is it to be human. And up above, in the high places of the comparison, there smiling vanity plays its false game, deceives the fortunate, so they get no impression of those elevated, simple first principles.

To be a ruler—aye, what a strife is not carried on about this in the world, whether it be to rule over kingdoms and countries, over thousands, or to rule over a single man— besides oneself, whom no one is greatly concerned in ruling over. But out in the field with the lilies, where every man who quietly and in solitude sucks the milk of those first principles is what he is according to the divine plan, he is ruler : moreover, there no one will be ruler ! To be a prodigy ! Ah, what strenuous efforts are not made in the world to attain this envied place, and how does not envy itself strive to frustrate them ! But out in the field with the lilies, where every man is what God has made him, the wonder of creation : aye, there no one will be a prodigy ! The better individual would certainly smile, the shrill laughter of the crowd would mock the fool who in such a sense could speak about being a ruler, and about being a prodigy.

And yet, what can the preacher really mean by those words : " that God separated the human in order to see whether he would regard himself as an animal " ? For the one who is not separated is willing to be soothed, consoled, edified and uplifted by the absoluteness of those first principles; the one who is willing to reconcile himself to disappearing and perishing in the insignificant service of the comparisons : he regards himself as an animal, whether in the comparative sense he was distinguished or humble. Therefore God singled out the human, made every man into this separate entity which is implied in the absoluteness of those first principles. The individual animal is not singled out, is not unconditionally a separate entity, the individual animal is a number, and belongs under what the most celebrated pagan thinker has called the animal classification: the herd. And the human being who turns away in despair from those first principles to plunge into the herd of the comparisons makes himself into a number, he regards himself as an animal, whether in a comparative sense he becomes the distinguished or the humble.

However, with the lilies the concerned one is set apart, far away from all human or perhaps better inhuman comparisons between man and man: moreover, the one who turned his back on the greatest city in the world, has not left such a varied herd, such a tremendously confused manifold behind him as the one who turned his back on the inhuman comparisons—in order humanly to compare his raiment with that of the lily.

By clothing then must certainly be understood the fact of being human. A pagan has earlier been aware of this. He did not know how to refer everything to God, but he believed it was the soul which, as he ingeniously says, like a weaver itself wove the body, the apparel of the man. And now in beautiful wonder he praised the ingenious creation of the human body, its glory, with which no plant and no animal can endure any comparison. In his thought he let it belong, as it were, to what is man's distinction: the erect walk, and when in thinking he imitated it, then was his mind uplifted. He wondered over the ingeniousness of the human eye, and even more at its glance; for an animal has an eye, but only the human has a glance, the human who therefore, also, in the beautiful mother-tongue of wonder, is called the erect, yet so that there is indicated the two-fold meaning, first the fact that the human form is erect like the straight trunks of the trees, and next, that in this way the erect one directs his glance upward; even if the straight trunks of the trees rise higher, the erect one by means of his glance proudly lifts his head higher than the mountains. Thus the man stands erect—commanding, and therefore the fact of that wonder was deemed so glorious that the human was the only created thing which had hands, for the ruler indeed stretches forth his hand when he commands.

And so too that wondering pagan knew many ways in which to speak gloriously about the human's glorious raiment. Many have perhaps spoken more learnedly, more skilfully, perhaps more scientifically about it, but, strangely enough, no one has spoken more wonderingly than that noble wise man, who did not begin by doubting everything, but, on the contrary, when he became older, when he had seen and heard and experienced much, really began to *wonder,* to wonder about that *simple first thought,* which usually no one troubles himself over, not even the scholar and the scientist, for it still fails to interest those —as an object of wonder. But this discourse of wonder is still imperfect in so far as it refers the clothing to the soul. Most imperfect, aye, the discourse is foolish, which absolutely forgets that solemn *first* injunction, so it takes as a matter of course and thoughtlessly the fact of being human for granted, as if it were nothing, takes it in vain, and immediately begins the foolishness about articles of clothing, about trousers and jackets, about purple and ermine. But the discourse is also imperfect which does take notice of the first, but is not really aware of God. No, if the human is to compare himself with the lily, then he must say : " All that I am is due to my being human, that is my raiment; nothing is due to myself, but it is glorious."

How are we now to speak about this glory? We could speak a long time without finishing, but this is not the place for that. Let us therefore rather speak briefly and concentrate everything in one single word, the word which the Scripture itself uses with authority : *God created man in His own image,* and yet again, for the sake of brevity, merely understand that word about one thing.

God created man in His own image; ought it not to be glorious to be thus clad! The Gospel says, in order to praise the lily, that it surpasses Solomon in glory—ought it not to be infinitely more glorious to resemble God! The lily does not resemble God, no, it does not do that; it has a little sign upon it whereby it reminds of God; it has a testimony, as God has indeed left nothing created without a testimony to Himself, but the lily does not resemble Him.

If a man sees his image in the mirror of the sea, then he himself sees his image, but the sea is not the man's image, and when he goes away, the image is gone. The sea is not the image, and it cannot even retain the image. How does this happen except because the visible form, precisely through its visibility is powerless (precisely in the same way that the physical presence makes it impossible to be omnipresent), so it cannot reflect itself in another in such a way that this other retains the image when the form removes itself. But God is spirit, is invisible, and the image of the invisible is in turn invisible : thus the invisible Creator reflects Himself in the invisibility, which is a spiritual determination, and God's image is precisely the invisible glory. If God were visible, aye, then there would be no one who could resemble Him or be His image; for *no* image of the visible *exists,* and among all visible things there is nothing, not even a blade of grass, which resembles another, or is its image; if such were the case, then the object itself would be the image. But since God is invisible, no one can *visibly* resemble Him. That is exactly why the lily does not resemble God, because the glory of the lily is the visible; and that is why the pagan still spoke imperfectly about the human, even when he spoke most perfectly about the glory of the human body, but said nothing about the fact that the invisible God created every man in His own image.

To be spirit, that is man's invisible glory. So when the concerned person stands out in the field, surrounded by all the witnesses, when every blossom says to him, " Remember God!" then the man answers, " I shall certainly do that, little children, I shall worship Him; you, poor things, cannot do that." The erect one is consequently a worshipper. The upright walk was the distinction, but the ability to cast one's self down in worship, is still more glorious; and all nature is like the great staff of servants who remind the man, the master, to worship God. It is this which is expected, not that the man is to come and take over the control which is also gloriously appointed to him, but that in worshipping he is to praise the Creator, which nature does not do, for it can only remind the human to do it. It is glorious to be arrayed like the lily; it is even more glorious to be the ruler who stands erect; but it is most glorious to be nothing through the act of worship.

To worship is not to rule, and yet worship is precisely that whereby the man resembles God, and the fact of being able in truth to worship, is the superiority of the invisible glory above all creation. The pagan was not aware of God, and therefore he sought the resemblance in the fact of ruling. But the resemblance does not consist in this; no, on the contrary, it is then taken in vain. It is in truth only within the infinite difference, and therefore the act of worshipping is the resemblance with God, as it is the superiority over all creation. Man and God do not resemble each other directly, but conversely : only when God has infinitely become the eternal and omnipresent object of worship, and man always a worshipper, do they then resemble one another. If a man wishes to resemble God through the fact of ruling, then he has forgotten God, then God has gone away, and the man plays ruler in His absence. And paganism was like this, it was human life carried on in God's absence. Therefore paganism was still like nature; and the hardest thing that can be said about it is : it could not worship—even that simple, noble wise man, he could keep silent in wonder, but he could not worship. But the fact of being able to worship is not a visible glory, it cannot be seen; and yet the visible glory of nature groans, it implores the ruler, it incessantly reminds the man that finitely he must not forget—to worship. Oh, how glorious to be human!

But so the concerned in his diversion with the lilies got

something quite different to think of than his own concern; he came really to consider how glorious it is to be human. If he again forgets that in the worldly intercrossing of the comparisons and the collision of the distinctions between man and man : then it is not the fault of the lilies, since, on the contrary, it is because he has also forgotten the lilies, forgotten that there was something he was supposed to learn from them, and something he must finally remember to do for them. That is, if we were to characterize the worldly concern in a single word, must we not say : it is a concern about clothing, a concern about being seen? Just for that reason the edification through the invisible glory is the highest exaltation over worldly concern : the fact of worshipping is the glory, and also a favour that is accorded the lily.

So much for the instruction of the lilies. We shall now consider how the concerned learns from the BIRD *how glorious it is to be human.*

"*The bird sows not, neither does it reap, nor gather into barns.*" The bird is without care for the necessities of life. But is this, then, really a perfection; is it a perfection to be carefree in danger, if one does not know it, does not know that it exists; is it a perfection to take assured steps—because one walks blindly, to walk confidently—because one is walking in his sleep! No. Then one must indeed say more truthfully that it is a perfection to know the danger, to see it before the eyes, to be awake : that it is a perfection *to be able* to have a care for the necessities of life—in order to overcome this fear, in order to let faith and confidence drive out fear, so that one is in truth without a care for the necessities of life in the unconcern of faith. For only this freedom from care on the part of faith is in the divine sense the soaring, whose beautiful but imperfect symbol is the easy flight of the bird. Therefore we also speak of lifting ourselves on the wings of faith, and this wing-beat is in the divine sense the perfect, the wing-beat of the bird only a weak, a figurative foreshadowing. Moreover, as when the tired bird with weakened wing-beat slowly sinks to earth, so even the proudest, boldest flight of the bird is only earthly and temporal languor in comparison with the lofty soaring of faith, a slow sinking compared with the easy rise of faith.

We shall now consider this more carefully. Why does the bird have no worldly care for the necessities of life? Because it lives only in the moment, hence because there is no eternity for a bird. But is this indeed a perfection! On the contrary, how does the possibility of an anxiety about subsistence come about? From the fact that the temporal and the eternal touch one another in consciousness, or rather from the fact that the human has consciousness. In the possession of consciousness he is eternally far, far out beyond the moment; no bird flew so far away, and yet precisely thereby he becomes aware of the danger which the bird does not suspect : when eternity came into being for him, then the morrow also came into being. Through his consciousness he discovers a world which not even the most travelled bird knows : the future; and when this future through the consciousness is withdrawn in the moment, then a concern is discovered which the bird does not know; for however far it flew and from however far it returned, it never flew to the future and never returned from the future.

Since now the man has consciousness, he is the place where the temporal and the eternal constantly touch one another, where the eternal interests itself in the temporal. Therefore time can seem long to a man because he has the eternal in his consciousness, and with this he measures the moments; but time never seems long to the bird. Therefore the man has a dangerous enemy which the bird does not know : time. An enemy? Aye, an enemy or a friend whose aspirations or whose intercourse the man cannot avoid, because he has the eternal in his consciousness, and must therefore measure it. The temporal and the eternal can painfully touch one another in numerous ways in the human consciousness, but one of the contacts at which the man particularly winces is the care for the necessities of life. Its distance from the eternal seems so infinite; there is no question of filling out the time with some glorious achievement, some great thought, some uplifting emotion, as in the hours of which one says that they are lived for eternity. Ah, no, there is only the question about the humble labour in the hours which are really absolutely lived for the temporal existence, the humble labour to produce the conditions for existing temporally. But, nevertheless, the fact of being able to have a care for the necessities of life is a perfection, and the expression of dejection is merely the expression for man's elevation; for as high as God lifts up, so deeply does He also depress, but consequently, the fact of being profoundly depressed also indicates the fact of being highly exalted. And as God elevated the human being above the bird through the eternal in his consciousness, so He depressed him again lower than the bird, so to speak, through his knowledge of the anxiety, the earthly, humble anxiety, which the bird does not even know. Oh, how superior it seems for the bird not to have a care for the necessities of life—and yet, how far more glorious it is to be able to know this care.

The human can therefore indeed learn from the bird, he can also call the bird his teacher, but not, however, in the highest sense. As the bird is without care for the necessities, so fundamentally the child is also; and who is there who would not gladly learn from a child! And when an imagined or an actual need makes a man in his concern despondent, depressed, and dejected: oh, then he will willingly be soothed, willingly learn from a child; willingly, in his quiet, thankful mind, call the child his teacher. But if the child wished to accept the title and to speak instructively, *then* the parent would certainly say gently: "Oh, my dear child, that is something which you do not yourself understand." And if the child then insisted, the parent would say that it was a naughty child, and perhaps would not even hesitate to slap the teacher, and perhaps with justice, and why? Because seriously the parent is the child's teacher, and the child only in a playful sense of jesting earnestness the parent's teacher. But thus it is indeed a perfection to be able to be anxious about the necessities of life, and the human is far superior, even if he willingly learns, according to the instruction of the Gospel, from the bird, and in his quiet, thankful mind calls it his teacher.

The bird that is without subsistence cares, is then the symbol of the human, and yet the human, through being able to have these cares, is far more perfect than the symbol. Therefore the human never dares forget that the One who referred him to the bird of the air, as to a primary, a childish instruction, that precisely He in earnestness and truth is the real symbol, the true, essential human symbol of perfection. For when it is said, " The birds of the air have nests and foxes have holes, but the Son of man has not where to lay his head," then there is mentioned a condition which is far more helpless than that of a bird, and is also itself conscious of this. But then, with the consciousness of this, to be without a nest, without a place in which to seek refuge, then—to be without anxiety : aye, this is the exalted image of creation, this is man's divine pattern. For the bird this pattern does not exist, nor for the child; but consequently the fact of being able to know this care for the necessities is a perfection. Is this not so?

We are accustomed to say that it is an advantage for a woman that as the weaker she cannot go to war; that it is an advantage for the prisoner that he cannot get out and risk his life; that it is an advantage for the sleeper that he sleeps unconscious of the danger; or we certainly say it is a perfection to be excluded from venturing to call the exalted his pattern ! But why then is it said otherwise about the care for the necessities, as if the women were more fortunate because it is particularly her husband who must earn the living; as if the prisoner were fortunate because the state supports him; as if that one were fortunate who acquired his wealth without effort; or as if that one were the most fortunate of all who, perhaps because of his wealth, was barred from calling the God-Man his pattern!

However, out in the field with the bird, the concerned cannot speak in this way; he looks at the bird and completely forgets his imagined concern; he even forgets the actual need momentarily; he is soothed, aye, he is edified, but if the bird were to presume to speak an instructive word, then he would certainly reply : " My little friend, that is something you yourself do not understand," that is, he would himself become conscious that it is a perfection to be able to feel a concern for the necessities of life.

" The bird sows not, it reaps not, nor does it gather into barns"; that is to say, the bird does not *labour*.

But is this then a perfection, not to work at all? Is it a perfection to steal the day-time in the same sense as sleep steals the night-time! For certainly the bird awakens early to song, and yet, yet when it has slept, it really awakens to dream; even its most beautiful song is indeed a dream about an unhappy love; and thus it sleeps and dreams its life away, a happy or a melancholy jest. But is this, however, really a perfection; is it a perfection in the child that it plays and gets tired—as a man gets tired from working —and sleeps, and plays again! It is charming in the child —ah, who would not willingly learn from a child! And if the parent sometimes indeed does his work, but is not happy in doing it, moreover, is perhaps even dejected : oh, then he will readily be soothed by the child, will gladly learn from it, will readily in his quiet, thankful mind call the child a teacher. But he will not hesitate, if it becomes necessary, to rebuke the teacher, and he will do it justly. And why? Because the parent in the serious sense is the child's teacher, the child only in the charming sense of playful earnestness the parent's teacher.

The bird does not toil; its life in an innocent sense is in vain, and in an innocent sense it spends its life in vain. Is this indeed a perfection? Then is it also indeed an imperfection in God that He works, that He works hitherto! Is it a perfection in the bird that in a time of scarcity it sits and dies of hunger, and knows nothing at all that it can do; that confused it lets itself fall to the ground and die? Ordinarily we do not speak in this way.

When a sailor lies in his boat and leaves everything to chance in the storm, and does not know anything at all to do, then we do not speak of him as a perfect sailor. But if the brave seaman knows how to steer, if with skill and energy and persistence he combats the wind and storm, works himself out of danger, then we admire him. If late in the forenoon we see a man who has arisen late, sluggish and yet hungry, waiting to get his food by chance, then we do not commend him; but if early in the morning we see the active worker, or even if we do not see him, see that he has already been there, that the fisherman has already been out with his net, that the herdsman has already put away his churn, then we commend the fisherman and the herdsman. To work is the perfection of the human. Through working, the human being resembles God, who also works. And if, then, a man works for food, we shall not foolishly say that he supports himself; we shall rather say, simply in order to recall how glorious it is to be human : " He works with God for food. He works with God, hence he is God's fellow-worker." The bird is not that; it gets its food, but it is not God's fellow-labourer. The bird gets its food, just as out in the country a tramp gets support, but the servant who works for his food calls the master his fellow-worker.

The bird does not work—and yet it gets its food : is this a perfection in the bird? Ordinarily we say that he who does not work shall not eat; and God too says this. If then God makes an exception of the bird, then it is because the poor bird cannot work. The poor bird cannot work—do we speak in this way about a perfection? Perfection then consists in working. It is not as we inadequately represent it, a hard necessity to be obliged to work in order to live. Oh, no, it is a perfection, not to be a child throughout one's whole life, not always to have parents to care for one, both while they live and after they are dead. The stern necessity which, however, still precisely recognizes the perfect in the human, is needed only to force the man who will not by himself freely understand that the fact of working is a perfection, and who is therefore unwilling to go to work. Even if, therefore, the so-called stern necessity were not there, it would still be an imperfection for a human being to refrain from working.

It is said about the medals a king distributes that some wear the medal as an honour to themselves, other honour the medal by wearing it. So let us cite a great example, who can really be said to have honoured the fact of working : the Apostle Paul. If ever anyone might have been justified in wishing the day and the night doubly long—then certainly Paul. If ever anyone could have given each hour significance for the many—then certainly Paul. If ever anyone could have permitted himself to be supported by the congregation—then certainly Paul : and yet he preferred to work with his own hands ! As he humbly thanked God that he could boast of the honour of having been scourged, persecuted, insulted; as he humbly before God proudly called his chains a badge of honour, so he also found it an honour to work with his own hands; an honour with respect to the Gospel, that with a woman's beautiful and an apostle's holy modesty he dared say : " I have not earned a farthing through the preaching of the Word; I have not married a fortune through becoming an apostle; " an honour, that with respect to the humblest man, he dared say : " I have not been exempt from any of the vicissitudes of life, nor have I through favour been excluded from any of its advantages; I have also had the honour of working with my own hands !"

Oh, in the desperate, brilliant or pitiful wretchedness of worldly comparisons, where one knows equally as little what honour is as what perfection is : there one speaks cowardly or treacherously in another fashion. But out there in the field with the bird, there the concerned understands how glorious it is to work, and from that how glorious it is to be human. For that which makes the distinction is not that one works for wealth, another for bread, one to accumulate a surplus, another to guard against poverty; no, that which makes the difference is—that the bird cannot work.

But in this way the concerned, diverted by the bird, got something absolutely other than his own concern to think of; he came rightly to consider how glorious a thing it is to work, how glorious it is to be human. If, under the strain of toil, he again forgets this, oh, then perhaps that lovable teacher, the bird, will fly past him and remind him about the thing forgotten—if only he looks at the bird.

XI

THE UNCHANGEABLENESS OF GOD

TEXT: The Epistle of James 1:17-21

Every good gift and every perfect gift is from above, coming down from the Father of lights, with whom can be no variation, neither shadow that is cast by turning. Of His own will He brought us forth by the word of truth, that we should be a kind of first-fruits of His creatures. Ye know this, my beloved brethren. But let every man be swift to hear, slow to speak, slow to wrath: for the wrath of man worketh not the righteousness of God. Wherefore putting away all filthiness and overflowing of wickedness, receive with meekness the implanted word, which is able to save your souls.

My hearer, you have listened to the reading of the text. How near at hand does it not seem now to turn our thoughts in the opposite direction, to the mutability of temporal and earthly things, to the changeableness of men. How depressing and wearisome to the spirit that all things are corruptible, that men are changeable, you, my hearer, and I! How sad that the change is so often for the worse! Poor human consolation, but yet a consolation, that there is still another change to which the changeable is subject, namely that it has an end!

And yet, if we were to speak in this manner, especially in this spirit of dejection, and hence not in the spirit of an earnest consideration of corruptibility, of human inconstancy, then we would not only fail to keep close to the text, but would depart from it, aye, even alter it. For the text speaks of the opposite, of the unchangeableness of God. The spirit of the text is unmixed joy and gladness. The words of the Apostle, coming as it were from the lofty silences of the highest mountain peaks, are uplifted above the mutabilities of the earthly life; he speaks of the unchangeableness of God, and of nothing else. He speaks of a " father of lights ", who dwells above, with whom there is no variableness, not even the shadow of any change. He speaks of " good and perfect gifts " that come to us from above, from this father, who as the father of " lights " or light is infinitely well equipped to make sure that what comes from Him really is a good and perfect gift; and as a father He has no other ambition, nor any other thought, than invariably to send good and perfect gifts. And therefore, my beloved brethren, let every man be " swift to hear "; not swift to listen to all sorts of loose talk, but swift to direct his attention upward, from whence comes invariably only good news. Let him be " slow to speak "; for our ordinary human talk, especially in relation to these things, and especially that which comes first over our lips, serves most frequently only to make the good and perfect gifts less good and perfect. Let him be " slow to wrath "; lest when the gifts do not seem to us good and perfect we become angry, and thus cause that which was good and perfect and intended for our welfare to become by our own fault ruinous to us—this is what the wrath of man is able to accomplish, and the " wrath of man worketh not the righteousness of God." " Wherefore put aside all filthiness and overflowing of wickedness "—as when we cleanse and decorate the house and bedeck our persons, festively awaiting the visit, that we may worthily receive the good and perfect gifts. " And receive with meekness the implanted word, which is able to save your souls." With meekness! In truth, were it not the Apostle speaking, and did we not immediately obey the injunction to be " slow to speak, slow to wrath ", we might well be tempted to say: This is a very strange mode of speech; are we then altogether fools, that we need an admonition to be meek in relation to one who desires only our welfare?—it is as if it were meant to mock us, in this context to make use of the word " meekness ". For suppose someone were about to strike me unjustly, and another stood by, and said admonishingly : " Try to endure this treatment with meekness " —that would be straightforward speech. But imagine the friendliest of beings, one who is love itself; he has selected a gift for me, and the gift is good and perfect, as love itself; he comes to me and proposes to bestow this gift upon me—and then another man stands by and says admonishingly: " See that you accept this treatment meekly!" And yet, so it is with us human beings. A pagan, and only a human being, the simple sage of antiquity, complains that whenever he proposed to take away from a man some folly or other, and so help him to a better insight, thus bestowing a benefit upon him, he had often experienced that the other became so angry that he even wished to bite him, as the simple sage said jestingly in earnest. Ah, and what has God not had to endure these six thousand years, what does He not endure from morning until night from each of mankind's many millions—for we are sometimes most wrath when He most intends our welfare. Indeed, if we men truly understood what conduces to our welfare, and in the deepest sense truly willed our own welfare, then there would be no need to admonish us to be meek in this connexion. But we human beings (and who has not verified this in his own experience?) are in our relationship to God as children. And hence there is need of an admonition to be meek in connexion with our reception of the good and perfect—so thoroughly is the Apostle convinced that all good and perfect gifts come from Him who is eternally unchangeable.

Different viewpoints! The merely human tendency (as paganism indeed gives evidence) is to speak less about God, and to speak almost exclusively and with sadness about the mutability of human affairs. The Apostle, on the other hand, desires only and alone to speak of God's unchangeableness. Thus so far as the Apostle is concerned. For him the thought of God's unchangeableness is one of pure and unmixed comfort, peace, joy, happiness. And this is indeed eternally true. But let us not forget that the Apostle's joy has its explanation in the fact that the Apostle is the Apostle, that he has already long since wholly yielded himself in unconditional obedience to God's unchangeableness. He does not stand at the beginning, but rather at the end of the way, the narrow but good way, which he had chosen in renunciation of everything, pursuing it invariably and without a backward look, hasting towards eternity with stronger and ever stronger strides. But we on the contrary, who are still beginners, and subject to discipline, for us the unchangeableness of God must have also another aspect; and if we forget this, we readily run in danger of taking the lofty serenity of the Apostle in vain.

Let us then speak, if possible to the promotion both of a wholesome fear and of a genuine peace, of Thee, who art unchangeable, or about Thy unchangeableness.

God is unchangeable. In His omnipotence He created this visible world—and made Himself invisible. He clothed Himself in the visible world as in a garment; He changes it as one who shifts a garment—Himself unchanged. Thus in the world of sensible things. In the world of events He is present everywhere in every moment; in a truer sense than we can say of the most watchful human justice that it is present everywhere, God is omnipresent, though never seen by any mortal; present everywhere, in the least event as well as in the greatest, in that which can scarcely be called an event and in that which is the only event, in the death of a sparrow and in the birth of the Saviour of mankind. In each moment every actuality is a possibility in His almighty hand; He holds all in readiness, in every instant prepared to change everything : the opinions of men, their judgments, human greatness and human abasement; He changes all, Himself unchanged. When everything seems stable (for it is only in appearance that the external world is for a time unchanged, in reality it is always in flux) and in the overturn of all things, He remains equally unchanged; no change touches Him, not even the shadow of a change; in unaltered clearness He, the father of lights, remains eternally unchanged. In unaltered clearness—aye, this is precisely why He is unchanged, because He is pure clearness, a clarity which betrays no trace of dimness, and which no dimness can come near. With us men it is not so. We are not in this manner clear, and precisely for this reason we are subject to change : now something becomes clearer in us, now something is dimmed, and we are changed; now changes take place about us, and the shadow of these changes glides over us to alter us; now there falls upon us from the surroundings an altering light, while under all this we are again changed within ourselves.

This thought *is terrifying, all fear and trembling.* This aspect of it is in general perhaps less often emphasized; we complain of men and their mutability, and of the mutability of all temporal things, but God is unchangeable, this is our consolation, an entirely comforting thought : so speaks even frivolity. Aye, God is in very truth unchangeable.

But first and foremost, do you also have an understanding with God? Do you earnestly consider and sincerely strive to understand—and this is God's eternally unchangeable will for you as for every human being, that you should sincerely strive to attain this understanding—what God's will for you may be? Or do you live your life in such a fashion that this thought has never so much as entered your mind? How terrifying then that He is eternally unchangeable! For with this immutable will you must nevertheless some time, sooner or later, come into collision —this immutable will, which desired that you should consider this because it desired your welfare; this immutable will, which cannot but crush you if you come into hostile collision with it.

In the second place, you who have some degree of understanding with God, do you also have a good understanding with Him? Is your will unconditionally His will, your wishes, each one of them, His commandments, your thoughts, first and last, His thoughts? If not, how terrifying that God is unchangeable, everlastingly, eternally, un-

changeable! Consider but in this connexion what it means
to be at odds with merely a human being. But perhaps
you are the stronger, and console yourself with the thought
that the other will doubtless be compelled to change his
attitude. But now if he happens to be the stronger—well,
perhaps you think to have more endurance. But suppose it
is an entire contemporary generation with which you are
at odds; and yet, in that case you will perhaps say to yourself: seventy years is no eternity. But when the will is
that of one eternally unchangeable—if you are at odds
with this will it means an eternity: how terrifying!

Imagine a wayfarer. He has been brought to a standstill
at the foot of a mountain, tremendous, impassable. It is
this mountain . . . no, it is not his destiny to cross it, but
he has set his heart upon the crossing; for his wishes, his
longings, his desires, his very soul, which has an easier mode
of conveyance, are already on the other side; it only
remains for him to follow. Imagine him coming to be
seventy years old; but the mountain still stands there, unchanged, impassable. Let him become twice seventy years;
but the mountain stands there unalterably blocking his
way, unchanged, impassable. Under all this he undergoes
changes, perhaps; he dies away from his longings, his
wishes, his desires; he now scarcely recognizes himself. And
so a new generation finds him, altered, sitting at the foot
of the mountain, which still stands there, unchanged, impassable. Suppose it to have happened a thousand years
ago: the altered wayfarer is long since dead, and only a
legend keeps his memory alive; it is the only thing that
remains—aye, and also the mountain, unchanged, impassable. And now think of Him who is eternally unchangeable, for whom a thousand years are but as one day
—ah, even this is too much to say, they are for Him as an
instant, as if they did not even exist—consider then, if you
have in the most distant manner a will to walk a different
path than that which He wills for you: how terrifying!

True enough, if your will, if my will, if the will of all
these many thousands happens to be not so entirely in

harmony with God's will : things nevertheless take their course as best they may in the hurly-burly of the so-called actual world; it is as if God did not pay any attention. It is rather as if a just man—if there were such a man !— contemplating this world, a world which, as the Scriptures say, is dominated by evil, must needs feel disheartened because God does not seem to make Himself felt. But do you believe on that account that God has undergone any change? Or is the fact that God does not seem to make Himself felt any the less a terrifying fact, as long as it is nevertheless certain that He is eternally unchangeable? To me it does not seem so. Consider the matter, and then tell me which is the more terrible to contemplate : the picture of one who is infinitely the stronger, who grows tired of letting himself be mocked, and rises in his might to crush the refractory spirits—a sight terrible indeed, and so represented when we say that God is not mocked, pointing to the times when His annihilating punishments were visited upon the human race—but is this really the most terrifying sight? Is not this other sight still more terrifying : one infinitely powerful, who—eternally unchanged ! —sits quite still and sees everything, without altering a feature, almost as if He did not exist; while all the time, as the just man must needs complain, lies achieve success and win to power, violence and wrong gain the victory, to such an extent as even to tempt a better man to think that if he hopes to accomplish anything for the good he must in part use the same means; so that it is as if God were being mocked, God the infinitely powerful, the eternally unchangeable, who none the less is neither mocked nor changed—is not this the most terrifying sight? For why, do you think, is He so quiet? Because He knows with Himself that He is eternally unchangeable. Anyone not eternally sure of Himself could not keep so still, but would rise in His strength. Only one who is eternally immutable can be in this manner so still.

He gives men time, and He can afford to give them time, since He has eternity and is eternally unchangeable. He gives time, and that with premeditation. And then there comes an accounting in eternity, where nothing is forgotten, not even a single one of the improper words that were spoken; and He is eternally unchanged. And yet, it may be also an expression for His mercy that men are thus afforded time, time for conversion and betterment. But how fearful if the time is not used for this purpose! For in that case the folly and frivolity in us would rather have Him straightway ready with His punishment, instead of thus giving men time, seeming to take no cognizance of the wrong, and yet remaining eternally unchanged. Ask one experienced in bringing up children—and in relation to God we are all more or less as children; ask one who has had to do with transgressors—and each one of us has at least once in his life gone astray, and goes astray for a longer or a shorter time, at longer or shorter intervals : you will find Him ready to confirm the observation that for the frivolous it is a great help, or rather, that it is a preventive of frivolity (and who dares wholly acquit himself of frivolity!) when the punishment follows if possible instantly upon the transgression, so that the memory of the frivolous may acquire the habit of associating the punishment immediately with the guilt. Indeed, if transgression and punishment were so bound up with one another that, as in a double-barrelled shooting weapon, the pressure on a spring caused the punishment to follow instantly upon the seizure of the forbidden fruit, or immediately upon the commitment of the transgression—then I think that frivolity might take heed. But the longer the interval between guilt and punishment (which when truly understood is an expression for the gravity of the case) the greater the temptation to frivolity; as if the whole might perhaps be forgotten, or as if justice itself might alter and acquire different ideas with the passage of time, or as if at least it would be so long since the wrong was committed that it will become impossible to make an unaltered presentation of it before the bar of justice. Thus frivolity changes, and by no means for the better. It comes to feel itself secure; and when it has become secure it becomes more daring; and so the years pass, punishment is withheld, forgetfulness intervenes, and again the punishment is withheld, but new transgressions do not fail, and the old evil becomes still more malignant. And then finally all is over; death rolls down the curtain—and to all this (it was only frivolity!) there was an eternally unchangeable witness: is this also frivolity? One eternally unchangeable, and it is with this witness that you must make your reckoning. In the instant that the minute-hand of time showed seventy years, and the man died, during all that time the clock of eternity has scarcely moved perceptibly: to such a degree is everything present for the eternal, and for Him who is unchangeable.

And therefore, whoever you may be, take time to consider what I say to myself, that for God there is nothing significant and nothing insignificant, that in a certain sense the significant is for Him insignificant, and in another sense even the least significant is for Him infinitely significant. If then your will is not in harmony with His will, consider that you will never be able to evade Him. Be grateful to Him if through the use of mildness or of severity He teaches you to bring your will into agreement with His—how fearful if He makes no move to arrest your course, how fearful if in the case of any human being it comes to pass that He almost defiantly relies either upon the notion that God does not exist, or upon His having been changed, or even upon His being too great to take note of what we call trifles! For the truth is that God both exists and is eternally unchangeable; and His infinite greatness consists precisely in seeing even the least thing, and remembering even the least thing. Aye, and if you do not will as He wills, that He remembers it unchanged for an eternity!

There is thus sheer fear and trembling, for us frivolous and inconstant human beings, in this thought of God's unchangeableness. Oh, consider it well! Whether God makes Himself immediately felt or not, He is eternally unchangeable. He is eternally unchangeable, consider this, if as we say you have any matter outstanding with Him; He is unchangeable. You have perhaps promised Him something, obligated yourself in a sacred pledge . . . but in the course of time you have undergone a change, and now you rarely think of God—now that you have grown older, have you perhaps found more important things to think about? Or perhaps you now have different notions about God, and think that He does not concern Himself with the trifles of your life, regarding such beliefs as childishness. In any case you have just about forgotten what you promised Him; and thereupon you have proceeded to forget that you promised Him anything; and finally, you have forgotten, forgotten—aye, forgotten that He forgets nothing, since He is eternally unchangeable, forgotten that it is precisely the inverted childishness of mature years to imagine that anything is insignificant for God, or that God forgets anything, He who is eternally unchangeable!

In human relationships we so often complain of inconstancy, one party accuses the other of having changed. But even in the relationship between man and man, it is sometimes the case that the constancy of one party may come to seem like a tormenting affliction for the other. A man may, for example, have talked to another person about himself. What he said may have been merely a little childish, pardonably so. But perhaps, too, the matter was more serious than this: the poor foolish vain heart was tempted to speak in lofty tones of its enthusiasm, of the constancy of its feelings, and of its purposes in this world. The other man listened calmly; he did not even smile, or interrupt the speech; he let him speak on to the end, listened and kept silence; only he promised, as he was asked to do, not to forget what had been said. Then some time elapsed, and the first man had long since forgotten all this; only the other had not forgotten. Aye, let us suppose something still stranger: he had permitted himself to be moved inwardly by the thoughts that the first man had expressed under the influence of his mood, when he poured out, so to speak, his momentary feeling; he had in sincere endeavour shaped his life in accordance with these ideas. What torment in this unchanged remembrance by one who showed only too clearly that he had retained in his memory every last detail of what had been said in that moment!

And now consider Him, who is eternally unchangeable —and this human heart! O this human heart, what is not hidden in your secret recesses, unknown to others—and that is the least of it—but sometimes almost unknown to the individual himself! When a man has lived a few years it is almost as if it were a burial-plot, this human heart! There they lie buried in forgetfulness, promises, intentions, resolutions, entire plans and fragments of plans, and God knows what—aye, so say we men, for we rarely think about what we say; we say: there lies God knows what. And this we say half in a spirit of frivolity, and half weary of life—and it is so fearfully true that God does know what to the last detail, knows what you have forgotten, knows what for your recollection has suffered alteration, knows it all unchanged. He does not remember it merely as having happened some time ago, nay, He remembers it as if it were to-day. He knows whether, in connexion with any of these wishes, intentions, resolutions, something so to speak was said to Him about it—and He is eternally unchanged and eternally unchangeable. Oh, if the remembrance that another human being carries about with him may seem as it were a burden to you—well, this remembrance is after all not always so entirely trustworthy, and in any case it cannot endure for an eternity: some time I may expect to be freed from this other man and his remembrance. But an omniscient witness and an eternally unchangeable remembrance, one from which you can never free yourself, least of all in eternity: how fearful! No, in a manner eternally unchanged, everything is for God eternally present, always equally before Him. No shadow of variation, neither that of morning nor of evening, neither that of youth nor of old age, neither that of forgetfulness nor of excuse, changes Him; for Him there is no shadow. If we human beings are mere shadows, as is sometimes said, He is eternal clearness in eternal unchangeableness. If we are shadows that glide away—my soul, look well to thyself; for whether you will it or not, you go to meet eternity, to meet Him, and He is eternal clearness. Hence it is not so much that He keeps a reckoning, as that He is Himself the reckoning. It is said that we must render up an account, as if we perhaps had a long time to prepare for it, and also perhaps as if it were likely to be cluttered up with such an enormous mass of detail as to make it impossible to get the reckoning finished : O my soul, the account is every moment complete! For the unchangeable clearness of God is the reckoning, complete to the last detail, preserved by Him who is eternally unchangeable, and who has forgotten nothing of the things that I have forgotten, and who does not, as I do, remember some things otherwise than they really were.

There is thus sheer fear and trembling in this thought of the unchangeableness of God, almost as if it were far, far beyond the power of any human being to sustain a relationship to such an unchangeable power; aye, as if this thought must drive a man to such unrest and anxiety of mind as to bring him to the verge of despair.

But then it is also true that *there is rest and happiness in this thought.* It is really true that when, wearied with all this human inconstancy, this temporal and earthly mutability, and wearied also of your own inconstancy, you might wish to find a place where rest may be found for your weary head, your weary thoughts, your weary spirit, so that you might rest and find complete repose : Oh, in the unchangeableness of God there is rest! When you therefore permit this unchangeableness to serve you according to His will, for your own welfare, your eternal welfare; when you submit yourself to discipline, so that your selfish will (and it is from this that the change chiefly comes, more than from the outside) dies away, the sooner the better—and there is no help for it, you must whether

willing or resisting, for think how vain it is for your will
to be at odds with an eternal immutability; be therefore as
the child when it profoundly feels that it has over against
itself a will in relation to which nothing avails except
obedience—when you submit to be disciplined by His
unchangeable will, so as to renounce inconstancy and
changeableness and caprice and self-will: then you will
steadily rest more and more securely, and more and more
blessedly, in the unchangeableness of God. For that the
thought of God's unchangeableness is a blessed thought—
who can doubt it? But take heed that you become of such
a mind that you can rest happily in this immutability! Oh,
as one is wont to speak who has a happy home, so speaks
such an individual. He says: my home is eternally secure,
I rest in the unchangeableness of God. This is a rest that
no one can disturb for you except yourself; if you could
become completely obedient in invariable obedience, you
would each and every moment, with the same necessity as
that by which a heavy body sinks to the earth or a light
body moves upward, freely rest in God.

And as for the rest, let all things change as they do. If
the scene of your activity is on a larger stage, you will
experience the mutability of all things in greater measure;
but even on a lesser stage, or on the smallest stage of all,
you will still experience the same, perhaps quite as painfully. You will learn how men change, how you yourself
change; sometimes it will even seem to you as if God
Himself changed, all of which belongs to the upbringing.
On this subject of the mutability of all things one older
than I would be able to speak in better fashion, while
perhaps what I could say might seem to someone very
young as if it were new. But this we shall not further ex-
pound, leaving it rather for the manifold experiences of
life to unfold for each one in particular, in a manner
intended especially for him, that which all other men have
experienced before him. Sometimes the changes will be
such as to call to mind the saying that variety is a pleasure
—an indescribable pleasure! There will also come times

when you will have occasion to discover for yourself a saying which the language has suppressed, and you will say to yourself : " Change is not pleasant—how could I ever have said that variety is a pleasure !" When this experience comes to you, you will have especial occasion (though you will surely not forget this in the first case either) to seek Him who is unchangeable.

My hearer, this hour is now soon past, and the discourse. Unless you yourself will it otherwise, this hour and its discourse will soon be forgotten. And unless you yourself will it otherwise, the thought of God's unchangeableness will also soon be forgotten in the midst of life's changes. But for this He will surely not be responsible, He who is unchangeable ! But if you do not make yourself guilty of forgetfulness with respect to it, you will in this thought have found a sufficiency for your entire life, aye, for eternity.

Imagine a solitary wayfarer, a desert wanderer. Almost burned by the heat of the sun, languishing with thirst, he finds a spring. O refreshing coolness ! Now God be praised, he says—and yet it was merely a spring he found; what then must not he say who found God ! and yet he too must say : " God be praised, I have found God—now I am well provided for. Your faithful coolness, O beloved well-spring, is not subject to any change. In the cold of winter, if winter visited this place, you would not become colder, but would preserve the same coolness unchanged, for the waters of the spring do not freeze ! In the midday heat of the summer sun you preserve precisely the same coolness, for the waters of the spring do not become luke-warm !" There is nothing untrue in what he says, no false exaggeration in his eulogy. (And he who chooses a spring as subject for his eulogy chooses in my opinion no ungrateful theme, as anyone may better understand the more he knows what the desert signifies, and solitude.) However, the life of our wanderer took a turn otherwise than he had thought; he lost touch with the spring, and went astray in the wide world. Many years later he returned to the same place. His first thought was of the spring—but it was not, it had run dry. For a moment he stood silent in grief. Then he gathered himself together and said: "No, I will not retract a single word of all that I said in your praise; it was all true. And if I praised your refreshing coolness while you were still in being, O beloved well-spring, let me now also praise it when you have vanished, in order that there may be some proof of unchangeableness in a human breast. Nor can I say that you deceived me; had I found you, I am convinced that your coolness would have been quite unchanged—and more you had not promised."

But Thou O God, who art unchangeable, Thou art always and invariably to be found, and always to be found unchanged. Whether in life or in death, no one journeys so far afield that Thou art not to be found by Him, that Thou are not there, Thou who art everywhere. It is not so with the well-springs of earth, for they are to be found only in special places. And besides—overwhelming security!—Thou dost not remain, like the spring, in a single place, but Thou dost follow the traveller on his way. Ah, and no one ever wanders so far astray that he cannot find the way back to Thee, Thou who art not merely as a spring that may be found—how poor and inadequate a description of what Thou art!—but rather as a spring that itself seeks out the thirsty traveller, the errant wanderer: who has ever heard the like of any spring! Thus Thou art unchangeably always and everywhere to be found. And whenever any human being comes to Thee, of whatever age, at whatever time of the day, in whatever state: if he comes in sincerity he always finds Thy love equally warm, like the spring's unchanged coolness, O Thou who art unchangeable! Amen!

THE JOURNALS OF KIERKEGAARD
ED. ALEXANDER DRU.
A unique combination of notebook and diary in which Kierkegaard's spiritual and intellectual development are intimately recorded.

WORLD WITHOUT END
ROGER PILKINGTON
A Christian examines his faith in the light of modern scientific discovery.

THE SECRET SAYINGS OF JESUS
R. M. GRANT with D. N. FREEDMAN
"An excellent little paperback. It should be bought and read by all who are interested in the development of early Christianity."   GUARDIAN

NAUGHT FOR YOUR COMFORT
TREVOR HUDDLESTON
"A noble book, a superb book to be read by anyone who cares about race or human relations."   MANCHESTER GUARDIAN

DYING WE LIVE
TRS. REINHARD C. KUHN
"I hope and pray that everybody at all concerned about the future of our human race will read this book."
                                                    TREVOR HUDDLESTON

DOES GOD EXIST?
A. E. TAYLOR
An essay arguing that it is unbelief, not belief that is unreasonable.

THE PLAIN MAN LOOKS AT THE BIBLE
WILLIAM NEIL
"A good popular guide book to the Bible, which is at the same time a book well worth the instructed Christian's reading for its own sake."   CHURCH TIMES

THE RESURRECTION OF CHRIST
DR. A. M. RAMSEY
An illuminating study by Dr. Ramsey, Archbishop of Canterbury, of the place of the Resurrection in Christian life and thought.